Dreaming
in
Real Time

D0424707

Dreaming
in
Real Time

The Shanti Shanti Story

Linda Forman

Blue Halo
PUBLISHING

North Atlantic Books
Berkeley, California

Published by
NORTH ATLANTIC BOOKS
P.O. Box 12327
Berkeley, California 94712

BLUE HALO PUBLISHING
1285 Baring Boulevard #210
Sparks, Nevada 89434

Cover artwork by John Rheaume
Book design by Jennifer Dunn
Printed in Canada

Dreaming in Real Time: The Shanti Shanti Story is sponsored by the Society for the Study of Native Arts and Sciences, a nonprofit educational corporation whose goals are to develop an educational and crosscultural perspective linking various scientific, social, and artistic fields; to nurture a holistic view of arts, sciences, humanities, and healing; and to publish and distribute literature on the relationship of mind, body, and nature.

North Atlantic Books are available through most bookstores. To contact North Atlantic directly, call 800-337-2665 or visit our website at www.northatlanticbooks.com.

LIBRARY OF CONGRESS CATALOGING-IN-PUBLICATION DATA
Forman, Linda, 1954–
Dreaming in real time : the Shanti Shanti story / by Linda Forman.
        p. cm.
    ISBN 1-55643-449-9 (pbk.)
    1. Shanti Shanti (Musical group) 2. New Age musicians—United States—Biography. I. Title.
    ML421.S49 F66 2002
    781.63'092'2—dc21
                                                            2002152454

    1 2 3 4 5 6 7 8 9 TRANS 08 07 06 05 04 03

to:

The Masters of the Tradition,
Who dedicate their lives to the pursuit of the Divine ...
Thereby preparing the way for all the rest of us to follow.

[c o n t e n t s]

THE BOUNDARIES BETWEEN EAST AND WEST are dissolving today, as many people in the West are becoming proficient in Eastern yogic practices and many people in the East are becoming proficient in Western science and technology. Paramahansa Yogananda once remarked that yogis from the East would start taking birth in the West to help guide Western countries spiritually in the coming planetary age, just as Western souls would take birth in the East to help develop their material cultures. It is perhaps a necessity that for such foreign teachings to flourish in this country—reflecting as they do a very different language, culture, and social system—that they literally take birth here and be adapted from within.

Yet of these many Eastern teachings very few people, particularly young girls in America, have ever heard of the Vedas, even though the Vedas are the root of the yoga tradition, much less have any desire to chant them. That anyone would take Sanskrit chanting up as their life's mission since childhood, and make it into a musical career, is without precedent. That two sisters could do this together is more surprising. This makes the story of Andrea and Sara Forman quite remarkable and one of the great spiritual adventures of modern America.

*   *   *

Sanskrit is said to be the language of the gods, or the higher levels of consciousness, reflecting the cosmic sound vibrations that create, sustain, and dissolve the entire universe. It is based on Sanatana Dharma, the eternal or universal dharma and natural law behind the universe. Sanskrit is perhaps humanity's oldest language and contains probably our greatest abundance of spiritual teachings, holding the core texts of both Hindu and Buddhist Dharma for thousands of years. It has provided some of our greatest mantras like OM, and some of our greatest prayers and highest aspirations as a species.

Yet Sanskrit remains an arcane language in the West, even though it has much in common with ancient Indo-European languages of all types. Few people in the West learn the language, much less are able to contact its power, the Divine Shakti that works through it. Those who study it formally in universities usually learn it as a dead language and don't even know how to pronounce it correctly. Even yoga students, who take on Sanskrit names, seldom try to understand the language that yoga has always used to express itself. Few people understand how musical and rhythmic the Sanskrit language is. Indian- or Sanskrit-based music has a tropical beat that can vie with that of any folk or rock music, at the same time preserving a spiritual energy and an ability to lift us beyond the body and the mind. Even the most abstract Vedic philosophy is chanted, and has been put to dance in many forms. The original Vedas themselves were such hymns and songs.

A modern Western version of such Sanskrit devotional chants (generally called Kirtan) is now becoming popular in the West. Many people are content to listen to it for its musical content alone, but there are deep meanings to these chants that invoke the gods and goddesses, the great powers of the higher Self or pure consciousness behind the universe. Such music is not intended simply to entertain but to transport the listener into a higher state of awareness in communion with the conscious universe and its many dimensions of light and joy.

Shanti Shanti has produced its own special blend of such Sanskrit, or chanting music, and is able to bring its Shakti out in their concerts. The two sisters can bring people through their music into the Sanskrit language itself, which is said to be the very voice of the goddess. They can connect people to the energy of the goddess that is the real transforming force in life.

* * *

I have heard Shanti Shanti sing at various events over the past few years and have watched Andrea and Sara quickly mature into seasoned performers. They have not only found their dharma—they are helping to create a new musical dharma for the planet. They are already touring the world with their music and sharing it with an amazing diversity of audiences, young and old, and from many different religious backgrounds. As their work is just beginning, it is likely to grow rapidly for years to come.

They have brought their parents along in their venture, with their father himself a skilled singer, musician, and song writer and their mother, herself an Ayurvedic practitioner, providing a well-written biography of her two amazing daughters. Their family provides a new model as to what families can become as we enter into a new age of consciousness no longer defined by old physical and geographical boundaries.

* * *

Clearly the story of Andrea and Sara Forman is an important chapter in how Eastern spirituality is moving to the West and taking roots here. As seemingly Western incarnations of the tradition of Sanskrit chanting, the two sisters hold a Saraswati energy that is bound to awaken many people to the reality of cosmic sound. Their enthusiasm, vitality, and inspiration are infectious. It captivates entire audiences and leaves a lasting impact upon the heart. Andrea and Sara have learned the esoteric art of Vedic chanting and can perform some of the oldest, most famous, and powerful Vedic chants like the Purusha Sukta, Sri Sukta, or Narayana Sukta in a style that any old Pandit from India would appreciate. Yet they can also sing in a contemporary American style and move contemporary audiences with their sounds and rhythms—as vibrant as any popular music today. They can even combine both styles in order to introduce Western audiences to the more subtle sounds of Sanskrit. They bridge East and West in a way that is both uplifting and entertaining for all. Their story makes wonderful reading for anyone who is looking for the spiritual magic that makes life really worth living.

As a Western Vedic teacher myself—who seldom finds anyone really interested in the older Vedic teachings—it is great to see such vitality and enthusiasm in the new generation. It is a sign of great hope for the planet in these difficult times that often leave us wondering what the way forward is. The way forward is to follow the energy of the chant that has always carried our species onward since its cosmic beginnings, if we but open up once to its power and its grace that comes to us in such ever-new forms and personalities.

—Dr. David Frawley (Pandit Vamadeva Shastri), author of
Vedantic Meditation, Yoga and Ayurveda, and *Wisdom of
the Ancient Seers*

. . . Connecting With the Divine

AT THE END OF THE DAY, over dinner or sitting on the couch in the living room, our family has a way of reconnecting with each other that is probably as old as the tradition of the very first people sitting around fires as protection from the night. We ask of whomever in the family seems like they've had the most interesting day, "Do you have any stories?" By that question, we aren't asking the person to just make something up, but rather to share something from the day that might be interesting or inspiring or thought-provoking. The story doesn't have to be dramatic or extraordinary, because good stories come in all shapes and sizes, but it's always the most fun when it's about something provocative. The story can stimulate thought or conversation, or make us sit forward in anticipation, but it is a given, in our family, that the best welcome of the day is reserved for the person who walks through the door saying, "I have stories!" It is my personal opinion that a good story, told while everyone is in "relax mode" and reveling in being together, is the best form of entertainment in the world.

I had not realized what an integral part of our lives this habit was until I heard one of my daughters say one night, when she was very young, "Do you have a story, Dad?" And Robert knew by that particular request, voiced in quiet anticipation, that she didn't want a fairy tale, but rather a tale of real life.

Thinking back, I believe I started the whole "story" thing because it had been a part of my childhood. My dad was a first-generation Italian whose parents had immigrated to the U.S. a year or so before he was born. Through copious amounts of hard work and perseverance, my grandparents carved a large working ranch out of a very remote, very lonely part of Nevada known as the Carson Valley.

My dad had three brothers and one sister, and his mother was stretched to the nth degree caring for her family, as well as being the cook for the cowboys who came to work on the ranch. During certain times of the year my grandfather had as many as fifteen hands to help out, and my grandmother built up such a reputation as an excellent cook that the men came from all over to work on the ranch, sometimes even forgoing work that paid better, just to eat the delicious food she put on the table.

A big ranch and all that responsibility left five children with a lot of time to get into mischief, and my dad accumulated some of the best stories that a child could ever hope to hear! As soon as he came home from work, I would climb up on his lap where he sat relaxing in his chair and ask him to "tell me a story." He always had a fascinating one to share.

My dad's stories were better than any TV show could ever be because they held the additional charm of being based on real circumstances, and as an added bonus, I knew most of the characters! They were the highlight of my day, and for me, no sitcom or drama held half the entertainment or excitement that his stories did. He had hundreds of them, passed on to me like little gold nuggets of family history. Over the years, he kept on sharing them with me even when I outgrew his lap and had to just sit on the couch beside him. Before he passed away at ninety-seven, my dad could still somehow find new stories to tell from his childhood. He would recall them from time to time, and whenever he did, I would feel a little rush of excitement when I realized that this was a brand new story, and not something I'd heard before.

As time passed, and I went on to establish my own family, the tradition continued, but the stories have changed considerably, and that is a huge part of the pleasure. Where my dad had tales of wild horses, cowboys, and runaway wagons on steep ravines, our family is now in the process of growing its own stories, but they are more like the odysseys of cosmic cowboys, rather than cowboys from the Old West! It's a different type of adventure, certainly, but I hope entertaining enough that our children's children will be satisfied when they climb up on my lap and ask me, "Do you have any stories?"

I never grew tired of hearing stories, and I have never outgrown the love of the art of storytelling. It is a way people have of remembering and preserving the lives of all the generations that have gone before. It enlivens and enriches our current existence by giving us the feeling of touching something that connects us to everything and everyone around us, on a level that is eternal.

I have honored that tradition by telling my stories to my own children, and I am now continuing the tradition once again by telling my family's stories to you.

chapter one

"LADIES AND GENTLEMEN, WE ARE SHANTI SHANTI." As those words rang out from the stage, the audience erupted in a spontaneous roar of sound that started someplace toward the back and moved steadily forward, carrying a joyous energy in its wake that grew and fed upon itself until the entire area vibrated.

The two young girls on the stage seemed startled at first by the intensity of emotion being displayed, but as the standing ovation went on and on, they seemed to relax into the audience's response, both of them looking out from the stage across the vast expanse of people and smiling so joyfully that their faces reflected the over-whelming sensations they were experiencing. I could tell by their expressions that they weren't taking the adulation of the audience and making it personal to them, but rather they seemed to be stepping into the larger meaning of the moment and becoming a part of the overall joy.

It had certainly been a long, strange ride. I could never have guessed that this was where we were headed when the whole thing started so many years before. Looking at my husband Robert, stand-ing beside our daughters, it was obvious he was just as amazed as I was. From the look on his face, I could almost read his thoughts. "What in the world are we doing here, on this huge stage in Edin-burgh, Scotland, with an audience that is going crazy over Sanskrit chanting and our songs?"

People have asked me over the years, in slight variations of the same question, if I, in any way, "saw this coming." The answer is yes and no. There were all kinds of little hints along the way that there was something different afoot, but as I have learned only too well, we can tend to ignore the unlikely obvious in our lives in favor of the more-easily-explained.

As I sat in the audience that day, my heart literally ached with a feeling of universal love for the huge gift Shanti Shanti was being allowed to share with so many people, and also with the knowledge of the awesome responsibility that had been revealed as a part of that gift. The journey had certainly not been an easy one but looking back, it was amazingly obvious to see how every step had been essentially guided for us, and the destination had always remained the same, no matter how many distractions were thrown in our path along the way.

I have heard some very interesting (!) versions of our odyssey but, being a lover of a true story, and truth being almost always stranger than fiction anyway, it seemed that the only logical thing to do was to set the record straight for all the people who want to know the way it really happened.

People say that there is usually a pattern to our lives and, if we sit back and look long enough, we can almost always find a constant thread that winds from event to event, effortlessly joining each apparently separate incident with unerring consistency. That can certainly be said about our journey.

When I was little, I had a regular experience recur that seemed insignificant, but in retrospect, I can see that it was actually much more of a central issue in my life than I would ever have guessed at the time. It eventually became an important strand of connecting thread that helped tie things together for me in a way that gave an interesting perspective to the question, "Did you see it coming?"

At four or five—or at least that's as early as I can remember having the experience—I used to wake in the middle of the night to find my room full of what I thought of as "line-people." Especially when I was small, their appearance was almost a nightly occurrence.

I remember lying in my bed, after realizing that something had awakened me but not certain what. Keeping my eyes resolutely shut tight, I would fight my own internal battle to not look at my darkened room. On the one hand I didn't want to have to interact with my nocturnal visitors because I was sleepy but, on the other, it was always kind of fun to see what they would be up to on that particular night. Curiosity would inevitably win out, and I would peek through one eye, only to find my room once again full of guests.

I called them the "line-people" because, in my mind, that was what they looked like—people outlined with iridescent, white chalk lines. They never spoke to me, but most nights one of them would come over to my bed, when they apparently realized I was awake, and reach out to put a hand on my head. There were always quite a few of them in my room, at least ten or so, and I would watch them moving about for quite a while before I finally drifted back to sleep.

I wasn't afraid of my line-people, but I did get weary sometimes of having company while I was trying to sleep. They had little regard for my desire to rest and seemed, in fact, to do their very best to disturb me. I didn't think there was anything unusual about their visits, and, in fact, regarded them as a normal part of my life. It never occurred to me that other people did not also have these nocturnal visitors in their bedroom. To put it in a clearer perspective, if anyone happened to comment about me looking a little tired the next day, and I would respond that the line-people had kept me up extra long, that person's resulting look of perplexity was completely lost on me. It would be years before I finally realized there was any connection between what I was saying and the strange looks I periodically received!

At some point in the latter part of my childhood, the line-people stopped their habit of visiting me regularly, or at least I couldn't see them as often as I used to if, in fact, they were still coming to see me. During my teenage years I would wake on occasion and find them in my room again, but after watching them for a while and receiving the requisite pat on my head, I would turn over and go back to sleep. By that time they had been consistent enough visitors in my life that there was no longer any element of surprise or disappointment involved. They were either there when I woke in the middle of the night, or they weren't.

When I married Robert, he and I went to live in his hometown of Dallas for a while because he wanted me to get to know his family, and vice-versa. One night, I woke up and was surprised to find that my line-people had apparently followed me all the way to Texas! I remember being pleased, and thinking that it was strangely reassuring that my relocation had not confused them, and after sleepily watching them for a few minutes or so, I turned over and went back to sleep.

In the morning, Robert told me he felt me lying awake beside him in the middle of the night, and asked if I was having trouble sleeping. I responded no, it had just been a visit from the line-people. When I saw the way his eyebrows shot up, I had my first glimmer of realization that maybe having the line-people as visitors was not a universal experience.

"The what?" he asked in a genuinely perplexed tone of voice. He was still a young and newly-enough-married man to want to think that his bride fit in with certain preconceptions—like not seeing invisible people in their bedroom in the middle of the night.

"The … line-people," I stammered slightly. My next thought was that maybe they didn't normally have line-people in Texas.

"Honey," he began, trying to appear patient but obviously leery of what I might say next, "I don't know what line-people are." He was sitting down by now and looking at me in such a way I could tell he was a little concerned. I tried for the next most obvious explanation.

"You probably call them something different," I tried, helpfully. "No one told me to call them that, it was just something I came up with because that's what they always looked like to me."

When he didn't answer, but instead just continued to sit and look at me as though trying to decipher some secret code that I was speaking, I tried again.

"So, what do you call them?" I asked this with what was, to me, perfect logic. If he didn't call them line-people, they obviously had a different name that I was not familiar with. Marriage was certainly going to be educational.

"I don't know what line-people are, Linda," Robert said evenly. "Tell me what you think they are."

By this time, I realized I had inadvertently stepped onto some very shaky ground, and tried to assume my best impersonation of a confident, mature woman ... who was not insane.

I started into a fairly detailed description of line-people, and I must have done a credible job because, at the end, Robert just looked at me and smiled.

"Well, that is really amazing," he said finally, and I looked at him closely to make sure he wasn't being sarcastic. Now that I had discovered that my nighttime visitors were an anomaly, it was very important to me that my brand-new husband, whom I absolutely adored, shared at least some understanding of my experience, and didn't regard it as too terribly strange.

"The next time they come, can you wake me up?" He asked this in total sincerity, and I knew at that moment I had definitely married well.

Over the years, during their periodic visits, I would try to wake Robert so he could see them. This proved a difficult task since he is such a sound sleeper, but even when I was able to quietly rouse him it became apparent that my line-people tended to fade with any disturbance to the environment, even something as subtle as having another person in the room observing them. Repeated experiments on my part with regard to this response always resulted in the same outcome, but it would be quite a few years before I would finally come across any type of explanation for this phenomenon. Quantum physics addresses it as the "act of perception having the ability to affect that which is being perceived." Apparently, my line-people responded to subtle changes in the environment, and perception alone was enough to alter their presence.

My descriptions of them were so vivid, however, that my husband came to believe, absolutely, in the reality of my experiences, and we would discuss them at great length whenever they appeared. (Do you have any stories!?) I believe we both came to think of them as some kind of cosmic oddity that, for some reason, I was able to perceive. I think my credibility was also helped by the fact that I did not display any other obvious signs of dementia!

Looking back now, it is as though this particular experience served as almost a kind of flexor for my consciousness. *Whatever* those white figures were, it was a result of their spectral companionship, and the fact that I grew up with them as such a normal part of my childhood, that I developed a totally unique set of parameters for the expectations of life's extraordinary possibilities.

My unusual guests were good preparation, at the very least, for what was yet to come.

[c h a p t e r t w o]

As is common for many people, high school was not "the best time of my life." I never really felt like I fit in with, much less understood, the reigning sentiments of the sixties and early seventies. I was too young to have much of an opinion about the Vietnam War, but I certainly did know what I thought about the other relevant topics of the day. The whole flower-child persona, and all the behaviors that implied, held little attraction for me. It seemed like a colossal waste of time to live a life so centered on drugs and sex, and I set out to find something much more tantalizing.

This is where things would get sticky, because in my pursuit of a more fulfilling lifestyle, I quickly learned that that particular concept could be, especially for a teenager, a bit of an oxymoron. I cast about and came up empty-handed when I looked in all the directions patterned by my friends and reflected in the social mores of that particular time. I grew frustrated with my attempts and was filled with an unrelenting desire to find something that would satisfy the intense longing for fulfillment I had had roiling inside me since my very earliest memories.

I kept myself open to all kinds of options and eventually, and serendipitously, wound up stumbling onto something that would actually prove to be a life-changing step, though I certainly had no idea of it at the time. My accidental experiment was the first step down a road to places far more intriguing and intoxicating than all those other activities that were really just pretenders to the throne.

One day, after begging to be excused from participating in my P.E. class due to one of the chronic headaches that plagued me for most of my high school years (exploring the source of these headaches would eventually be done through Ayurveda, but I'm jumping ahead), I was sent to the school library. Hanging out by myself, bored but thrilled to be missing P.E., I came across a book on yoga and found myself transported for the next hour or so while I studied the poses (*asanas*) and read about all the seemingly magical experiences yoga could impart to the devotee of this ancient knowledge.

After school, I drove straight to the bookstore and bought a small paperback book by Richard Hittleman, and my life, as the saying goes, would never again be the same. That yoga book would become a well-loved, dog-eared friend that went with me everywhere for the next several years.

Up to that point, I had never really thought of myself as an "athletic" individual, even though, as a result of growing up on a farm, I could ride horses (like the wind, my dad would say), ice-skate (fairly smoothly) on the pond, and climb the steep Nevada mountains like a goat. I even took up bike riding in a serious way.

But I always felt like the finer sporting arts eluded me, and it didn't help that I thought myself clumsy and uncoordinated, which was probably why P.E. was my least favorite class. The six-week session my school devoted to gymnastics was an experience in utter humiliation for me, and the day I hit the springboard too hard, over-shot the pommel and landed on my head sort of sealed the deal.

With yoga, I suddenly had something that I connected with in a very profound way. It liberated me from any feelings of physical inadequacy, and I adored the control yoga gave me over my body. The breathing (*pranayama*) and meditation techniques transported me to a place where the stress of high school dissolved, and peer pressure receded to a deserved level of non-importance. From the moment I began the yogic pattern that I adopted as my "program," something very powerful came into play for me.

The actual meditation part of my now-daily routine took me a little longer to feel as comfortable with as the actual yoga postures, even though I had almost immediate results from the contemplative process I was using. It took me a while to stop trying so hard, to learn that success results from simplicity, and that the mind could only relax if I didn't try to make it happen. Even though I felt wonderfully refreshed and rejuvenated after meditating, I still wanted to experience that "cosmic high" I kept reading about.

Before I even recognized that I was, in fact, already having enormous experiences, my little yogic ritual became something that I couldn't wait to get back to each day. The truth was that I enjoyed that time so much because, without even realizing it, I was slowly but surely penetrating the layers of surface thought, and plumbing the depths of deeper consciousness. With regard to the fact that I thought I was not having a "cosmic experience," I eventually was able to realize that I was missing the point completely. While I was busy looking for that huge explosion of spiritual fireworks, I was ignoring the steady, bright sparkler of infinity I was already holding in my hand.

To deal with my school conundrum, I eventually came up with what I thought was a brilliant idea. Why couldn't I do yoga during my P.E. class every day, instead of the requisite high jumps and hurdles? It was good exercise, it got rid of my headaches, and, most important, I would actually show up for class!

I worked up the courage to approach my P.E. teachers with my excellent plan, and I was a little shocked when they immediately agreed. I had prepared a huge list of reasons why this was such a good idea, and I didn't even get to use one of them. I think my poor teachers were thrilled at the prospect of not having to deal with me (and my athletic recalcitrance) anymore.

So, while the other kids played volleyball and grimaced through hundreds of sit-ups, push-ups, and jumping jacks in the auditorium, I was up on the school's stage at the very end of the huge gymnasium, hidden behind a velvet curtain. While everyone else shouted and jumped about with varying degrees of exuberance, I quietly went through my yogic series that included pranayamic breathing exercises, asanas, and then, finally, meditation.

Though I didn't fully realize the significance at the time, the velvet curtain that separated me from the noise and chaos in the auditorium would come to symbolize the lifelong struggle we all are confronted with to maintain our inner quiet amid the turmoil of everyday life. I remember my first Divine conversations as having started on that exact stage.

Initially, I was overwhelmed with the booming voices and various noises that ricocheted off the walls of the gymnasium, threatening to shatter every hard-won peaceful moment I was able to achieve. The loud sounds overwhelmed my concentration, and I discouragingly thought I'd never reach that celestial place of yogic bliss that Richard Hittleman talked about with such familiarity.

Then one day something changed. I remember sitting quietly on the stage, and I had just closed my eyes in preparation for the meditation sequence at the end of the asanas. I found myself not really fighting the noise anymore, just being resigned to its presence, because I had been dealing with it for many weeks, and it had become inescapable if I wanted to continue to do my private "yoga class."

Suddenly, it was as though my thoughts were physically being pulled away from me and I had an experience of actually witnessing my mind thinking. Then, from my position behind this huge curtain that separated me from the rest of the gym and all the boisterous activities going on, I realized that I wasn't hearing a single, solitary sound. All the noise had stopped and time seemed to just stand still, and I was everywhere and nowhere at the same time. I was me, but in a much larger sense. I was an expanded, much more fully aware version of myself.

I'm not exactly sure how long I was allowed to experience this heightened sense of awareness, probably not more than a few seconds. But the memory of those moments has remained with me to this day, propelling me toward a path where that transcendental aspect of myself has become familiar to me as my connecting lifeline to the Divine.

*   *   *

Sometime in my senior year of high school, one of my older brothers returned from a long trip to Europe with a very special mission. He was going to give everyone in my family a special meditation technique that he had received, personally, from the Maharishi Mahesh Yogi. He had been told to do just that by the Maharishi, and since my brother Dan was so enamored with the results of his meditation, he was determined to pass along the joy.

My brother had been involved with some of the less positive aspects of the sixties, and he escaped to Europe when he felt himself being pulled into a dead-end lifestyle. He wanted a fresh start. While in Europe, Dan became acquainted with the Transcendental Meditation Program, and he quickly became as zealous a convert to that lifestyle as he had previously been to the destructive one he left behind. He felt renewed, and was infectiously excited about this technique that removed stress and brought peace and joy to the practitioner.

"You don't even have to believe in it for it to work," he would say over and over again, as my parents looked at him dubiously every time he tried to give them his meditation lecture. "All you have to do is just do it."

After much pushing on my brother's part, which I was happy to join in on since I was already such a happy advocate of Eastern knowledge, our parents finally relented and we were all instructed. One of my favorite memories is of my Italian dad standing at a *puja* (an East Indian ceremony of thanks) in his stocking feet, holding a flower. The look on his face spoke more about a parent's loving desire to do whatever it took to help keep their child off drugs than a million commercials with a broken egg ever could.

For myself, I loved everything about TM. This was just a continuation of what I'd already started in the gym, on my own, and I thought it was just great to now have personalized instruction of a more structured technique integrated into my existing practice.

By this time, I had a very full spiritual calendar going, because though yoga and meditation were a regular part of my life, I was also still very much involved with the Catholic Church I'd been brought up in. I loved the traditions of the Church and was able to observe many similarities between the Indian pujas and the Catholic celebration of mass. The truth was that I was completely enamored with anything that had to do with God. I even toyed with the idea of becoming a nun at one point, but after a visit to a Carmelite monastery realized that I also wanted the freedom to pursue my own unique path. The nuns were wonderful to me, and I loved the peaceful joy of vespers, but I found myself missing the sounds of daily life while at the monastery, especially the rambunctious voices of children. I thought I would probably want to get married some day and have a family with whom to share my love of the Divine, in my own special way.

So, I continued to pursue this strangely diversified path I had started out on. I would sit in church and do TM. I would reflect on the relationship between "sins" as described in the Church doctrine and the reaction to all actions known as "karma" in the East. I would look at the Eastern deity known as Brahma, the all-great God, and think how much less different religions were than one might first suppose. It all made perfect sense to me, and I never felt any conflict between philosophies, because all the different belief systems really just had, at their basis, humanity's overwhelming desire to know God.

The years that followed included the requisite dating, but as I progressed down that particular path, I left something considerably more lasting than broken hearts in my wake. Most of the boys I dated wound up starting TM, and it became a kind of joke that if a guy was doing TM, he had probably, at some point, dated me! I certainly ran no risk of being considered a femme fatale, because not only were there no broken hearts involved, but I seemed to leave my boyfriends happier than I found them.

At the exact right time and place, which happened to be a Fourth of July celebration in Reno, Nevada, I inadvertently caught the eye of a musician from Texas. He was destined to become my husband and partner in the cosmic adventure that is our marriage.

chapter three

ABOUT FIVE YEARS INTO OUR MARRIAGE, and as the result of a very unusual experience, Robert and I found that we were suddenly dealing with the reality of having a child. During the first few years there had not been any huge urgency to have children. We were both young and inexperienced in just about every area of life, but we were smart enough to realize that we needed some growing-up time before attempting to try to raise a child.

We were busy discovering the mixed joys of being responsible adults, as well as the pleasures and challenges of being married. There was also the enormous area of career choices to be explored. Robert's main occupation had revolved around the music business since his college days in Texas. He half-jokingly said that the day he lost interest in school was the day he realized that he was making more money playing his guitar than his professor was teaching university classes!

The siren song of a musician's life proved too strong to resist, and Robert found himself touring in a bluegrass band. Always precocious when it came to music, he became proficient at new instruments as he went along, playing guitar, bass, five-string banjo, and fiddle as the group continued to tour.

He stayed with the band for a time after we married, and even after we moved from Texas back to Reno, but at some point it occurred to him that our options would be expanded enormously if he and I performed together. He saw it as a way to increase our personal flexibility, at the same time allowing us to branch off and explore new avenues of musical expression. We would also be able to continue the path of spiritual exploration we had started on right after meeting, because we would control our own work timetable.

When Robert first broached the idea of putting together a band, I didn't take the concept all that seriously. Even though we both sang, I did not play any instruments, and aside from choir and a brief drama stint in high school, had never performed on stage. Imagine my surprise when he came home one day with an expensive Fender bass, made of gorgeous dark wood, but smaller in size than the one he already owned.

"What's this?" I asked with total innocence.

"Your new instrument." He said this as though the fact that I had never played even an "old instrument," or any instrument at all, was irrelevant to the issue at hand.

This was very early in our marriage so I figured I hadn't discovered the full range of my husband's sense of humor.

"I don't play an instrument," I said unnecessarily, since he knew this as well as I did.

"But you will."

After my initial (strong) rejection of any notion that I would start performing with him, he dropped the subject, but left the bass lying around where I could see it as he sat rehearsing his music. At first, I totally ignored the ploy, seeing it for exactly what it was, but after a time, the sheer beauty of the instrument, along with the intriguing thought that I might actually be able to play it, drew me in as I'm sure he knew all along it would.

The bass guitar was gorgeous and small, so it fit my hands perfectly, and when I picked it up and touched the heavy strings, I loved the deep, mellow sounds that issued forth. But performing? I thought not.

This was one of those times when it seems that life can just pick us up and carry us along to places we had no prior thought of going. I had always loved music, and before I had time to actually think about what I was doing, I began to play bass with Robert as he practiced in our living room. Then we were singing together, and that was followed by auditions for actual performances. At one point, we were hired to do three sets a night, six nights a week, starting in about twelve weeks. The only songs I could play, though, were the three (!) we did for the audition. Looking back, I have no idea how we actually pulled it off, but by the time we started the job three months later, we had a repertoire of more than eighty songs.

As time passed and our band continued to coalesce, the musical responsibilities started being divided up in such a way that audiences would eventually exclaim about our extraordinary versatility. In reality, it was simply resourcefulness brought on by need. Since Robert was the group's producer, it was also a great illustration of his own personal "musical vision," which was, in a nutshell, if he liked the way something sounded, there had to be a way to do it! There was basically nothing he would not try (or make me try), and I learned to dread coming home and finding a new instrument sitting on the kitchen table. It usually meant he had found some new sound he wanted to incorporate into our show, and I probably had about two weeks to learn to play whatever it was he had brought home as a "surprise." I was nowhere near the level of talent he enjoyed as a musician, but Robert had such a positive attitude about my abilities that I didn't have the heart to tell him I couldn't do it. So, two weeks later, I would be onstage with a brand new instrument, winging it, with more bravado than actual aptitude. Ah, the power of love!

In any given performance, we were a virtual cornucopia of musical diversity. Robert played his six- and twelve-string guitars, five-string banjo, violin, and harmonica, and I was assigned electric bass, kalimba (an African instrument), auto-harp, and any additional percussion such as tambourine, shakers, etc. We hired a drummer who was flexible enough to also play bass, so I could be in musical "rotation" for certain songs. For instance, in one particular musical trilogy, I recall that I started the first part off on a kazoo, moved on to auto-harp, then played bass with one hand and tambourine with the other! And all of this (except the kazoo) was done while singing! In retrospect, this description makes us sound like a circus act, but the whole thing actually worked quite well and gave audiences the impression of extreme musical versatility! They thought it was amazing, but we knew it was mostly just exhausting.

For the next several years, with this configuration as a basis for performing, we were immersed in a plethora of new artistic experiences, including our initial foray into the recording business. Things were very busy, and there was a lot of traveling and performing, but we also still made it a priority to continue to explore our spiritual interests. This had been one of the initial impetuses for Robert to have us form our own band, and I quickly saw the advantages of being so independent. At every opportunity between bookings, we were either on a meditation retreat, taking classes, or studying on our own.

There was so much to do in those early days, the topic of having children rarely came up, except as a concept to be looked forward to, and even then only at some time in the comfortably distant future. The vision of me standing on the stage in front of a microphone with a Fender bass balanced on my big pregnant belly was more startling than inspiring, and we were having too much fun to give much thought to the more serious business of settling down and raising a family! That was a topic we had definitely filed in the "later-on" category.

One day, though, I had a very peculiar thing happen while I was doing my daily meditation practice. It was an experience that was destined to instantly, and dramatically, change what had been a very casual attitude toward having a baby into something that was considerably more of an imperative.

I was sitting cross-legged on my bed and reveling in the luxury of being able to enjoy a long, peaceful meditation. Our musical group was not performing anywhere for at least a week, so my entire day was filled with a feeling of total relaxation. There were no work pressures or related stresses clouding the horizon, and I had settled in to enjoy my afternoon respite.

Robert was gone for a few hours, our house was still and quiet, and I was relaxed enough to have some very deep experiences ... at least that was what I later told myself must have been the case when I tried to make sense of what happened next.

I'm not exactly sure how long I sat there because time had, at some point, done a sort of slow dissolve for me. It was a feeling I had had before, because during particularly deep experiences in meditation, it is common to have the boundaries of time and space soften and even disappear completely.

That must have been exactly what did occur, because one minute I was residing in a blissfully peaceful state, and the next I was aware of the presence of someone else in the room with me.

At first I thought Robert had come home and slipped in quietly, but when I opened my eyes and glanced around, I found myself still alone. I closed my eyes again and resumed my meditation, but the strange feeling returned, and it was stronger this time. Now I was not only aware of a presence in the room with me, but I could also feel something specific about that presence. I realized that I *knew* whoever was in the room with me, and a sensation of loving familiarity followed immediately on the heels of that realization.

As I continued to sit quietly on my bed, I had a tremendous feeling rush up from the center of my being, and the intensity of it was completely overwhelming. I felt as though I were involved in an internal struggle to remember something very important, and the effort of stirring that memory caused an accompanying flood of emotions to course through me. Most strongly, I was acutely aware that I had been painfully missing something, or more accurately someone, for my whole life, but until that very moment, I had not been consciously aware of the source of the feeling. It felt as though something had been stirred to life deep inside me, and the end result was like an overpowering, aching joy.

As I sat on my bed, trying to grasp the myriad sensations that were sweeping through me, understanding suddenly came blazing through in a fiery trail of white light. With crystalline clarity, I knew exactly who my celestial visitor was, and I knew my understanding was real because it came to me in that lightning-quick shorthand of comprehension that I had felt before. I think it's the way our soul helps us to instantly see what our mind is too cluttered to understand. And it was as obvious as a flashing neon sign!

The presence in my room that day was the subtle energy of my future child. And it was paying me a visit, at this particular time, for a very specific reason. I was being given a summons … a kind of heavenly demand … a maternal call-to-arms! There are not enough metaphors in the world to convey the overwhelming feeling of blissful reunion I experienced at that moment. I knew this child, and this child knew me.

Apparently (!) it was time for Robert and me to have a baby. And it looked like my little cosmic visitor, our child-to-be, made this surprise visit to help get the process rolling along. I assume that we must have seemed to be frustratingly reluctant future parents.

And sure enough, I could feel myself instantly respond with an overwhelming sense of loving anticipation. How wonderful! We were going to have a baby! In that moment, I was just like people who always swear they don't like surprises, only to reluctantly show up at their own surprise party and find themselves the delighted recipient of a perfect gift. And this was more than perfect. It was a cosmically wonderful gift!

Boy, was I ever going to have a story for Robert when he got home that night! Some part of my mind was mildly curious about what he would think of my news, especially since we had not ever really talked seriously about having children. Whenever the topic did lightly come up, we could both always think of a million reasons why "right now" was not the right time. Suddenly, though, none of our previous reasons for parental procrastination mattered one whit, and as I sat on my bed feeling the unbelievably clear presence of this little soul still in the room with me, I knew with great certainty that I would be pregnant sometime very soon.

I had enough presence of mind to try to get a "fix" on the way my little cosmic guest felt to me, personality-wise, before the whole magical event was over. I had always believed that the stamp of a person's being is indelibly imprinted on the soul, and I couldn't help but wonder if I would recognize this visitor as being the person who would arrive at some future point in the form of our baby.

Later on that night, I greeted Robert with the news that I had something very exciting to tell him. As I related the incident in full detail, he didn't bat an eye, but just sat listening intently. The longer I spoke, the more his face took on a look of complete focus. When I finished, he said, very simply, "Well, it must be time to have a baby."

I wasn't all that surprised to find him so instantly amenable to the idea because I knew it really wasn't my idea to begin with. Robert and I had begun to experience, with increasing frequency, the subtler influences in our lives. We were starting to understand that there were always larger forces at work within a person's existence, and when knowledge and understanding come to us in such a special way, there is not much to argue about. Whether we choose to acknowledge them or not, these influences in everyone's lives are not any more or less real than "real" experiences. In instances like this one, it really just felt like we were along for the ride, and there was not a whole lot more for us to do right now beyond sitting back and enjoying it. We knew the hard stuff would come later on, when it was our turn to take on the responsibility of caring for our little celestial messenger.

Only a short time later I found myself with a positive pregnancy test balanced on our bathroom counter. I remember sitting on the edge of the bathtub, looking at the results, and having the full impact of its significance actually hit me. Even though the whole adventure had started with a very blissful, ethereal experience, the end result would be an extremely real, extremely corporeal baby. What I was looking at so intently as I sat in my bathroom was not a subtle perception; this phenomenon had an arrival date and everything!

It was one of those moments when I experienced a definite letting go of my own sense of ability to control and manage my destiny. It was amazing what a little pregnancy test could do, but I suddenly felt a deepening of maturity in myself that was sobering. And also a little terrifying. Fortunately, the experience I had had during that spectacular meditation a month or so earlier was still very much with me, so I had an overall feeling that everything was going to be just fine. My little visitor was coming to stay, and we had about nine months to get ourselves prepared.

[c h a p t e r   f o u r]

It was now time to immerse myself in the wonders of pregnancy, and I approached the process with alacrity. I started reading prenatal books, saw a doctor, became mindful of my diet, and made sure I structured time for exercise and meditation. I was the quintessential neophyte of pending motherhood, as I congratulated myself on having everything in hand. This was actually the beginning of never, ever having anything under any semblance of my control again, but I was blissfully unaware of that fact at the time.

In the midst of this laid-back state of maternal complacency, I woke one morning with a shock of realization that something very important had completely slipped my mind. I had only about eight weeks before I would be ineligible for the Vedic study program.

About two years earlier, Robert and I started an Eastern educational program that was based on meditation, yoga, and the study of the *Vedas*, the ancient books of the Indus Valley civilization. It had, so far, been a fascinating learning experience, and very appealing to the parts of both of us that loved spiritual anthropology. Because the *Vedas* are also considered to be the oldest intact scriptures in the world, and recognized to be at the basis of many religions practiced today, this study course, with regard to Robert and me, was a match made in heaven.

I had almost completed the entire series and was missing only my last segment, but this particular one-month session was the most important of the series. It contained some very exciting knowledge that I had been waiting patiently to learn. Now that I was pregnant, however, I wasn't sure I would be accepted into the final phase. One of the special techniques we were to learn was something called the "flying sutra," and though the name alone was enticing, I knew the practical application to be very far-reaching.

The "flying sutra" sounded very dramatic, but the basis of the knowledge was actually quite simple. The techniques we'd been studying were all from *Patanjali's Yoga Sutras*, an ancient book of advanced meditation practices intended to assist in, and accelerate, the spiritual experiences of the student. The sutras, or "stitches" as the word directly translates from Sanskrit, help the mind to "connect" with itself on the deepest level, in that area which is also, not coincidentally, the source of all thought within oneself. A side benefit of this connection is enhanced spiritual awareness and development of subtle acuity.

Patanjali is the founder and father of yoga, but in this case the term does not refer to the well-known pretzel positions we see on the front of health magazines at the checkout counter of the grocery store. It is rather the body of Eastern knowledge that incorporates the entire study of mind, body, and spirit. Patanjali lived around three centuries before Christ and was considered a great philosopher and grammarian, and was a respected physician as well. The particular discipline outlined in his most famous book is often referred to as "the sovereign path" because of the regal, noble method by which the self is united with the Self.

> *Yoga is the process of becoming free from limited definitions of the field of consciousness,*
> *Then the abiding of the seer, in my own true nature.*

— Patanjali's Yoga Sutras

Thoughts are introduced into the awareness, through the use of special mantras, during meditation. If the sutra "to fly" is introduced, for example, while a person is grounded in a deep state of "restful alertness," the physiology experiences a great leap in awareness, both mentally and physically. There is a rush of energy up the spine when the technique is employed, and at that moment, the person practicing the technique seems to literally "leap-frog" through the air. It would probably look silly to watch, but to the person experiencing the "leap" it is anything but. Countless studies have documented the phenomenon, and though there are mixed interpretations as to what is actually happening, scholars can agree there is definitely a change in the brain wave patterns at the moment of "take-off."

Skeptics might say that anyone could simply jump across a mat without help from any special advanced technique. Actual practitioners would say that it is an incredibly unique experience to be sitting cross-legged (a very difficult position to be able to jump from, if we are talking about just a matter of muscular control) and to suddenly find yourself six to ten feet or more across a mat, all in the blink of an eye. Simply put, one moment the practitioner is sitting in one place, and the next, he has moved through the air and landed a substantial distance away! And during this external process, a corresponding internal "leap" gives the person practicing the technique the feeling of an exponential increase in spiritual energy.

I've tried mimicking the experience by simply "hopping" from a seated position, using no special meditation techniques, and I can say, first-hand, it doesn't work. All I'm able to do are little jumps across the mat, which leave me feeling tired; I'm certainly not able to leap many feet in one effortless motion, let alone feel energized by the activity.

Anyway, this was the dilemma I was faced with, and it might be easy to understand why I didn't want to miss this last phase of instruction. The course sounded like fun, not to mention educational in an unconventional sort of way. Then there was the fact that I wanted to observe the actual phenomenon, and to experience for myself if the practice was do-able!

After much discussion, Robert and I finally decided that I should just go to the course and see what unfolded. We knew there was a chance I would be turned away, but at the worst, we would have had a beautiful drive through Northern California.

As we drove in the car together, I made the observation that this could be my last opportunity to do something so carefree for quite a few years. Even though we'd never had the responsibility of a baby, we both assumed that time and energy were going to be in seriously short supply. This excursion felt a bit to me like a last metaphysical fling before settling down to the more sober endeavor of being parents. (It would turn out that I was completely wrong on this point, but I had no idea what kind of a strange odyssey it was that we were actually getting ready to embark upon!)

Arriving at the Instructional Center in Northern California, I was apprehensive as to whether or not I would actually be allowed to stay. Even though I was only about three months into my pregnancy, I was already starting to show a little round belly, and as I walked up to the registration table, the instructor took one look at me and shook his head.

"It does not say on your application that you are pregnant," he said, looking down at my paperwork, then over his glasses at my tummy. And then, as though belatedly realizing he could have just made an embarrassing mistake, he nervously cleared his throat and quickly added, "If you are, in fact, pregnant."

Quick save. I thought about saying as much to him, but it looked as though any attempt at humor would be lost on this fellow with his thick, dark-rimmed spectacles and serious demeanor. Instead, I just responded in a way that matched his no-nonsense tone.

"No, it doesn't say I'm pregnant, because I wasn't at the time I originally filled out those papers. But I don't see that as any obstacle to my being here." I even thought about asking if there was an economy "flight" course for expectant mothers—fly one, get one free. I restrained myself from displaying any levity, though, as he continued to glower at me over the top of his glasses.

"It's too dangerous to learn this particular part of the instruction while you're pregnant. Besides, you won't be able to actually do the technique anyway."

"Why?" I asked.

"Because being pregnant would keep you from having a clear enough meditation experience to effectively do the flying sutra. Pregnancy is such a huge distraction for the body that it's hard for anything else to go on." With that, I found myself being summarily dismissed as this very stern young man turned his attention to the next person standing in line.

I was disappointed. Robert was waiting to see how my registration went, and when I told him the news, we retreated to a corner of the room and sat down to evaluate my situation. I knew that I was too early in my pregnancy for a little bouncing around on a soft mat to present any problem, not to mention the fact that I had really been looking forward to this. A month-long retreat of studying and meditation would be a wonderful kick-off for what lay ahead. Pregnancy and childbirth were trying, at best, and I knew this program of enforced rest and study would be extremely rejuvenating. As Robert and I had already discussed, we could not foresee a time in the near or even distant future when I would be able just to pack myself off for a month of spiritual R&R. It was apparent from my observation of friends and relatives that after a baby arrived, any discussion of month-long vacations disappeared from a parent's lexicon. We decided that I should make another run at the registration line, but this time my luck changed when I wound up at a table with a woman sitting behind it.

"Didn't I already see you in the other line?" she asked, looking first at me with a sweep of her eyes, then down at my paperwork. She was scanning my application with an air of no-nonsense competency. Unfortunately, at that particular moment I was looking for a little less efficiency, and a little more empathy. Where was this woman when I was trying to register my car at the DMV?

"Yes, you did," I answered, matching the straightforward tone she had used. "What are the rules regarding pregnancy?"

Looking down at my subtly rounded belly, she answered, "No one past the first trimester is allowed to register for the final phase because of the 'flying' sutra."

I couldn't help thinking that this conversation sounded more like I was trying to get on a thrill ride in an amusement park than attempting to enroll in an advanced meditation program. I once again controlled the impulse to share my sense of humor, however, and pressed on.

"Well, there you go, then," I asserted. I was speaking with considerably more confidence than I felt. "I won't technically be three months along in my pregnancy until after the course is under way. So really, I'll still be within the first trimester rule." I put my hand on my belly and gave her my best "sister-in-arms" smile.

She just said "hmmm" in such a noncommittal way that it would have made an IRS agent proud, and looked back down at my papers. I glanced over at Robert, who was watching me from across the room, and shrugged my shoulders in response to his questioning look.

When the woman looked back up at me, it was with an attitude of impatient irritation, making it clear she was not going to respond to my blatant attempt to solicit her solidarity. I hadn't actually thought she would, but felt it was still worth the try.

"So, you've been studying and meditating a long time," she finally stated. "Do you do yoga? Exercise?"

"Yes, I'm very active, and I wouldn't be applying to this program if I thought it would, in any way, be a problem." She had provided me with a window, and I was determined to squeeze in as far as I could to present my case. "You couldn't possibly be more concerned about the health of my pregnancy than I am, and I wouldn't push on this if I didn't think this program would be great for both my baby and me."

I had spoken with total sincerity, but now I felt it was time to just sit back in my chair and resign myself to accepting whatever decision she made. If I were not intended to be in the course, no amount of bowing and scraping could change that. I would accept it gracefully, get back in the car with Robert, and enjoy the scenic drive home.

She looked down at the paperwork again, then back up at me.

"Did they tell you that you probably would not be able to have any dramatic response to the meditation techniques?"

With the posing of that question, I realized I had somehow moved from the position of standing in front of a window that was barely open, to one that was now open half-way, and I could feel the fresh air of opportunity beginning to waft over me.

"Yes, they told me all that, and that's just fine. I'm really here for the relaxation and knowledge." With that, she nodded her head briskly, and picking up the "accepted" stamp, slammed it down on the paperwork.

Robert could tell from my face that the news was good, but we had no time for celebration because course orientation started in about fifteen minutes. After retrieving my bags from the car, he gave me a big goodbye-hug and kiss, and then, saying he'd see me in four weeks, got in the car and headed off for the long drive home. This would be the first time we had ever been apart for so long, and I missed him already. I walked inside the building to begin my lone month-long study of Vedic knowledge.

The course was wonderful. Hours of meditation and yoga each day, with classes on the Vedas interspersed throughout. There were about fifty other course participants, and they came from all different walks of life. It was fun and interesting to hear how each person incorporated meditation into their busy schedules, and I became good friends with several of the other women in the course. A couple of them had children already, and another one had definite plans to have a baby soon, so when they realized I was pregnant, they took me under their wings like a flock of mother hens. (There's probably a joke in here about hens not being good at flying ... and that's why they were taking "flying" lessons ... Sorry.)

The weeks flew by and it seemed hard to believe when our instructors informed us that it was time to begin the final portion of our course. We had covered all the other aspects of the different techniques and had now reached the home stretch, or the "flying" sutra portion of our education.

As was explained by our instructors, all of the special mantras we had been practicing over the past couple of years were for the specific purposes of increasing mental awareness and deepening spiritual experiences. The flying sutra was designed for the exact same reason, no matter how exotic and flamboyant the name sounded. The point of all the meditation and yogic exercises we'd been doing was, specifically, to help us learn how to achieve a restful state of deep awareness. No easy task, and that was why the program was taught so carefully. Functioning from that state of deep consciousness, we had learned how to introduce "instructions," or sutras, into our quiet state of restful alertness, thus giving the mind the powerful experience of learning how to integrate deep awareness and activity.

The entire concept was very brilliant, and therefore it was no surprise that it was cognized by ancient sages, or seers of wisdom, thousands of years ago. It was fascinating to me that the knowledge was certainly no less relevant now than when the concept was first developed. In fact, in today's hectic world, peace and calm might be considered the ultimate currency of our busy realm.

The whole point of learning how to enliven this ability in the mind is so we can maintain equanimity in the midst of chaos and confusion, or, daily life! Everyone has had the experience of having a wonderful night's sleep and waking up feeling incredibly good. In that state, everything seems possible. The day couldn't look better, and we don't want anything to disrupt our prevailing sense of well-being. We optimistically tell ourselves, as we start into our normal activities, that we're going to feel this good all day, no matter what happens to us. We're not going to let *anything or anyone* influence us to the contrary.

Unfortunately, there is also the reality of the dismal experience of watching that wonderful sense of peacefulness slip quietly away as we get further and further into the ups and downs of our day. The ancient scholars of consciousness knew that true peace of mind is real only when it can stay with us through thick and thin, and that knowledge is the entire basis of the teaching underlying the sutras.

Living the inner reality of peace is the goal, no matter how tumultuous life on the outside becomes.

By the time the actual day of instruction approached, I was nowhere near as excited as I thought I would be. I was somewhat curious about what we would be covering, but to my surprise, I found I was mostly just preoccupied with being pregnant. I'd had my share of bouts with morning sickness during the month-long course, and had even left a couple of classes to slip back to the privacy and quiet of my room until the intestinal turmoil subsided. All in all, I had been enjoying my sabbatical, but I was definitely looking forward to getting back home to Robert and sharing all that went on during the month. I was amazed when he told me on the phone about all the home projects he'd done while I was gone. Apparently, he'd painted our bedroom, built storage shelves for the kitchen, and re-arranged all the furniture, but it was when he said he'd gone out and bought a new car that I felt a little startled. This was my clue that it was definitely time to go.

I had decided, over the past few weeks, that I was going to take it really easy when the time actually came for us to learn the "flying" instruction. I had no idea what to expect from the actual session, but I had a fairly substantial belly by this time and no desire to physically push myself, particularly with regard to something I was completely unfamiliar with. I decided that I would listen to the instructions, and then go back to my room and rest. I was more excited about going home and focusing on my pregnancy now than I was about receiving any new techniques. The words from the staff at the beginning of my course regarding the distraction of being pregnant seemed almost funny to me now, and I smiled at my own naiveté as a first-time mom. Of course I would be distracted! I was making a brand-new little human being! Who cared about some new meditation technique? It was amazing how nature had shifted my priorities.

During this part of the instruction, we sat on soft mats on the floor, cross-legged. There were about ten or twelve other people in the room with me. We sat in a semi-straight line across the front of the room, and as the instructions were given out, we were told to quietly close our eyes and meditate. At the moment we felt ourselves to be residing in a very quiet, deep place inside, we were to silently repeat the sutras we had just been given.

Since I had already determined that I would probably not be able to fully experience this technique until after my pregnancy was over, I was not very intense as I sat listening to the instructors. I closed my eyes, relaxed, and then quietly repeated the sutras we'd been given.

I was suddenly sitting about eight feet from where I'd been just a moment before!

It took a moment for me to comprehend what had just happened. As I'd repeated the sutras to myself, there had been a moment of absolute silence inside, and then I felt an enormous burst of energy race up my spine. When I opened my eyes, I was no longer in the same place, but somewhere clear across the other side of the mat!

The other women in my group were staring, mouths slightly agape, but the instructors didn't seem surprised, just pleased, and they motioned for me to turn myself around so I would be facing the other way. My "leap" had taken me to the very edge of the mats, and if I continued in that direction, I would be heading straight into the wall.

I turned and re-situated myself so that I was once again sitting comfortably, all the while thinking to myself that whatever had just happened was truly amazing. No sooner had I closed my eyes again, though, and started to think the sutras, than suddenly, WHOOSH! I was back in the spot I'd started from.

This time when I looked at the instructors, they were grinning at me, and one of them even made the comment, "Well, so much for pregnancy being a problem!"

Apparently not! At least not with this baby!

Later, I would reflect on my experience that day as having been a sort of cosmic preview of events to come. As the years clicked by and I was able to watch my daughter's destiny begin to unfold, the feeling I experienced at that moment would return to me many times—the initial, bright burst of energy that started somewhere at the base of my spine, then the swelling rush upward, like a great explosion of cosmic voltage. The fact that I was suddenly propelled eight or so feet through the air was the least of it; the true phenomenon was the internal "leap" that simultaneously took place, the experience of the power of subtle consciousness. Apparently, not only was my pregnancy not an impediment or hindrance to this type of experience, but having a "baby on board"—at least *this* baby—actually seemed to enhance the entire episode.

It would come to be revealed, through the perspective that only time can provide, that this child and I were, even then, getting ready to embark on a very special journey together. She certainly would prove to be a great co-pilot to have along.

chapter five

From the beginning, I had envisioned having my baby at home, but as delivery day drew nearer, circumstances conspired to change my best-laid plans. First off, a lab test came back with a result that hinted at high blood sugar levels, and my midwife immediately requested that I see a doctor for a more extensive check-up. The part of me that was destined to become an Ayurvedic Practitioner balked at the notion of turning myself over to a Western medical doctor for a process as normal and natural as a pregnancy, but this was the late '70s, after all, and the concept of pregnancy as a "health issue" was still a prevalent attitude in traditional medicine. There was the very real concern that I could be risking my baby's health, however, which immediately negated any objections I might have had. My midwife assured me she knew of a wonderful OB-GYN from South Africa, whom I would really like.

This was the second event that contributed to the overall change in delivery plans. I just loved the doctor she recommended. He and his partner were newly arrived in this country and in the process of establishing a clinic that would be the launching pad for their ground-breaking new approach to delivering babies … *they would let the mother do it!*

Unless circumstances dictated otherwise, these doctors did not believe in unnecessary interference, and it was clear from the moment I walked into the office that I had found kindred spirits. They had posted a huge graph over the front door tracking the number of deliveries, along with the percentage of caesarians performed. That number was indicated by a tiny red line on their chart that I knew was well below the national average. We were going to get along very well.

After running a series of tests and determining that everything was fine with my pregnancy and that the other result had been an anomaly, the doctor came into the room where I was sitting in my little paper gown to talk with me. We discussed everything, from the dismal state of modern medicine to the state of the Union. When I left his office an hour later, a lasting friendship had been made.

The night my daughter Andrea Devi was born, my new friend and my husband were by my side as I labored through my first delivery, and it was with great relief that I heard one of them finally announce that her head was crowning. A few moments later, the doctor was handing Robert the shears and telling him to (gulp!) cut the umbilical cord. My husband had been a real trooper throughout the past twenty-four hours, but I knew as I watched his face blanche, then turn red, then white again, that he had just reached the end of his tolerance for medical activities. The doctor must have seen it too, because he reached over and grabbed Robert's hand and placed the scissors gently but firmly in his palm.

"Go ahead, Dad."

With those words, Robert got a grip on both himself and the scissors, and helped bring his first child into the world. For someone who turns the TV off when a program shows any kind of surgical procedure, this was a big step for him. But that was by no means the end of the excitement for the night.

As the doctor picked up our new baby and wrapped a blanket around her, Robert glanced up at me with a perplexed look on his face, and I knew the exact reason why. From the moment she slipped into the world, there had been a noise building in the room, and now, as the doctor leaned across the bed to hand our baby to us, it was as though our room had suddenly filled with a million bumblebees. The buzzing sound was resonating so loudly I could only watch with amazement as the doctor's lips moved, because I could hear nothing of what he said. The atmosphere was absolutely alive, and it felt as though the room had been "zapped" with a huge dose of high-voltage electricity. It was with fascination that Robert and I watched as the doctor and the nurses continued with their after-delivery business, while he and I could only sit there on the bed, stunned. Apparently he and I were the only ones who could hear it!

As we looked down at our baby, we were already caught in the suspended amazement that naturally surrounds childbirth, but now we were both captivated by the sudden realization of the origin of this mystifying noise. Our little daughter was the sound! Or rather, she was the reason we were hearing it.

We were actually experiencing a phenomenon that Robert and I have since experienced two more times, with the birth of each one of our children. Over the years I have talked with other parents and listened to some of their hesitant descriptions as they try to convey the sense of celestial wonder that accompanies the birth of a child. There appears to be a "cosmic moment" that takes place as a child draws its first breaths, and Robert and I were able to actually experience it up close for the first time when Andrea was born.

In Eastern philosophy there is an understanding of this process that expresses the mysterious phenomenon in very interesting terms. When a person is born, it is the beginning of a kind of contract, so say the ancient seers. We come into our life with a specific amount of life energy, or *prana,* and that amount is determined by a delicate cosmic combination of past actions, or karma. The goal of a life is, simply, to progress toward God. Hence the desire to extend our prana to the longest possible measurement, thus extending the length of time we have to attain our goal. That is done through right action in life.

It is because that first breath, the first use of prana, is such an important moment in a person's existence that we can experience it as a true cosmic moment. When Andrea was born, Robert and I were surprised witnesses to the amazing energy that accompanies a child into this world, and we literally could hear the "sound" of the beginning of her life. This would be one of the first instances where, at a loss for adequate words, we would simply refer to the whole incident as a "God thing." And both of us would know, from that moment on, exactly what that meant.

*   *   *

As the years went by, the huge impact of Eastern philosophies and beliefs, particularly those of India, on our family became very clear, illustrated over and over again. The episode with the doctor was one such moment, but there were many more. The influences at first were so subtle that it took quite a few years before I could see the connecting thread that was consistently being woven through our lives, and the great overall effect each seemingly small event would eventually have on the overall picture.

One such event occurred when Andrea was just a couple of months old, in a department store in Reno, where I was having one of my first memorable shopping experiences with an infant. I was doing my best to keep her peaceful by crooning quietly to her, rocking her in one arm while flipping through a bargain rack with the other, trying to find some post-maternity clothes. I was oblivious to everything except the task at hand.

All of a sudden, I found my attention being inexplicably drawn away from my preoccupation with the clothes rack to a group of people standing all the way across the store. It was one of those instances when something beckons us so subtly, yet so strongly, that it takes a moment to realize our attention has even been engaged. This was certainly the case here, because I suddenly found myself gazing at a small group of East Indians and—the oddest thing—they were staring back across the store at me. It was a strange moment, as we stood considering one another, and nothing else seemed to exist for just that brief span of time.

An unusual feeling washed over me, then I mentally shook myself as Andrea's fidgeting brought me back to the moment. I had a potentially fussy baby in my arms and still had not found anything to wear to an event Robert and I were supposed to attend. Moments later, I was re-immersed in the task at hand and had completely forgotten about the odd little encounter. Suddenly, something caused me to look up again, and to my surprise I found myself in the center of the same group of Indians that had been standing across the store just a few moments before.

I gazed around, slightly taken aback, but it was hard to feel too uncomfortable when everyone in the group was smiling at me warmly, and talking all at once. I couldn't understand a word but just shifted Andrea to a more comfortable position in my arms, and smiling slightly, shook my head, wondering if perhaps they had mistaken me for someone else. Just then, one of the men disengaged from the rest of the group and stepped forward. Everyone suddenly grew very quiet. He smiled at me with gentle tenderness and gestured toward Andrea.

I have to say here, to the reader, that it will probably seem strange that a new mother, protective as a mountain lion over her baby cub, would be so trusting with a group of total strangers. As explanation, I can only say that these people were as familiar to me as relatives at a family reunion. I felt nothing but love and infinite good-will coming from them, and such genuine warmth I could not have summoned an uneasy sensation within myself even if I'd tried.

The gentleman, taller than anyone else in his group and dressed in soft flowing fabric, gently reached out his arms in a gesture that indicated he wanted me to hand Andrea to him. The women in the group were all smiling at me as though I should be completely delighted by all of this, and as I hesitated, intuition fighting with common sense, he suddenly just reached over and lifted her out of my arms. As I started to voice my protest, he smiled the gentlest of smiles but made no move to give her back, just situated her more comfortably, holding her as though she were the dearest of babies.

The man then began chanting softly in an East Indian language.

Without taking his eyes from her little face, he reached with one hand for a small bag that was hanging from his waist. Still continuing the chant, which had now become more intense and melodic, he dipped his fingers into the pouch and, lifting his hand to Andrea's forehead, gently touched a finger to her soft skin. When he moved his hand back, he had left a red powdered mark right above her eyes.

By this time, she was gazing at him in absolute adoration, and he smiled at her as his words trailed off, apparently at the end of the recitation. He held her for just a moment longer, looking as though he didn't want to have to hand her back at all, but when he finally looked up at me it was with large brown eyes that were slightly teary.

"She's a wonderful baby, very special," he said, in heavily accented English. "I have blessed her."

Feeling a confusing mixture of emotions, I reached out my arms to take my baby back. Now that it was over, I found myself feeling relieved, yet inexplicably sad, as though some important moment had passed that would never come again.

Not quite sure what was expected of me, I looked around at all the smiling faces.

"Thank you," I said, and now soft laughter rippled through the group as they stood gazing at both of us in the most loving way.

"No. Thank you," the man said, and smiling again, he bowed to me slightly, formally, before turning and starting to move off, with the entire group following him. They glanced back, nodding and smiling at me, as I continued to stand there, somewhat bemused, with my baby.

I looked away from them and down at my daughter, who was lying completely peaceful in my arms. She gazed back at me, red spot on her forehead gleaming brightly, and we both, suddenly, smiled at each other, her little toothless grin a baby echo of the look on my own face at that moment.

"Well, what in the world was that?" I said quietly, suddenly aware now of the other shoppers around me. It occurred to me then that I literally had not seen anyone outside our strange little group once the entire incident began, even though the store was actually quite busy.

When I glanced up to see where our new friends had gone, I was surprised that I could not see them anywhere in the store. Thinking they must have gone in a different direction from where I saw them headed, I turned all the way around with Andrea still in my arms. Even though I had a good vantage point and could see clearly in any direction they might have chosen, their entire group was nowhere to be found. And there was no door near enough for them to have exited that quickly. Since by this time the whole episode was starting to feel very dreamlike to me anyway, it did not come as that great of a surprise to find that this fairly large group of people, vividly dressed in easy-to-spot clothing, had basically "disappeared."

Feeling a kind of curious fascination, I walked to the door, still holding Andrea, to see if I could catch a glimpse of any of them walking across the parking lot or getting into a car. I was searching for something "normal" here, and apparently I wasn't going to find it no matter how hard I looked. The parking lot was empty except for one or two other shoppers.

I approached the nearest cashier and asked her if she saw where the group of Indians went. I knew she must have seen the whole episode, because her cash register was not far from where we'd been standing.

"I'm sorry?" she said.

"The Indian people," I explained, aware that a note of exasperation slipped into my voice. There was just no way anyone could have missed such an obvious group. "There was a large group of East Indians, in beautiful clothes, standing with my daughter and me, right over there." I pointed to a place just a couple of aisles over.

The girl shrugged her shoulders, then gave me a look that said she was probably re-evaluating her initial impression of me.

"I haven't seen anyone around here like that. There was just you and those people over there." She pointed a well-manicured nail in the direction of some teenagers and an older couple who were shopping in the same vicinity. Curiouser and curiouser!

I mumbled my thank you, and as I turned to walk away caught a glimpse of the clerk looking at me a little suspiciously. I made a point of moving in a way that could only be interpreted as sober and dignified. After all, mystifying incident or not, I still had shopping to do.

This was a wonderfully strange, truly bizarre incident, but it was just one of a series of many odd things that began to happen with increasing regularity. Before Andrea was even a year old, another unusual encounter occurred with an older couple that evoked a strange sensation in both Robert and me, and caused me to remember the incident in the store and think of them as being somehow related.

We were living in Southern California at the time, having moved there from Reno for business reasons, and were out for an early Saturday morning stroll with Andrea in Malibu. This was a regular part of our routine since, as young parents, we were always looking for something inexpensive to do on the weekends, which was no mean feat in Los Angeles. A long walk through a pretty area, with the beauty of the ocean close by, fit the bill perfectly.

It was one of those indescribably beautiful California days, with blue sky and mild temperatures, and the ocean was particularly radiant, sunlight shimmering across the endless expanse of breaking waves. We had wandered into one of those quaint little shopping centers that seem to dot coastlines everywhere. Peeking in and out of the various stores as we pushed Andrea along in her stroller, we slowly made our way along the boarded sidewalk.

After a time, my attention was drawn to the presence of an older couple strolling the mall with us who, with strange but consistent timing, always seemed to be just a step or two behind us. Or, looking up, I would find them watching us intently from a bench as we sauntered past.

They were memorable to me, and I kept noticing them, because they were striking in an ageless sort of way. They both had lovely eyes, and soft expressions to their faces, as though their seemingly long lives had left just the gentlest of imprints.

After about an hour of this sort of serendipitous game of tag, during which we'd all exchanged smiles and nods several times, Robert, Andrea, and I finally found ourselves standing face to face with the couple on a walkway that was too narrow for anyone to be able to pass. I started to move to the side with the stroller so they could move around us more easily, but the man, smiling gently, stepped in front of me and stood in such a way that I had to stop again as well. His wife stepped to his side then, taking his arm, and just as I thought we were all going to squeeze by each other, the two of them just stood there, looking down at our baby.

They each had a sort of look on their faces that parents everywhere would recognize, and Robert and I both smiled at them. We were enjoying our new roles as parents tremendously, and thoroughly understood the kind of nostalgia that older parents might feel. We were delighted to share the joy of family with this lovely couple, for a moment or two. But then the old gentleman surprised us.

"She's a very, very old soul. Do you know that?" He asked this gently, glancing up at us. Then, smiling, he looked back down at our baby and his surprisingly vivid blue eyes held a look of intense admiration and unmistakable kindness.

I have to admit that he caught Robert and me a bit off guard. Even though we were familiar with Eastern philosophy, it was still a little disconcerting to have the topic broached in such a casual way, between strangers, in the middle of an outdoor shopping mall.

His comment was in reference to the Eastern belief that a soul is on a journey of discovery and it returns to the Earth as many times as it takes to complete the process. An old soul is considered to be someone who has passed through eons of experiences, accumulated through many lifetimes, and can be at a point of great accomplishment in the cosmic wheel of incarnations.

This man and his wife, who looked like the quintessential Western couple, were speaking to us about a very metaphysical topic. And this was occurring during a period that definitely pre-dated all the "New Age" usage of jargon that has become so familiar to us now. What was most striking about the whole encounter was the couple's obvious intense desire to make us understand something about our own baby, and this feeling was palpable as we stood together on the walkway. I realized then that it was no coincidence that they were observing us and staying close by since we'd first seen them at the shopping center.

Robert and I were both processing the situation and trying to figure out what, exactly, this whole thing was all about. We both laughed a little then, self-consciously, and murmured our acknowledgement that we thought our baby was, in fact, very special. We had apparently both decided to take his comments at face value. Since I did not then, and still do not now, personally know any parents who do not think of their baby as sublimely special, this was an entirely appropriate response. But the man was apparently not going to be easily placated by banal pleasantries.

"No, she's really very, very special. Do you know what I'm trying to tell you?" He asked this while looking at us both now, with something that almost resembled urgency in his eyes. By this time he certainly had our attention, and I saw a little flicker of concern pass over Robert's face. The only thing that argued against any notion of questionable sanity was the fact that he and his wife were the epitome of genteel respectability. They were reassuringly normal in every aspect of their mutual demeanor, and the only irregularity lay in the overly focused manner in which he was trying to convey something to us.

As he still made no move to let us pass and continued to look at the three of us so intently, it was obvious, whatever he was about, that the old fellow meant business. It occurs to me now that other shoppers had to be making their way around us, but in an eerie recurrence of my other shopping experience, I don't recall anyone but these two people standing with us as we shared some strange moment in time.

Something must have clicked for Robert and me at about the same time, because the significance of the situation finally registered for both of us. We looked at them with as much respectful regard as they'd been directing toward us, and with undiluted sincerity gave them the indication of acknowledgement they had apparently been waiting for.

"Yes," Robert finally said. "We know what it is you're trying to say to us."

The husband turned and looked at his wife and she smiled and nodded at him as though satisfied by our response.

"Good," he stated with emphasis, satisfied at last. And looking back down at Andrea one last time, "So special."

With that, the man bowed gently to us, then they both turned and walked slowly off down the path, in the same direction they had come from.

Robert spoke first. "Well, that was certainly strange."

I was aware now of all the people milling around us on the walkway and wondered where they had been just a moment before. We both turned and looked in the direction the older couple had walked away toward and, predictably, did not see them.

"Where'd they go?" Robert asked, genuinely perplexed, as he turned and glanced in both directions. "How'd they move away so quickly?"

I smiled lightly and took hold of the stroller handle and began to push it along. "They're gone."

For the rest of that morning, our path never again crossed with that of the old couple, but they certainly left a large imprint of their presence on both our minds. The whole episode had also served to provide us with the experience of a different kind of cosmic "leap."

chapter six

WE FOUND OURSELVES in Southern California when Andrea was about ten months old because of a number of issues that necessitated a fundamental change in some parts of our lives. With a new baby, we had been shifting from one idea to the next in a search for some type of work that would not include constant traveling. The economy had taken a dip around this same time, and it was definitely a challenge trying to find a career niche. Now that we were no longer performing together, Robert's heart was not into going out and putting together a new band, so when an opportunity arose for him to take a position at a television station in Los Angeles, we decided to take the plunge. Before we had an opportunity to change our minds, we were packed into a moving van and heading to Southern California.

For the next couple of years, we had a bit of a struggle learning to adapt to the change of moving from a fairly small community like Reno to the enormous metropolis that is L.A. While Robert was busy learning all about the media business, I did part-time work at the station in the public relations department. The company was forward-thinking enough to allow me to bring a playpen to the office, so I did not have to leave Andrea with a babysitter.

She was keeping me very busy, and I was quickly learning why new mothers always have the same exhausted look on their faces. It didn't help that Los Angeles can feel pretty lonely, and we found that making new acquaintances with a new baby can be a challenge. While potential friends without children wanted to party the night away, we could barely keep our eyes open.

There was also the fact that the sheer number of people in Southern California, even at that time, tended to create an insular type of environment. A clear example of this phenomenon was the fact that even though we lived on the same street for two years, we did not know even one (!) of our neighbors. People never stopped for a chat or strolled over to an adjoining yard on a warm summer evening, and no one encouraged neighborly familiarity. It was very isolating, and hard to get used to.

I took Andrea for a walk around the neighborhood every day, and I was always amazed that no one seemed to have the slightest interest in talking to either one of us. The only time I recall anyone actually speaking to me was one day when Andrea, with her little, unstable, toddling steps, accidentally wavered onto a lawn before I could reach down and steer her in the right direction. Immediately a door was thrown open and an older women proceeded to shout at us with righteous indignation: " No trespassing! Get off my grass!" I quickly picked Andrea up and got us out of earshot.

Needless to say, it didn't feel like a very hospitable environment in which to raise a child. I had grown up on a large farm with my Italian relatives all living within (pleasant) shouting range, and L.A. felt huge and unfriendly to me.

All these factors made me very receptive when I received a call one day from an acquaintance made through the television station. I thought she was a very pleasant person, and I responded readily when she told me she had met someone whom she thought I might also enjoy, especially when she provided me with a few details.

The person she wanted me to meet was a doctor, visiting from India, who, as my friend related, had the extraordinary ability to discern a patient's health through just feeling the pulse.

It happened that, a few days before, Robert and I had found out that I was pregnant with our second child. We had told no one since I was only about six weeks along, and we were still adjusting to the concept of this surprise addition to our family. Since I have always been interested in any issue concerning health, my friend's visitor was intriguing, but the fact that I was pregnant at that particular time made his visit all the more relevant.

That afternoon, I met my friend at an office where several other people were also waiting to see the doctor from India. At our inquiry, the woman at the desk told us we were welcome to make a small donation to help defray some of the expenses incurred through the doctor's visit to the U.S., but other than that, there would be no fee. After speaking with her, there was nothing else to do while we waited. No forms to fill out, no nurse to take your weight and history. It was all so different from what I was used to with traditional medicine, but my friend assured me this would be an experience I would remember.

I was soon shown into a smaller room and directed to a chair. My friend was going to wait for me outside. Before long, the doctor came in, and nodding pleasantly, he shook my hand and took a seat across from me at a desk. He was a small Indian man, dressed nicely in a business suit, with a white medical jacket over that. Since I had been told his English was limited, I was originally a little concerned about how we would communicate, but he had such an air of confidence about him from the moment he walked into the room, I relaxed and figured we would somehow work it out. He had a very kind face and I liked his manner immediately.

He raised his hands and, gesturing, indicated that I should lift my arms onto the desk. He took both my wrists and held them gently, with his fingers at specific points, and not really knowing what to expect, I waited for the next instructions. To my surprise, there didn't seem to be any. He just sat very quietly and closed his eyes. I tried willing myself to relax so that whatever he was feeling from my pulse would be positive and not influenced by nervousness, but it was somewhat disconcerting to just sit in the chair, perfectly still, with this man holding my wrists and not saying a word to me.

Eventually he sat straight up and, opening his eyes, let go of my wrists. He rubbed his hands together and smiled at me, but this time his smile had lost a little of the original confidence. That was a bit unsettling to me and, even worse, as I noticed the expression in his eyes, I realized that the good doctor was now looking downright uneasy!

Needless to say, I felt more than a little trepidation. I frantically cast about in my mind for exactly what my friend had told me to expect from my visit with this doctor. I nervously remembered that she said he was an Ayurvedic physician with more than thirty years' experience, and that he could tell what your health was from just feeling your pulse. Considering the look he'd just given me, what did that mean? Was he feeling something bad? When I had entered the room, I felt so confident, but now I was definitely experiencing a growing sense of uneasiness. This was not at all the way I'd envisioned my visit going.

Motioning for me to once again raise my arms, the doctor felt my pulse when I lifted my wrists. After what seemed like a very long time but was, in fact, probably only a few moments, the Indian doctor's face suddenly cleared, and with a huge sigh of relief he let go of my wrists and sat back in his chair.

"You're pregnant!" he stated, in heavily accented English, but his tone left no doubt that I was being mildly chastened. He had a slightly scolding look on his face, as though I had tried to keep something from him, but he had figured out the puzzle. It was as though I, as one of his first American patients, tried to intentionally discombobulate him with my unusual pulse, until he realized I was pregnant, and then everything once again made sense.

I was absolutely astonished. This slight, quiet man, with his neat dark suit and soft mannerisms, was able to tell that I was pregnant by simply feeling my pulse? What kind of medicine was this? It seemed like magic, more than medicine, so different from the type of medical treatment I was accustomed to, with the sharp needles, prodding hands, and aggressive, invasive exams.

But he did seem slightly irritated with me, and I explained, very simply, that I didn't know my early pregnancy would have any effect on his diagnosis. He nodded his understanding and resumed his original composure, as he smiled and proceeded to write down some herbs and diet adjustments he was suggesting for the remainder of my pregnancy, as well as afterward.

I, meanwhile, was flabbergasted by the powerful subtlety of the healing art this man practiced with such competence. If this doctor could tell I was expecting a baby by something as simple as feeling my pulse, I was definitely interested in what else he had to say. He saw my genuine astonishment at his diagnosis and realized that I had not intentionally omitted information.

As my "exam" continued, he demonstrated an amazing knowledge of my past health history. He could tell things from my pulse that a doctor of Western medicine would not have been able to see even with a battery of tests. It was as though, almost instantly and with amazing accuracy, he knew things about me on a level I barely understood myself.

It was funny, actually, that the doctor initially acted as though I had tried to pull something over on him, when he was the one who pulled a fast one on me! I had certainly not expected a medical demonstration of such subtle brilliance when I walked into the room that day. I had not expected to have my interest in the type of medicine he practiced piqued to the point where I immediately went out and searched for every book I could possibly find on the subject. I did not expect that, as a result of our brief encounter, I would begin to study Ayurveda in earnest and would eventually completely incorporate that knowledge into my family's lifestyle.

In other words, I had no idea that this man from India was going to be responsible for introducing me to a life path I would be walking down from that point on.

[c h a p t e r   s e v e n]

LIFE EXPERIENCES COME IN MANY FLAVORS, and not all of them have that obvious dash of drama that seems to change one's life in such sensational ways. A lot of what life does offer, though, can have a quality of plain old hilarity to it, affecting and changing our lives through the subtle influences of laughter and amusement. This just also happens to be the stuff of which great stories are made, and I have one, in particular, that is a personal favorite.

A specific incident stands out in my mind surrounding the birth of Sara Anjuli, our second daughter. We had moved back to Reno by this time, because we both wanted to be in a more nurturing environment with our new baby. Just negotiating a visit to the obstetrician was a daunting task in Los Angeles, and the thought of being able to drive around a town without having to sit on a freeway for most of the day was extremely appealing. I also missed my South African friend and couldn't imagine having a baby without him in attendance.

By this time, I felt about as big as the proverbial "house," and as my due date drew nearer, I think there was more than a passing resemblance to one, too. It was disconcerting that, during my prenatal checkups, the doctor would shake his head and mumble something like "this is going to be a ten-pounder for sure." It always made me feel as though I were on a fishing trip, rather than lying on a hard table with a nurse smiling down at me in empathy.

59

On my exact due date, my reproductive system proved to be as reliable as a Swiss clock, because my pains started early in the morning and I labored with increasing intensity through the rest of the day. I felt no sense of panic, having been through this whole thing once before, and my pains remained about five minutes apart for most of the time so I could still function fairly well. I helped Andrea pack her little overnight bag for her visit to her grandparents' house, and even drove with Robert to drop her off. It had been prearranged that my parents would take care of her when the time came for me to deliver, so, satisfied with big hugs, kisses, and our promises to call, she disappeared inside.

We finally reached the hospital about 6:00 P.M. Considering the fact that I'd been in labor since early that morning, I was feeling very pleased with my lack of urgency, and my calmness conveyed itself to Robert because he was acting like a comfortable old hand with this expectant father thing. No frantic drive to the hospital for us, with both parties hysterical with stress! We were doing all of this in a very civilized fashion, and I congratulated myself on our combined aplomb. I had no idea that events were getting ready to go ricocheting off in some very unexpected directions, and my sense of calm capability was about to do a sharp U-turn.

By the time I pulled myself onto a bed and lay waiting for someone to "check" me, I had started to feel pretty worn out. There had been no meals since morning because of the rules about eating while in labor. The concern had to do with whether anesthesia would need to be administered on a woman with a stomach full of food, should an emergency C-section be required, so I'd been sparse with my snacks. I was now feeling the loss of all the expended energy from my many hours of labor. There was also the very real concern about my "ten-pounder," and as I rode labor pain after labor pain and felt my body preparing for the ordeal of birth, I was happy to be at the hospital instead of at home, risking the possibility of a C-section.

When a nurse finally came into the room, my sense of fatigue was really settling in, and I was definitely ready to get the whole thing formally under way. I was not prepared for the nurse's next comment, however, nor for her extraordinary bedside manner.

Taking one look at me, she glanced at the other nurse who had walked in with her and, not bothering to address her comments to me at all, mumbled something about first-time mothers, shaking her head with apparent disdain.

I protested, in a somewhat muted voice since I was in the middle of another contraction, that this wasn't my first time.

To which she responded with barely veiled hostility, "Well, honey, then you should know better than to get so worked up about a couple of pains."

I tried to tell her that I had been in labor since early that morning, but she wasn't listening. She gave me a cursory exam, snapped off the glove, and declared that I wasn't having this baby today, or anytime in the next twenty-four hours. Period. I should go back home and wait until "something real" happened.

I couldn't believe what I was hearing, and Robert, who had been standing quietly at the side of the room, tried to talk to the nurse while I grimaced through another pain.

"She's been in labor all day," he said, starting to get a little nervous now, because he fully realized exactly how tired I was. "Are you sure we should go home? My wife is pretty good about this kind of thing, and we didn't even come here until she felt it was absolutely necessary."

To which the nurse replied, her voice oozing impatient sarcasm, "I'm sorry if she can't take the discomfort of a few pains. But she's not having a baby now, so you should just take her home."

I was in no shape to argue, much less to analyze the situation, and felt that it was possible I had, in fact, misgauged the whole thing. I took umbrage at the "she can't take a few pains" part, because I felt I had been extremely stoic about my discomfort throughout the long and arduous day, but it was no more than a fleeting feeling as I was once again riding a wave of pain. As the pain crested and receded into a haze of tiredness, I gathered together my remaining reserves and prepared to head home. I told Robert that she might be seeing something, with her vast experience, that wasn't clear to me, because I was so involved in the actual process.

Robert picked up my maternity bag, and we left the hospital, moving very slowly the whole time. Walking was pretty miserable by now, and I thought about going back, but the nurse's parting comment—"You really should know better if you've been through this before"—was enough to stiffen my resolve to not return until it was completely necessary.

We drove home in silence: me, because the pains were getting really intense, and Robert, because he could tell I was conserving my energy. If I wasn't even close to having this baby, and I was already so worn out, it was going to take every bit of strength I had to get through the next day or so.

We didn't go pick up Andrea since it was almost her bedtime, but instead just phoned my parents to tell them it was a false alarm. With both of us tromping slowly and dejectedly into the house, dread of the long night ahead reflected in both our attitudes, Robert set down my bag and turned on the TV, trying for some distraction. Realizing we had nothing in the house for dinner, he jumped up and said he would quickly run out and get something at the grocery store. I went into the bedroom to change into my pajamas.

Within two minutes of Robert leaving, it became apparent that I was in very big trouble. The pains were so intense I couldn't stand, and I was literally caught with my pants down. With no way to even make it to a phone, I realized through a foggy wall of discomfort that I was going to be on my way back to the hospital right away, so I should try and get my clothes back on. The pains were now hitting about one minute apart, one wave ending as the next was beginning, and I realized it was not even a possibility that I could dress myself.

There was also the very dismal realization that I was completely alone until Robert returned from the store. I fought to control the feeling of panic that was threatening to overwhelm me, and tried to slow my breathing, repeating, "he'll be back, he'll be back" over and over again, like a life-saving mantra. I watched the door intently, willing it to open, with the words sounding more like a prayer with each passing minute.

When Robert finally walked through the door, the relief on my face must have told him everything because he just set down the grocery bag and came to help me. I gestured toward my clothes, but he shook his head and took my arm. I was having an awful time walking, with the pains coming so fast I could barely move, so he tried, with an admirable dose of husbandly optimism, to pick me up. Unfortunately, the operative word here is "tried." Robert is a good-sized guy, but I was a very ungainly load, all belly and misery. Finally giving up, he half-dragged, half-carried me to the car and helped me squeeze inside.

It was then that I noticed the snow. Big, billowy clouds of fluff descending on our car so fast that the windshield was already covered over in the couple of minutes since Robert arrived in the driveway. The conditions were a virtual whiteout.

By the time we reached the freeway, Robert was in a state of frantic self-control, leaning so far forward to try and see that his nose was practically touching the windshield. Every few seconds his head would swivel toward me before returning quickly to the difficult task of driving, as it was becoming extremely doubtful that I was going to make it to the hospital in time to deliver this baby.

"The … baby … is … coming" was all I could manage to squeeze out between clenched teeth. With such intense contractions demanding 100% of my focused attention, it was a battle trying to keep this baby from being born on the freeway, in one of the worst blizzards I'd ever seen. The snow was swirling down around us, enveloping our car as we fought our way down the road, only able to crawl at ten miles an hour. Even though we were barely able to see a foot in front of us, it felt as though we were the only souls on Earth at that moment, since the road was completely deserted. Robert fought to control his own panic, and we both struggled to maintain a semblance of calm.

"Don't you dare," he said, in reference to the bleak prospect of having to help me manage a birth in the middle of a blizzard, on a freeway. "You can do this, Linda." He tried saying this with forceful conviction, attempting to override the fear. "You can keep that baby from coming out." Even through the haze of pain I managed a grim smile, his comment striking me as something that could only be uttered by someone who'd never actually tried to keep a ten-pound watermelon inside his body after the signal had been given for it to get out!

After what seemed like an eternity, the barely visible exit for the hospital finally loomed ahead. It sounds trite, but that was such a welcome vision, I felt weak with gratitude. The baby was pushing so hard to get out that, by that time, I was practically turning blue from the effort of trying not to bear down. We pulled around to the back of the hospital and frantically tried to find the emergency doors though the snow.

By this time, Robert was literally in a cold sweat, in spite of the temperature outside, and he strained to find the entrance, driving slowly and even rolling down the window to swipe at the snow the overworked wipers were leaving behind. At some point he started looking for any entrance that we could use. The hospital was under remodeling construction, so none of the existing signs were accurate, and the construction signs weren't visible in the storm. He finally saw something, and pulling the car as close as he could, jumped out to get help. He couldn't find his footing on the snowy pavement but ran anyway, and wound up doing a first-base slide up to the door. He put his hands up to the glass and peered in, but it was obvious, even through my fog of discomfort, that he wasn't happy with what he saw.

At this point something must have snapped for Robert, because he suddenly threw all sense of decorum aside and started to yell at the top of his lungs, while pounding hard on the door. Every aspect of the circumspect man I married completely vanished, and was replaced by a very resolute person who was going to get through that door, no matter what it took.

It was simply unbelievable to me that, after all this, we could not find a way to get into the building. It was a mystery how the hospital had suddenly turned into a fortress that a person had to fight to get into. Where was that dastardly nurse, I wondered, as I spiraled into yet another contraction.

Somewhere along here, I must have entered into that special place where reality gets suspended because the body starts releasing serotonin in response to the pain. Suddenly, as I focused my blurred vision on my distraught husband and realized what he was actually doing, it all became too much. Dissolving into helpless laughter, interspersed with low groans of agony as each labor pain rolled through, I tried pounding on the windshield, but Robert didn't hear me.

I even tried to reach over and honk the horn but I couldn't seem to make it work from the angle I was at. The harder he pounded and the louder he shouted, the more I laughed, and the more I laughed the more the pain fought for control. I couldn't communicate the reason for my helpless hilarity until he finally turned frantically around, his face painted with a miserable look of "what do I do now?"

At that point, I was finally able to point at the door he'd been pounding at with such desperation. Confused at my signals, at first he just looked frustrated, but then, when he turned and actually looked at the door, he caught the full impact of the futility of his actions. Posted on the door, in large letters, were the words HOSPITAL MORTUARY. Well, that certainly did explain the lack of response.

Sliding back to the car, his face beet-red from frustration or embarrassment, or probably a combination of both, Robert threw the car into reverse and backed out, all the while nervously glancing at me as I wiped the tears of laughter off my face. It occurred to me that he was afraid it had all been too much and I'd finally lost it, but every time I tried to explain how ridiculous this whole thing was starting to look to me, a fresh onset of pain silenced my words.

Once again we started looking for the emergency room door. The healthy dose of laughter must have had some kind of rejuvenative effect on me, because I decided that something had to give and it wasn't going to be me. That nurse would not be the reason I gave birth to my baby in a car.

"Drive to the front of the hospital," I told Robert.

"Why? What? What good is that going to do? You can't make it up the steps! And there's no place to park!"

"Yes, I can. Just get me to the front of the hospital." It's amazing what feats we feel we can accomplish when adrenaline starts surging.

Robert pulled up to the curb. The front doors to the hospital were just barely visible through the blizzard, but I rallied all my confidence and remaining strength, and hoisted myself out of the car.

"What are you doing? I can't carry you! Hey, what are you doing?! You're going to have that baby on the front lawn!" I could hear Robert's voice, rising with hysteria, even as I steeled myself for the task ahead. Those few hundred feet looked like Mount Everest from where I stood. But I knew I had no choice. I couldn't sit in that car, helplessly, for one more minute.

"Go park the car and come upstairs," I shouted over my shoulder between contractions. Then I gave my full attention to the task at hand. Step, step, stop. Wait for the pain to pass, then step, step, stop, and so on, and so on, all the way to the stairs. I won't say those fifteen or so steps didn't look impossible to me from where I was standing, but I gritted my teeth, took a deep breath, and started up.

After about four stops, and so much deep breathing I thought I'd faint from hyperventilation, I was shocked to find that I'd actually made it to the doors. Opening them and stepping inside, I was assailed by an overwhelming sense of relief and accomplishment. The woman at the front desk took one look at me and yelled to someone I couldn't see, "We have a baby coming! Get a gurney!"

Following a quick ride upstairs, during which time I felt a true sense of peace come over me that I was not going to expose my baby to the dangers of a snowstorm birth, I was wheeled out of the elevator, only to have my newfound sense of equanimity quickly destroyed. The very same nurse who'd sent me home less than an hour before stood looking down at me, clucking her displeasure.

"You're back again? Didn't you believe me when I said that baby was not coming tonight?"

The orderly pushing the gurney asked for help transferring me to a bed, and the nurse continued to shake her head at me, even while helping the attendant. Too exhausted to say a word, I knew it was way past the point where explanations were necessary. The truth of the situation would rise to my defense with far more eloquence than I could possibly muster at that moment.

The nurse did not even have time to examine me. Finally focusing on the situation rather than on the need to reprimand me, she took one look and her head went shooting up, as she shouted to anyone who could hear. "We need a bassinet! RIGHT NOW!"

As circumstances would have it (!), my doctor was walking by at that exact second. He was dressed in his street clothes, ready to head home for the day, when the nurse literally grabbed him by the arm and pulled him into the room.

I could hear her frantic whisper, "The baby's head is already crowning!" At this point, I had only been in the hospital for a total of maybe three or four minutes.

Robert finally came running in, snow-covered and anxious, and the nurse looked over at him nervously. He glared back at her.

My doctor, who was true to his philosophy of "least interference," even under circumstances that could have induced a more exaggerated response, walked into the room with an air of quiet competence that immediately stilled the nurse's nervous prattling. Even though she obviously felt responsible for almost having me drop the baby out as I walked into the hospital, it was clear to him that the situation was taking care of itself, and he would just assist.

When he saw who it was that was actually in the situation, he just smiled broadly at me and rolled up his sleeves. There was no time to even put on a pair of gloves, so he literally reached up and just caught the baby's head as it practically came shooting out.

And this was where my doctor's reputation as a very caring physician really came into play. He loved the entire birthing experience so much that he always let the parents be as involved in the process as possible, and even under such rushed circumstances, he still wanted us to savor the specialness of the moment.

"Linda! Look down!" His voice came to me from the side of the bed. There hadn't even been time to detach the bottom part of it, as is normally done for childbirth, so he was positioned a little awkwardly, leaning over. At this point, there were several other nurses in the room, including the one who had heard the initial comments when we'd first been sent home. I noticed her giving the other, older nurse looks of extreme displeasure when she walked into the room and realized who we were.

"What?" I asked, from my exhausted position on the bed. I was reveling in the blissful post-labor state, which was even more pronounced due to my grateful happiness that things had turned out ok.

"Look down. Your baby's looking for you." Not really understanding what the doctor was saying, I pushed myself up onto my elbows and proceeded to have one of the most surreal experiences of my life. With just the head and shoulders delivered, and the doctor's hand beneath the baby's head, our daughter was, literally, looking me right in the face.

No crying or screaming, just a lovely little face gazing serenely back at me. I could only smile through the haze of tears, but I will never forget the experience of that moment. There was something about the sweetness of her face with its unnervingly peaceful expression that made the moment intensely poignant. We could clearly feel that this baby was going to have a very special role to play in our lives, but she was announcing her entrance into this world in the most strikingly calm fashion. That characteristic would remain her signature in all that was to come.

Aside from falling in love with our new baby, Robert and I were also having to assimilate the fact that we were re-living the same phenomenon as when Andrea was born, but this time, there was the clarity of past experience. Robert and I looked at each other, then back down at our baby, and I knew he was hearing that buzzing sound again, just as I was. The whole place vibrated with the intensity of it, and I found myself wondering if anyone else could hear it.

All the people in the room seemed to be moving with a kind of elevated grace, smiling and laughing softly, as though subconsciously reacting to the feeling permeating the surroundings. There was a soft glow of joy, and it was clear that we were experiencing the sound of a new spirit coming into the world and observing a sort of heraldry of heavenly vibrations.

Everyone was responding to the magic of the moment. The feeling of love in the room was palpable, and the sensation of joy was full to overflowing. I felt as though when the door opened, the entire hospital would be bathed in its residue.

The doctor looked at me and smiled.

"What's her name?"

"Sara Anjuli," I answered, my voice husky with overwhelming happiness.

"Well, Sara Anjuli," he said, looking down at her sweet face. "Welcome to the world."

chapter eight

ONE OF THE MANY SURPRISES that parents experience is that their offspring bring their own life agendas along with them when they arrive. As parents, we tend to think of our child as an extension of ourselves, but that is accurate only up to a point. They may have our DNA and be linked to us through genetic codes, but that only means they'll have hair like Grandpa, or maybe our walk or a few of our gestures. The really important parts of their being will be uniquely theirs, and it is our job to recognize our children's special life expression and help them discover for themselves what that is. This is the true joy of raising children.

Who will these children grow up to be, and what gifts will they bring as their contribution to this world? The most important question parents can ask themselves is what they can do to help their child realize the potential they came into this life with. The parents' accumulated knowledge can be shared to help the child on his or her own journey.

With all the concerns over finances and time-management that have to be addressed, these are some of the more philosophical questions new parents find themselves contemplating during the long wait of pregnancy, but especially after, when the new baby arrives.

It isn't long, however, before the busy reality of dealing with an infant, then a toddler, and then a precocious older child pushes the time for luxurious contemplation to a very far-removed back burner!

The day-to-day effort to take care of children, make a living, run a house, as well as the struggle to find an extra bit of energy to invest back into the marriage, not to mention the spare two or three minutes to squander on yourself, quickly becomes a familiar balancing act.

Raising children is, flat-out, a huge amount of work. But how fortunate for us all that Nature, with its infinite ability to create balance, also makes a child the largest reservoir of joy a person can experience within a lifetime.

With all that must be addressed daily in a family, it is amazing how most parents still somehow manage to function with the prevailing awareness that it is not just our job to grow a child, but to also nurture a spirit. We give our children vitamins and make sure they get good food and exercise, but it is crucial that we also remind ourselves that there is a little soul inside that growing body that needs nourishment as well. Overextended parents may not think about that aspect of their child's growth as constantly as they think about schoolwork or soccer practice, but it is an unacknowledged truth that parents do contemplate the subtler aspects of their child's development more often than busy schedules might indicate. Most parents have an inherent desire to help their children be all they can, both physically and spiritually.

That desire may manifest in unexpected ways. We may not think of our actions as being spiritually motivated, but every time we try to give our children an example of correct behavior or right action, we are also trying to establish in them some kind of moral compass to serve as a guidance system later in life. This is usually done automatically, without the parent being completely cognizant of this mechanism of support.

The practice of religion or the sharing of spiritual philosophies can be some of the ways parents help children formulate thoughts and ideas and concepts that will help them grow to be strong adults. This was the case in our house, and the topic of God was certainly a major part of many early discussions in our home as Robert and I tried to lay the groundwork for a rich and well-rounded family life.

That practice has stayed consistent for us through the years, and as our family has grown, our children became active participants in discussions that ranged the globe with regard to cultural and spiritual anthropology. It was an endless source of fascination to them to learn how various peoples worshipped and honored God.

It became quickly apparent that Robert and I both enjoyed the process of exposing our children to a rich variety of philosophies, and, for them, some aspect of each and every day was tied to the contemplation of God. We certainly had no desire to confuse them, but rather to make them comfortable with the concept that there was more than one way to honor the Divine, and we found that as our family allowed that aspect of life to overlap our more mundane pursuits, the happier everyone was. It provided a fullness and richness that fostered acceptance and tolerance. The intention, I suppose, was to discuss everything and to be afraid of nothing. Our loose philosophy was that no point of view should be feared or considered threatening. Rather, we hoped that discussion and understanding would serve to strengthen our children's sense of belonging, and along with the resulting confidence, give them a sense of security with regard to their own place in the world.

There was a concerted effort to never let any discussion lapse into an attitude of "preaching," because it had been our experience that children as well as adults become quickly disenchanted and begin to think of God as a burden when spirituality is packaged in an overbearing manner. Also, since there is probably nothing more destructive one can do to a child's spiritual growth than to instill in them a feeling of self-righteousness, our goal became to just have fun while embracing the vast richness of spirituality that is present everywhere, and our children responded with characteristically youthful exuberance.

In the pursuit of diversity, it was easy enough to expose the girls to the Western religious viewpoint. I was raised as a Catholic, so it was natural for me to familiarize them with that aspect of Western religion. Robert's father was in the military, so he had spent some of his childhood in the Far East, and because of that experience, Robert had developed a fairly extensive background of Eastern knowledge.

We made great events out of religious holidays, with special meals and attendance at the various religious functions, followed, as always, by lots of discussion and stories. Andrea and Sara loved the tradition and pageantry of the Catholic mass, but they also loved the exotic beauty of the Eastern traditions. We found that the exploration of spirit enriched the holidays in immeasurable ways. We still observed the giving of presents and candy, but the spiritual foundation was always something that stayed around far longer than the melted chocolate or the broken train.

On a regular basis, various Eastern teachers and priests came to town to officiate at various celebrations and functions, and we were regularly invited to attend. We discovered that there is nothing people love so much as sharing their own cherished traditions, so our family was given access to many different positive religious experiences, and each one became a part of the mosaic of our family's spiritual journey. Many, many of the people we met at that time are still a part of our lives today.

It seemed there was always some lavish celebration or prayer of thanksgiving going on, and the girls loved the pageantry and joy present at the different functions. There was one particular event, though, that distinctly stands out in my mind, because it actually was a marking post on the path of the odyssey that is still ongoing.

An Eastern ceremony of thanks, called a *puja*, was to be performed, and we were invited because some friends of ours were going and had put in a good word for us with the people who were hosting the event at their home. It was a lovely ceremony, really an interesting exposure to Eastern traditions, but about halfway through, the East Indian gentleman who was officiating invited the girls to come up and assist him. That small act was the beginning of a lifelong love affair for the girls.

The girls thoroughly enjoyed being part of the ceremonial process, handing the holy man the requested flowers and oil, but as cute as their participation was, that was not what most stands out in my memory. The really startling thing was the way Andrea responded to the language that the ceremony was being conducted in.

As soon as the pundit, or priest, started speaking in Sanskrit, the ancient language usually used for these types of Eastern religious events, she was completely enraptured. Sara was still very little, only about four, so she was mostly concerned with keeping her footing and not falling with the flowers, but Andrea, who was six at this time, couldn't stop staring at the pundit, her eyes round with fascination. She had a look of complete absorption on her face, and seemed genuinely disconcerted by the chanting the priest was doing.

After the ceremony was over, she ran to me and breathlessly tried to convey just how much she loved "those words." Andrea simply couldn't contain her excitement, and she seemed almost upset with the urgency of expressing to me how beautiful she thought the whole thing to be. She kept saying how much she "loved hearing him chant that language" and asked repeatedly, on our way home, when we would come do it again.

I found myself laughing a little at her reaction, and answered that we could probably come again sometime soon, but I was slightly taken aback by her exuberance. Given that the event had been a fairly long affair, taking up most of the afternoon, I fully expected her to be tired and ready to go home, rather than so anxious about repeating the experience.

Our next surprising exposure to Sanskrit occurred about a year later. We were contacted because a group of East Indian musicians was touring the United States. These musicians were experts at playing the musical form of the *Vedas*, known as the *Gandharvas*. The pundits the girls met at the puja were scholars of the written form of the *Vedas*, or Sanskrit. Both Vedic musicians and pundits have chanted or played the *Vedas* in an ageless repetition of tradition that extends from father to son for generation after generation.

By this time in our lives, Robert had given up on doing anything besides music for a living and had put together the financing to build a recording studio. The goal was to be able to record his music without always having to leave town, and as an added benefit, the studio was large enough to rent out space for other musicians.

It was because of the studio that we received the call telling us that there were holy men from India in town, and they were requesting a recording session. Apparently, they wanted to record some of the ancient material they were playing at concert appearances throughout the U.S.

Indians are extremely family-oriented, so we didn't think the musicians would mind if our own two girls were in the studio that day. Given how much Andrea and Sara had loved the puja experience, we thought they would really enjoy getting to hear a private recital by this particular group.

When the Indians arrived, the girls found it all very exciting, especially when the musicians unpacked their traditional instruments. As we had correctly assumed, the gentlemen loved having children running about, and the family environment seemed to put them instantly at ease. They were enjoying the girls' company so much they even insisted that Andrea and Sara stay right in the recording studio with them while the recording session was going on.

This was a completely foreign approach to us, and in such direct contrast with the intense attitude we were used to from most Western musicians during recording sessions that we had to laugh. In fact, the pundits loved the girls so much, they had them sit right with them on cushions while they were playing their music, and the flutist even wound his arm around Sara so she could feel herself to be an actual participant in the music he was playing!

Andrea and Sara were enchanted by these kind men, as was everyone in the studio, and it made the experience of listening to their beautiful playing that much more enjoyable. The fact that they were so loving and relaxed about the whole recording process, displaying charming mannerisms and humble attitudes, made us all regard the session as a valuable cultural experience.

The hours spent with those musicians produced some of the finest examples of Indian musicianship we've ever had the pleasure to hear or record. It made me think that some part of their attitude must have transferred itself to the actual recording, because the sounds were unbelievably good. I'm sure there's a truism in there that we could all benefit from … less awareness of the self, and more enjoyment of the actual process, can give us the best possible results in all our endeavors.

After the recording session was done, we all sat around the control room chatting like old friends. They invited us to a concert they were giving that night at the local university, and we accepted with pleasure.

That night, we joined faculty, students, and other guests in the auditorium for a wonderful evening of traditional Indian music, and the girls, as well as the rest of the audience, sat transfixed as the musicians wound a powerful musical spell around everyone in the room. They played *ragas*, or pieces, from the *Gandharva Vedas*, and it was fascinating to watch how the musicians effortlessly followed one another, the goal always seeming to be to elevate their part of the whole rather than focusing the attention on themselves, individually. Interestingly, that selfless attitude only seemed to accentuate their individual talents, and the audience was mesmerized by the combined display of artistry. The overall impression was further enhanced by the feeling that the musicians were playing for something, or Someone, larger than themselves.

As the last note died away, we all sat perfectly quiet for a moment, reluctant to have the experience end. No one was quite ready to let it go, but we all expressed our appreciation of the concert with thunderous applause. The musicians smiled graciously and stood to accept the unabashed approval of the American audience.

In the car on the way home, Andrea and Sara raved on and on about how wonderful the music "made you feel," and though I didn't realize it at the time, the seeds of our future pathways had been nurtured just a little further along.

[c h a p t e r   n i n e]

IT WAS ABOUT NOW, in the family timetable of events, that things started to get really interesting around our house. I had been studying Ayurveda, the ancient healing art from India, since my first appointment with the Ayurvedic doctor years earlier, and I was constantly on the lookout for books on the subject wherever I could find them.

All that effort it took to gather information on Ayurveda back then makes me appreciate how much things have changed. I was eventually able to go on to study Ayurveda formally here in the U.S. It is easy to observe how drastic the societal change has been when one walks into any bookstore today and can find an entire cornucopia of Ayurvedic books, not to mention the huge assortment of Ayurvedic lotions, oils, and body care products offered in department stores everywhere.

Even with all these developments, I still found myself somewhat amazed the day I opened my e-mail and found a general solicitation from *The New York Times*, asking me to subscribe. One of the articles they included as an enticement promoted the benefits of Ayurveda! If someone had shown me that e-mail twenty-some years ago (well, in all fairness, if they'd shown me *any* e-mail!), I would have been totally shocked, and now here it was, just sitting in my in-box as part of a mass promotion!

I'm digressing a little, I realize, but it is fascinating to take a moment to look back at ideas that were once considered so exotic and strange that it was impossible to imagine them ever becoming a part of mainstream awareness. To realize that those same concepts have now become a broadly accepted aspect of everyday life is a definite challenge to what can sometimes be, for all of us, rather rigid notions of boundaries. The widespread acceptance of Ayurveda as a health support system is one such example of this phenomenon, but the larger point is an instance of obvious foreshadowing. If anyone had told me that Sanskrit, in such a relatively short period of time, would move from virtual obscurity to the astonishing position of becoming the world's language of spirituality, I would not have believed them.

Incorporating aspects of Ayurveda's wisdom was something I attempted to do whenever possible, and it was always fun to watch how the effort to make even small adjustments in daily habits could bring about such positive results. I used *abhyanga*, or Indian-style massage, on all of our babies, starting right after they were born, and continued with this practice for many years because they all loved it so much they just wouldn't let me stop!

Prior to pursuing Ayurveda in a classroom format, I made it a regular practice to read all that I could about it. I wound up collecting a fairly impressive selection of books on the subject. I kept the books on a shelf in our bedroom as I was constantly referring to one health question or another and wanted the books handy for easy reference.

One day when Andrea was nine years old, I came into my room and noticed that several of my books had "gone missing," and my first thought was that Robert had taken them for some reason. Everyone in the family knew how much I cherished my hard-found books on Ayurveda, so it didn't even occur to me that one of our children would be my book bandit.

One can only imagine the surprise I felt when later that same day I passed by Andrea's bedroom and saw her sitting on her bed, cross-legged, with one of my books opened across her lap. Her attention was completely captured by whatever she was looking at, and she didn't notice me, but I saw that some of my other books were scattered around her in casual disarray.

"Well, hello there." My voice probably had a little annoyance in it as I asked, "Andrea, what are you doing, honey?"

She seemed to take a little long to look up at me, her attention obviously still on whatever she'd been so engrossed in, and it took a moment before she actually focused on me standing there, in her doorway.

"Oh, hi, Mom," she said, slowly closing the book. "What's up?"

"Andrea, why do you have my books?" I asked, clearly concerned that she was so casual with the books that had been such a struggle for me to find.

I should clarify here that Andrea had never been one of those children that just loved to sit around for hours and hours, reading. *I* had been one of those kids, so I knew the symptoms, and was, in fact, a little frustrated that she didn't ever seem to want to get lost in a book for an afternoon. Robert and I were constantly reminding her to read, and her teachers in school wrote those dreaded notes in her report card margins insisting that we "make sure Andrea reads more." We both had come to the conclusion that the "reading gene" was on vacation when I got pregnant with her. Now the oddity of seeing her sitting on her bed, transfixed by a book, was enough to take the edge off my irritation over the fact that the book was one I really didn't want her to have! Especially considering that these particular books were Ayurvedic textbooks that could be boring for an adult to plow through, not to mention a child, and my ultimate goal was to get her to read something interesting if she was actually going to make the effort. There was also the fact that half of each page in the book she was holding was written in Devanagari script. I really could not imagine why she'd decided to go into my room and get these particular books, but the fact that she thought she was so interested in them was even stranger.

"Well, I'm reading them, Mom. They're really neat books," Andrea replied with a little impatience in her nine-year-old voice.

She somehow managed to convey the attitude that I was the one coming up short in this exchange, because I even had to ask why she was reading these books in the first place!

"OK, well, yes, they are interesting," I said, trying not to sound discouraging about any reading attempt she was willing to make. "But you shouldn't be reading those books, they're too hard. There are dozens of books in your bookcase that are perfect for you if you're in the mood to read." And then, seeing again how casually the books had been tossed onto her bed, "I don't want anything happening to those, honey, so go put those back in my room, please."

Andrea got up from her position on the bed reluctantly and, picking up the books carefully, made a great show of returning them to my room. I was not trying to be unfair with her, I simply thought that if she were finally going to make motions toward reading for entertainment, I wanted it to be with books that were enjoyable enough that she'd want to do it again and again. It never occurred to me that there was something else going on.

A few weeks later, almost the exact same tableau played itself out. I found the books missing, only this time I went directly to Andrea's room, and there she was, on her bed, again totally engrossed in one of my books.

"Andrea, what are you doing, honey? We just went through this! Why are you reading these books again? You put those back in my room right now. It's a beautiful day, anyway, and you shouldn't be holed up in your room. You go outside and play." I might have spoken a little sharply to her, but this was all getting to be a little annoying, not to mention somewhat strange.

I still had not observed her taking any interest in any of her own books, and she certainly had displayed none of the apparent relish she held in reserve for mine, so I knew there hadn't suddenly been an "I love reading" transformation in her. I even flipped open the book to the section she'd been looking at, and sure enough, the material was as dry as the desert air. The pages were full of factual Ayurvedic information that a nine-year-old child could not possibly find intriguing enough to stay inside for on a clear, sunny day at the beginning of summer.

I didn't think much more about it, though, as it was a busy day, and there was a lot to keep my attention away from Andrea's unusual reading predilection. That night, however, it all returned with a strange new twist.

"Mommy, which side of the page do you read?" Andrea asked me, coming into my room all wide-eyed and questioning, and once again holding one of my books open in her small hands.

I was putting lotion on my face, getting ready for bed after a long, tiring day, and I admit I wasn't in the mood for a debate with my precocious daughter about my "special books." Plus, I had no idea what she was asking me, and my exhausted mind could make no sense of her question.

"What? What do you mean 'what side'?"

"Well," Andrea responded, pointing to the page, "Do you read this side ..." then, moving her finger to the opposite columns on the page, "or do you read this side?"

My heart sank. Oh, my gosh, I thought to myself. This little girl is such a poor reader, she doesn't even realize that half of the page isn't in English. What made this fact more frightening to me was that the Devanagari script she was pointing at looked nothing at all like English, so she couldn't be accidentally mistaking the words the way, say, we might quickly look at a page of Italian or Spanish and see some recognizable word forms. My mind immediately jumped to thoughts of reading lessons and tutors for the remainder of the summer. I kept my voice level, but I was more than a little concerned at what I saw as blatant failure in Robert's and my roles as parents.

"Andrea, honey," I said calmly, while gently trying to extricate the book from her, which just caused her little hands to squeeze harder on the cover. "I read the side that's written in English, of course."

She looked at me indignantly, hearing in my response a not-so-subtle commentary on what I took to be a reading problem.

"Well, I *know* that part is English," Andrea said, in a tone of voice that reflected her thought that she might be the adult here, and I the child, but her voice was also very insistent. I sat down on the bed and gave her my full attention, since she was so intense in her behavior I realized it was not going to be a quick journey to bed.

"Why do you read that side if you want to study about Ayurveda?" she asked me, her face reflecting total sincerity. "You should read the language it was written in. Otherwise, you're just relying on someone else's translation. What if they didn't do it right?"

I sighed, and tried again. The day was feeling longer to me by the moment.

"Andrea, Ayurveda is hard enough to understand if I'm just reading it in English. And honey, that side of the page is written in Devanagari script," I said, pausing for emphasis here so Andrea would realize the obvious, "and Mommy [with an unspoken 'and you'] can't read it." I now pointed to the ancient script that was on one side of the page, then I moved my finger to the opposite, which was written in English, so she would see how very different the languages were.

I am probably starting to make myself seem pretty dense here, but my only defense is that a parent's expectations of their child, lofty though they may be, still usually fall within the framework of "normal." I was still definitely functioning in that mode. I had not yet made the transition to the "everything is possible" place that would, later on, become a familiar state in which to reside.

But right then, all that was about to change.

"I can read it, Mommy. You could, too, if you just tried. You should want to be able to, if you're going to study Ayurveda. That's the language it was written in, and you should read it for yourself, not have someone else read it for you, and then tell you what it says!"

"Andrea. You can't read this," I stated emphatically, gesturing toward the Devanagari script. I was going to make this point clear, once and for all. "No one could possibly read that by just looking at it a few times."

"Mommy," Andrea said, and she seemed to be every bit as impatient with me as I was with her. "I can read it."

With that as her closing statement, she took the book and put it on my shelf. She walked out of the room and left me staring after her, feeling completely bemused by whatever it was that just occurred. I stood there thinking, "What in the world just happened here?" And then, as an afterthought, "And what did she *mean* she could read it?"

For a moment I had a glimpse into the magical "field of all possibilities," but that was immediately followed by saner, less exalted thoughts, and I shook myself slightly, as if to return to the safety of more familiar terrain.

I crawled into bed thinking, "This child is going to have a concerted effort focused on her to help her read better. If Andrea actually thought she could read Sanskrit, a foreign script from a dead language, we are clearly in a lot more trouble than I originally thought." Fortunately for Robert, he was recording and would not come to bed for a while, or he would have received an earful about what we should have been doing for our daughter's horribly inadequate reading skills.

The months passed, and the family was preoccupied with warm-weather projects as we moved into the familiar rhythm of summer days. The yard needed attention, rooms required painting, and the days flew by. I was too busy to think any more about my conversation with Andrea on that night (at least that's what I told myself), but I think I mostly just felt a little uncomfortable when the topic unexpectedly drifted through my mind. I did encourage her with her reading on a regular basis, and picked up new books that I thought might interest her.

Andrea spent an inordinate amount of time in her room that summer, but I attributed it to the respite from the stresses of school because she seemed happy and had an air of pre-occupied busyness about her. She never once complained about being bored as the summer heat wore on, and I was grateful to have her so engaged with whatever it was that had captured her interest. I think it was at some point in here that I was even mildly congratulating myself on the fact that I must have finally provided her with some books that she was finding appealing.

There were occasions when I did get exasperated with her for spending so much time in the house, while the other kids were outside playing. She would not exactly just hop up then, and do something completely ordinary, however. When Andrea was not engrossed in whatever she was doing in her bedroom, she and her little sister were exploring a fascinating (!) discovery they'd made. If they dressed up in gauzy, bright fabrics, took a stereo from the house for musical accompaniment, and stood on a big raised electric box we had in our front yard, they could "perform" for the entire neighborhood.

I was often caught completely off guard as, opening the front door to go get the mail or something out of the car, I found a large majority of neighborhood parents and children gathered together on our front lawn. They would be sitting on folding chairs they must have toted from home, and watching whatever new "performance" the girls were doing. The first time, I just looked at all these people sitting in our yard, and they, in turn, looked back at me as if to say, "Ssshhhh! Don't you see there's a show going on?" and immediately returned their attention to whatever the girls were doing on the box.

It struck me as incredibly weird, even at the time, that these people kept coming to our house for these little impromptu concerts, but since I couldn't come up with any logical explanation, I just shrugged it off to the idiosyncrasies of bored families and hot summer days. (I know that this probably seems like a sign of great dullness on my part, but just remember what I said about the tendency of busy parents to be very preoccupied with normal family responsibilities!)

Right before school began, I started the annual routine of cleaning the kids' rooms, top to bottom, and sorting through clothes that had stopped being worn because they didn't fit anymore or had grown holes in the knees. I had almost finished with Andrea's room, but, as always, left the worst part for last ... the area under her bed. She loved to "store" things under there, and I was never quite sure what I'd find. Certainly nothing could have prepared me, though, for what I was going to discover that day.

At first, it just looked like a bunch of papers, and I knelt down and started pulling them out, piece by piece. I marveled at how one child could find so much stuff to hide under her bed, and shook my head as I kept pulling out more pieces of paper. After several minutes of this, though, it dawned on me that there was something else going on. There was a problem with what I was doing. The more paper I pulled out, the more there seemed to be, until I had pulled out so much I was basically floating on an island of hundreds of pieces of paper.

What in the world was this all about, I asked myself as I continued to pull out still more sheets. I finally sat back on my heels and actually took a close look at the papers, and realized, with a start, that there was something "off" about all of this. It wasn't possible that all of these pages were some scribblings or childish drawings, and I tried to understand what in the world Andrea had been up to.

To my shocked surprise, as I started to closely examine first one page, and then another and another, I realized that each one of them was covered in Sanskrit lettering! To be specific, the same Devanagari script we had been talking about at the beginning of the summer! And even though I had no way of knowing for sure at the time, next to each Devanagari letter was what looked like its English counterpart.

I was absolutely stunned. I just sat there on the floor in my daughter's bedroom, quietly shifting through the hundreds of pages and finding a meticulous consistency to all of the letters. I must have sat there sorting through the enormous pile of paper for a very long time, because I was trying to make sense of the logic behind how much effort it must have taken that little girl to put all of this together. When I finally looked up, it was to see Robert watching me from the doorway.

"You have to come in and see this," I said, as he continued to stand in the doorway looking at me with a puzzled expression. I must have appeared a little strange to him, sitting on the floor amidst the hundreds of pages that were piled up around me like a small mountain of snow.

He walked into the room and knelt down, picking up one of the sheets of paper.

"What's all this?" he asked, as he unknowingly repeated my actions of some time before, picking up page after page and looking with amazement at the combination of Sanskrit and English letters.

"When did she do all this?" Robert said, voicing one of my first thoughts, even while he continued to move pile after pile of papers lying on the floor, and finding more of the same buried beneath.

By this time, there must have been a little bit of shock setting in for both of us, I think, because I remember just sitting there on the floor together, continuing to go through the papers. We were trying to make sense of what it was we were, in fact, sitting in the middle of, all the while acting as though some key to this mystery could be found if we just sat and looked at the pages long enough.

Finally Robert said something, and it was one of those defining comments that is immortalized the instant it's uttered.

Looking up at me with dozens of sheets of paper squishing out of both hands, he said, very quietly, "I think we have a major problem."

...THE CAT IS OUT OF THE BAG

[c h a p t e r   t e n]

SO, THE CAT WAS OUT OF THE BAG, at least as far as our family was concerned. It seemed we had a daughter who could read an ancient, dead language that clearly no one else in the family spoke, not to mention few other people in the *world*—and she was doing it without the years usually (!) necessary for learning any foreign language, let alone a complex one from thousands of years ago. When faced with uncooperative parents who kept insisting she go outside and play, this same child took it upon herself to hole up in her room and spend her entire summer constructing her very own Sanskrit dictionary! And when she finally did go outside to play, it would be to perform on a pretend "stage" with her sister!

Suffice it to say, our family was starting to be considered odd by the kindest terms, and people even started to treat us like we were a little "different" from them, which I found interesting since *they* were the ones showing up for impromptu concerts on our lawn.

By the time Andrea reached middle school, she had begun to realize that she was definitely out of step with her peers with regard to her interests. No surprise to us, but she found it difficult to accept that no one wanted to sit around with her and talk about a language that was popular about 10,000 years ago, and Andrea found nothing notable in the typical pre-teen discussions held on the school grounds. Why, she reasoned, would anyone want to talk about drinking, drugs, and sex when there was Sanskrit?

Around this time, we enrolled her in a Catholic school, hoping to tone down some of the harshness that seems to be so prevalent in most schools. We were hoping a smaller, religious school that provided closer supervision would give a respite from the awful language and over-the-top behavior that seem to flourish in the halls and classrooms at a typical public school. We were also hopeful that Andrea would find it a more comfortable learning environment. Not to mention that the whole Sanskrit experience had not quite computed for us, yet, so we were still trying to help her establish some version of "normal."

And she did, but only up to a point.

No matter how hard she tried to fit in, nothing seemed to work. In fact, the harder she worked to seem "average," the stronger the level of rejection from her classmates. Every day ended with a teary ride home from school, and I tried to offer typical parental advice about "not trying so hard," and "relaxing" more. I recalled my own middle school years as an exercise in discomfort, so I didn't think her experiences were all that strange. At least, I didn't until she started coming home with some unusual stories.

Remembering the lack of interest that the students at her old school showed toward Sanskrit, Andrea had refrained from even mentioning it at the Catholic school. She was determined to fit in, and at her previous school that subject had just created divisiveness whenever she tried to talk to her friends about what she liked to do in her spare time. They did not understand anything she was talking about, and had no concept of why she would seriously study *anything* on her own, let alone a dead language!

The fact that Andrea had intentionally kept her mouth tightly closed on this particular subject made the stories she started relaying to us about what the kids at the school were saying sound very strange, indeed.

First, she told us, came the comments like "There's something weird about you, isn't there, Andrea?" When she would look at them puzzled, they would elaborate with "There's something about you that you're not telling anybody, isn't there?"

That could, of course, be easily attributed to the truth that she was not, in fact, sharing something with them that she was very interested in, and they were just picking up on that vibe. If the comments had stopped there, that would certainly be an easy enough explanation.

But there was more.

"What country are you from, Andrea?"

When Andrea, totally perplexed, answered, "This country," the kids would shake their heads and say, "No, before that."

Then one day, a young girl who had been nice to Andrea since her first days at the new school came onto the playground at lunchtime and announced, "Andrea, I had a dream about you last night."

This was said in a loud enough tone that several of their classmates heard, and they all gathered around to hear about their friend's dream.

"What did you dream?" they asked.

"I dreamt that I saw Andrea, and she was dressed in beautiful, flowing robes, like from India," the young girl related, savoring the attention.

"Ohhhh," they all said, and then, looking at Andrea, collectively nodded their heads, as though to convey their beliefs that something was strange and this dream just verified their opinions.

"What else?" they asked.

"Well," Andrea's friend went on, "she was in a place, a holy place, but it didn't look like our church. Like a temple or something."

The group looked at Andrea as though all their suspicions about her had been well founded, and poor Andrea could not believe that she was once again going to be singled out as "different," but this time the ostracizing was going to be based on a dream, no less!

She came home from school that day in misery, and after a long discussion with me, resolved to put her head down and just get through the remainder of the school year in whatever way caused the least discomfort. I actually thought about, and discussed with Robert, the option of home schooling, but we both felt that this was one of those life lessons that could be the source of valuable strength for her later on.

Her friend did realize, after Andrea talked with her the next day, the uncomfortable position she had placed Andrea in, so when she continued to have similar dreams, the friend told Andrea about them privately.

The academic year ground on, and Andrea studied hard at school, but when she came home, she studied Sanskrit even harder. By this time, I could laugh with her about the fact that she read Sanskrit a whole lot better than she read English. It seemed to just flow from her, and she had a unique way of studying the various Sanskrit text-books that she now owned. (After that revealing day in Andrea's bedroom, Robert and I had contacted various universities that had Sanskrit as part of their curriculum, and based on department rec-ommendations, purchased books for her.)

One of the things that seemed so fascinating to us about Andrea's extraordinary ability in this area was that she told us she would read the Sanskrit writings once at night before going to sleep, and when she woke in the morning she knew the piece by heart. When Andrea showed me the length of some of these writings that she had learned by this unusual method, I was flabbergasted. Given the fact that she couldn't do this with any subject except Sanskrit, I was completely blown away.

The truth was, the abilities our daughter was exhibiting with regard to this ancient language just didn't seem real or possible, par-ticularly given the fact that Andrea was not that great of a student in all of the other subjects she studied. She was fairly average in apti-tude as well as attitude, but when it came to Sanskrit, all of her reg-ular traits morphed into an astounding gift that actually gave me goose bumps to observe.

Andrea made a comment regarding this phenomenon one day after I exclaimed with amazement that she could so beautifully chant a long piece of Sanskrit that she had just started studying.

In response to my incredulity, she quietly said, "It's not like I'm learning this language, Mom. It's really more like I'm just remembering something that I already know."

* * *

As time went on and the school days slipped into a reasonably comfortable rhythm, Andrea became somewhat resigned to the fact she would never really have a "place" among her classmates. She fully accepted the idea of not being accepted, and that was what made the next series of things that happened so remarkable. The events would also prove to be pivotal in that we began to see a clear pattern emerging, and this would serve as a kind of cosmic compass for us in the months and years to come.

Each student in the seventh and eighth grades (this school included grades one through eight) had been given the assignment of finding a piece of written work they particularly liked, and then orally presenting that choice to the entire school. In seventh grade, doing anything for a large audience can seem daunting, and Andrea was in a quandary as to what her choice should be.

We discussed the dilemma all the way home from school one day, and then later that evening. Andrea's problem, as she saw it, was that she already felt so terribly unaccepted, the thought of having to pick some particular writing and then, in her nervousness, stumble through the reading of it and possibly embarrass herself was too terrifying a scenario to even contemplate.

After hours of witnessing her escalating adolescent discomfort, I came up with a plan.

"Andrea, instead of making yourself miserable about this, why don't you just do whatever it is that you would really like to do, and forget about the kids' reaction since you can't control that anyway. Think about what you would truly enjoy sharing, maybe something that would be a personal expression for you, and forget what anybody else thinks."

After about two seconds of contemplation, her answer came with complete surety.

"Sanskrit," she stated, without hesitation. "I'd like to do my presentation in Sanskrit."

Well, the way I saw it, this solved the problem we were dealing with on a number of levels. First off, she would be reading her piece in Sanskrit, something she could do better than in English. Second, the kids would probably be so stunned they wouldn't know what to think, and it might take a day or two for them to gather together their collective pubescent opinions, and by that time the event would be over.

And then there was the fact that, since this particular cat was pretty much loose and running around the place, and certainly not about to go back in the bag anyway, what did she really stand to lose here?

"Is there any rule that it has to be in English?" I asked, thinking that "no Sanskrit" probably wasn't a rule the teachers had considered including when they put together the project outlines for their students.

"No," Andrea answered, and I could see by her face that something had hit home. She hated the assignment, but the thought of getting to do it in Sanskrit was such a huge enticement it was almost enough to make the whole, dreaded event seem fun.

"What if they think I'm really weird for doing this?" she asked, after taking a moment to think about the possible repercussions. I could hear the trepidation sneaking into her voice as the reality of the situation hit her.

"Honey, they already think that, don't they? So, who cares! You should just do this because you want to, and stop worrying about what might happen as a result. Do this because you love it, and forget about everybody else."

With that as a final thought, Andrea went running off to her bedroom and her Sanskrit books to find her piece. (Also her 'peace,' though I had no idea of that at the time.)

When the day of the event arrived, the entire church was filled to capacity. All the parents turned out in force to see the children take their anticipated turns at the microphone. Camcorders hummed throughout the large, cavernous room, and as I looked around at the audience, I felt jittery in spite of the brave speech I'd made to Andrea a few days earlier. My heart was in my throat as I saw her waiting in the wings, her little face tight with nervousness as she scanned the crowd, looking for me. I waved and smiled, ordering myself to curb my own apprehension and give her my most encouraging front.

One by one, the children approached the microphone. The assignment was to explain a little bit about the piece they'd chosen, and then give the actual delivery.

Parents beamed as each child read from their chosen material or recited a poem from memory, and I squirmed with nervous discomfort as each name was clicked off, and Andrea continued to wait.

Finally it was her turn, and Andrea approached the microphone with much more composure than I could ever have predicted. She looked around at the full house, overflowing with students, parents, teachers, and priests, and then bent the accordion neck of the microphone down to her level and began to speak.

Her voice was light and clear and, to my shocked surprise, amazingly calm. Andrea told the audience that she was going to recite a prayer from India, and this prayer was directed to that aspect of God that removed obstacles from our path, in order that we might experience all the wonderful things that life can offer.

And without a moment's hesitation, she began.

I remember the chills that went up my spine as she started into the actual Sanskrit, her voice becoming more strong and forceful with each word. When the impact of what she was doing actually hit the audience, they reacted to it as though with one mind. First, they seemed surprised; then they regarded her with mounting interest; and finally, everyone in the room sat staring at her with absolutely rapt attention.

As the prayer continued, there wasn't a sound in the entire room except for Andrea's voice as she stood at the front of the large Catholic

Church and recited in Sanskrit. At the end, as the last clear notes of the ancient verse rang through the room, the audience just sat completely still, and then, almost as though shaking themselves from a spell, they burst into loud applause. I will never forget the look in my daughter's eyes at that moment. She stood at the podium, gazing out upon the crowded room, and as the exuberant clapping continued, Andrea's face absolutely and completely relaxed. It was as though all the tension that she had been experiencing for the past several years dissolved away, and I was watching as the full realization hit her that she had finally discovered her place.

In the days following the school event, Andrea's position among her friends took an abrupt turn. Where before she was considered "strange," now she was exotic; if she had previously been regarded as un-hip, now she was the epitome of cool. Kids started showing up at school with portable recorders, which they abashedly pulled out at recess and asked Andrea to do "that weird language thing again" so they could record her. Overnight she found herself the center of attention, and to her most profound amazement, it was all because she had done a few lines of Sanskrit!

The invaluable lesson here was that she had found the experience of joyous peace in the sharing of such a special part of herself.

Andrea's eighth-grade year proved to be a much more comfortable experience all the way around, with the turning point having been that pivotal Sanskrit demonstration. The other kids now had a reason as to why they felt Andrea was so unusual, and they were fascinated that she had studied this extremely old language all on her own. There was also the fact that they loved it when she periodically chanted a little Sanskrit for them. Her unusual "study" methods, however, could continue to remain just a quiet little family secret.

There was a priest at the school that Andrea had always felt a particular affinity with, and as she became more comfortable around him and their friendship grew, she began to talk with him about how her interest in Sanskrit developed into something that, for her, was completely enthralling. He gave her a kind and interested ear while she talked with him about the linguistic origins of the language, and how Latin was derived from Sanskrit. Whether he responded so kindly because he just felt her need to talk about this subject, or because he was actually interested in what she was talking about, I have no idea. But he had his own role to play in the developing odyssey.

"Andrea, why don't you do some Sanskrit for the church at our special Christmas Mass?" he asked one day as the school was preparing for the seasonal festivities.

Andrea was ecstatic, but a little cautious at the same time. This was a very unusual opportunity, and the implication of what he was asking her to do was huge. A Catholic priest, suggesting she do an East Indian prayer, in Sanskrit, at a Christmas Mass, was almost too much to take in all at once!

Her hesitation, however, lasted only a few moments. The prospect of actually getting to do a Sanskrit prayer during a mass proved too enticing to resist. Once she agreed, plans flew back and forth between Andrea and the priest, and before she could fully analyze what it was she was agreeing to, arrangements had been made for her to chant Sanskrit in the large Catholic Church, on a microphone, as part of a special Christmas celebration.

The reality of the situation she had agreed to in the excitement of the moment reared its head over dinner, later that evening.

"Oh … my … gosh," Andrea said, fork suspended in mid-air, apparently not actually processing, until that very moment, the huge implications of what it was she was about to do.

"This is a Catholic Church, and this is a celebration for Christ. All the texts I study from were written way before Christ, so I don't have anything I can chant!" Her voice had a note of rising hysteria in it.

"And besides, the *Vedas* are based on Eastern philosophies. Are they going to be furious with me, and think this is all some sort of pagan worship thing or something?"

Robert and I tried to introduce a little bit of clarity into the situation.

"Sanskrit is a language, not a religion, no more than Latin is a religion," Robert said, applying logic to the problem. "Just because people use a particular language to express their religion does not make the language a religion."

"No, it does not," Andrea replied, also with perfect logic, "but the books I chant from are all religious books, and they reflect the beliefs of the Vedic civilization they originated from."

She had us there.

We all continued to sit quietly around the table, mulling over the situation. There was certainly no desire to be disrespectful to any religion, and her concern was valid. By chanting Vedic scriptures that originated in an ancient Eastern society, were we in conflict with any of the sacred beliefs of the Catholic Church? Christianity is regarded as a monotheistic form of worship, and Westerners would probably think of any Eastern-based religion as polytheistic. The *Vedas* are the oldest written scriptures in existence, and they are the basis of many modern religions' philosophy and theology. But they are also considered most closely linked to polytheistic religions, such as Hinduism. Were we stepping into murky theological waters by integrating prayers that most closely tie to an Eastern religion into a Western church?

"Andrea, Father Martin did not seem to think this was a problem, or he wouldn't have asked you," I finally pointed out. "And the Principal of the school has said it would be fine for you to do this, right?"

"Right," Andrea responded. "But Mom, these priests understand Latin, and since Latin derives from Sanskrit, they'll be able to hear that I'm asking for blessings. They'll also hear the names of different gods, since all the ancient writings are really just prayers from the *Vedas*, and are addressing different aspects of God."

"You just said it yourself, Andrea," I said, seizing on her last words, "different aspects of God. I mean, didn't the Vedic civilization acknowledge that there was one God, but wasn't the point of giving names and personas to various aspects of creation a way of defining and honoring specific manifestations?"

"Yes, that is exactly what it was," Andrea answered, slightly more confident as she caught on to where my tho taking me.

"That's where the Romance Languages all developed the male and female references," Robert added. "Those ancient people saw everything as a reflection of God, so they incorporated a prayer into every aspect of their lives. In time, as language developed, those traditions continued on without most of us understanding why. For instance, I had no idea, in my high school French class, why a house was reflected as having a gender. The reality is, though, whenever we use a gender-specific noun we are referencing those Vedic beliefs."

"Is it any different, really, when we say 'Mother Nature,' or 'Father Time' or the 'Goddess Within?' Aren't those just examples of how we use terms to help describe the indescribable aspects of creation? How is that so different from what you're describing in these religious verses, Andrea?" I asked, realizing I was honing in on something that was larger than the issue of her little Sanskrit performance at the Christmas Mass.

Andrea's face started to lose a little of the tightness it held a few moments before, and her eyes started to shine a little, as the larger meaning of what we were discussing began to sink in for her.

"I could just explain that when I say 'Ganesh,' I am referring to that aspect of God that removes obstacles from our path. Or when the verses talk about 'Sarasvati,' it is in reference to the female aspect of God that bestows beauty and artistic talent." As she warmed to the idea, her thoughts tumbled faster and faster, one right over another. "I could make sure I correctly say Christ's name in Sanskrit, so it is a proper reflection of His Holiday!"

"The point here is to honor God. That is all Sanskrit does. As long as you clearly explain what you're saying, no one should take exception to that." Even though we might have felt as if this sentiment should be self-evident, it is also true that all of us have our own fears to cope with when we feel our fundamental beliefs threatened. To make anyone listening to Sanskrit feel uncomfortable would be the complete opposite of the entire point of chanting it.

"Also," I continued, while Robert and Andrea sat there mulling the situation over, "there's a much larger point here. The *Vedas* were the beginning of religion in the world, as we know it today, so if everything our society is doing, currently, derives from this ancient knowledge, how can anything that honors God in such a loving way as Sanskrit does ever really conflict with anything else? Isn't it all just a matter of perspective?" It's not that I was naïve about religious xenophobia, but in an effort to help my child find her way in what can sometimes be an overly judgmental world, I was allowing the innocence of her own sincerity to simply shine through and take precedence.

When the day of the school's Christmas celebration arrived, I was once again filled with nervous angst as I waited for Andrea to step up to the microphone. I was by myself in the audience since Robert was watching our son, Micah, and he also had to pick Sara up from another school. Even though the whole matter had been sufficiently debated and put to rest at home, I still found myself scanning the church and wondering what the priests' response to the Sanskrit might be.

As the mass unfolded, it quickly became clear that we shouldn't have worried about the outcome for even a moment. In fact, had I been able to fast-forward through time and see the significance of this particular event, I would have been celebrating the beginning of an incredibly special time in all of our lives.

Andrea did the sign of the cross to begin her piece, saying, "In the name of the Father, and of the Son, and of the Holy Spirit" in Sanskrit. That seemed to catch the whole crowd's attention, and even though they had been quiet before, all of the people in the church seemed to suddenly become very still, and an air of expectation filled the room.

I glanced at the priest who had been instrumental in bringing this whole thing about, and he was smiling at Andrea from the sidelines, encouraging her on. She smiled back at him, then closed her eyes and began chanting. The church had wonderful acoustics, and the place seemed to vibrate with almost a hypnotic intonation of the ageless words.

The congregation was entirely focused on Andrea. No baby cried, and the restless rustling of young children stopped. In fact, the stillness in the church was so palpable it was as though the entire room was holding its collective breath.

As Andrea approached the end of the prayer, she intoned a beautiful Aum, and then, silent now, continued to stand at the podium with her eyes closed, and the final sounds washed over everyone gathered for the Christmas service.

No one stirred. They all just sat perfectly quiet, as though soaking up the last essence of the words as the final notes floated out across the room and drifted hauntingly away.

When Andrea finally opened her eyes, she looked out across the room full of people and smiled. Her face was transformed with a look of joy, and her eyes were literally dancing with happiness.

Suddenly everyone seemed to wake as though from some sort of enchantment, and though no sound was actually audible, it was as if a huge, collective sigh moved through the crowd before the mass quietly continued on.

I was delighted and surprised by the reaction, and visually I sought out the priest Andrea had worked with, who was now seated in an area near the other priests. To my amazement, even from where I was sitting, it was clearly evident that the priest's eyes, which he was blinking rapidly, were filled with tears. He was smiling with heartfelt approval, and the other priests were looking at Andrea and nodding enthusiastically. The Sanskrit prayer was a total hit!

The rest of the mass continued in a sort of delirious blur for me. I had a difficult time containing my excitement, and not jumping up and running over to where Andrea now stood. It was a struggle, but I managed to maintain a semblance of decorum for the rest of the service. As soon as it became possible, I was out of my seat and moving through the crowd toward Andrea.

I found it fascinating that the whole Sanskrit episode had felt so absolutely magical, and when I was finally able to wind through the crowd and get to Andrea, it became quickly apparent that the feeling was not just a mom's biased impression. Many people were struggling to make their way over to talk to her. Mothers and fathers, as well as their children, were clamoring to ask her what the beautiful prayer was she had done, and where they might be able to get a copy of it.

Andrea seemed slightly overwhelmed by all the attention, but she was smiling and responding as best she could, even as I was trying to pull her toward the front doors and the cool air outside. As soon as we cleared the threshold and the crowd started to thin out, I turned to her, my own amazement clearly reflected on her face.

"What in the world was that?" I asked, slightly out of breath.

"They loved it!" she said, stating the obvious.

"Yes, they certainly did, but why? Why did they love it so much?"

We walked to the car, jabbering in amazement the whole way. We were both excited to get home and tell the rest of the family what had happened. Great stories tonight!

As we drove and talked, it was apparent we both experienced the exact same reaction to the crowd's response—total shock that a Western religious group would have such a positive reaction to a prayer in an Eastern-based language. The audience had reacted so strongly, in fact, it was almost as though they had all experienced some sort of "happiness buzz" while Andrea was chanting the Sanskrit!

This was a momentous occasion for us, and particularly for Andrea, because it had, in its unfolding, opened a completely new understanding of the individual's relationship with the Divine. Even though we hadn't realized it as we sat around the dinner table just a few weeks earlier, the conversation we had that night, during which we debated the finer points of Eastern and Western beliefs, would be the genesis of something very far-reaching.

We had unwittingly laid the foundation for a lifelong aspiration as well as an inspiration, and we would continue to add to it, one brick at a time, for many years to come. It would be some time later that a wise priest, and dear friend, whom at that point we had yet to meet, would call that foundation our family's "ministry." The desire to unite people in their fundamental beliefs would be, for all of us, the driving force of the next decade and beyond, and the seeds of the future were sown that night as we discussed the ramifications of doing Sanskrit at a Christmas Mass.

Little did we suspect the size of the effort we were about to undertake, and even if we had, there was probably very little we would have done to alter the coming course of events.

. . . Curiouser and Curiouser

[c h a p t e r   e l e v e n]

THE ASTUTE READER will have noticed by now that there has been little mention of the other critical portion of Shanti Shanti, that being Andrea's younger sister, Sara Anjuli. Time-wise, Sara would already have to be involved in Sanskrit for the developments over the next several years to make any sense and, in fact, she was.

This particular part of the story, and the fascinating revelation of Sara's own innate gift for learning Sanskrit, seems like such a wonderful saga unto itself that I wanted to make a special effort in recounting it. And, sisters being sisters, I'm sure Sara would agree that I should!

The outstanding issue here is that we were already dealing with one child who showed a phenomenal ability to basically cognize a 10,000-year-old language, with apparently little effort. Yet, at the same time, that child seemed to be remarkably, indeed almost perversely, unaware that everyone couldn't just do this. Since we had tried, on numerous occasions, to impress upon Andrea the understanding that a person simply could not, in fact, manifest a knowledge of an ancient language, I was actually a little relieved when she revealed her determination to find someone to chant the *Vedas* with her.

I thought that, at long last, reality was going to triumph, and our daughter would be faced with a fundamental truth: that just because Sanskrit was something she seemed to magically "know," this was not a universal ability! It's unclear to me why I thought that this particular revelation would somehow clarify how it was that Andrea knew what she did about Sanskrit. I'm sure that, at the time, this was some last grasp at trying to find a rational explanation for the whole thing, but the logic of it eludes me now.

Anyway, the search for a Sanskrit partner started with Andrea listening to pundits who were visiting from India and marveling at how beautiful the *Vedas* sounded when recited in perfect unison by two people. This technique resulted in a kind of stereo effect that bathed the listener in the beauty of the pure Sanskrit tones. After that experience, Andrea immediately began her search for someone to chant the *Vedas* with her.

Her first impulse was to try and persuade me, but my initial reaction to her suggestion was frustration that she thought someone should just be able to start chanting the *Vedas*. It took all of my patience to try explaining, once again, that people could not automatically read and speak Sanskrit, even though it was something she could do with such an apparent lack of effort.

Then there was also the fact that I wasn't quite sure what the reaction would be from other people when Andrea explained her desire to have a Sanskrit partner. I didn't want her to be made to feel uncomfortable in her effort to describe something that even her own family was having a hard time grasping.

I was also filled with concern that her quest would end in certain disappointment. There wasn't anyone in our near field of exposure that already knew how to speak Sanskrit or, more to the point, seemed the least bit inclined to suddenly start cognizing the language.

One day while standing in the kitchen, I heard ten-year-old Andrea corner Sara, who was eight at this time, in an adjoining room and begin the process of trying to convince her little sister why she should chant Sanskrit with her. I have to say that I definitely had the sensation that we were approaching a critical juncture at this time. As I saw Sara sitting on the floor, playing with her Barbie dolls and glancing up with distraction as her older sister continued to present her case with such obvious passion, I really felt that this was going to be a turning point for Andrea. It was a virtual certainty that Sara would demonstrate to her, once and for all, that the ability to chant Sanskrit was not a given, and thereby some normalcy would be brought into this whole strange phenomenon. At least that was the convoluted scenario my mind laid out.

One can only imagine the sense of total disconnect that I experienced when, a few days later, I passed by Sara's bedroom door and heard the soft sound of both my daughters chanting Sanskrit.

I shook my head in complete disbelief . . .and just kept walking. I swore I could hear Scarlett O'Hara murmuring in my ear as I decided that I would, indeed, think about this tomorrow.

A few days later, Andrea came running up to me in a huge state of excitement. I couldn't quite catch the drift of what she was saying, as she was speaking so fast and with such exuberance, but when she finally managed to slow down a little, I practically froze at the implications of her words.

"Mom! You're not going to believe this! Sara can read Sanskrit better and faster than I could at first!"

As if what we'd already been dealing with regarding Andrea and this particular topic wasn't enough to come to grips with, now Sara apparently read Sanskrit as effortlessly as Andrea.

"Sara, can you read this?" I asked later that evening, holding up a page covered in the Devanagari script. I was fighting an overwhelming feeling of genuine bewilderment as I realized I was once again dealing with some bizarre phenomenon involving one of our children, a dead language, and an extremely unusual, if not "impossible," ability.

"It's really easy, Mommy," Sara tossed over her shoulder to me as she ran outside to play. "If you just look at the words, you already know them."

I was beginning to feel like my entire life was turning upside down and inside out.

The two sisters, from that point on, spent every free moment learning all the nuances of the ancient language, and the sounds of their voices and their Sanskrit chanting filled the house throughout the evenings and weekend days. It was really astonishingly beautiful, and Robert and I would linger outside their bedroom doors and marvel at the complexity of the pieces they seemed able to chant so effortlessly. We couldn't help but ask ourselves, as we stood quietly eavesdropping in the hallway, "What in the world is going on here?"

This was actually the beginning, for Robert and me, of letting go of every preconception we'd ever had about life, and learning to deal with what it had now become. In other words, we had to accept as fact what the mind automatically rejected as fantasy.

We were totally without understanding as to how we could have not just one daughter, but two, who could read and write and speak a ten-thousand-year-old language! To live in a home where your children are fluent in a language that you, the parent, do not speak or understand can be a very disconcerting experience. When your offspring, untaught, can pick up a book filled with a foreign script that you can't read, and read it aloud to you, it is definitely time to sit back and re-think your definition of reality.

There is obviously no connection here to a situation where children have learned a language through school or tutors, as that would be easy to understand and the progression would make sense because the road to knowledge is traceable.

Instead, this is a circumstance where one's children manifest a knowledge that has no direct route, but rather seems to simply appear one day without precedence or fanfare. This can be a very difficult experience to digest, especially given that in the normal progression of things, we are accustomed to having a reasonable explanation for most everything that happens. We are educated to think in concrete terms, and even if we clearly witness an event that might seem inexplicable at the time, our minds will quickly find a "reasonable" way of regarding it. We will tuck it away in our mental filing cabinet, and in time we'll have all kinds of explanations for the mysterious occurrence.

A very different set of circumstances was in play for both Robert and me, since we were living the phenomenon every day, and it was far more difficult to explain it all away. We were dealing with something that was completely mystifying, and the experience was up close and personal. There were times when circumstances were so difficult to comprehend and digest that we would be completely exhausted by the process.

It is certainly easy enough to acknowledge how much the human mind likes clear explanations for whatever it encounters. It is a natural reaction that helps keep life neat and tidy, resisting the mental and emotional pull toward entropy. Well, there was nothing neat and tidy about what we were going through at this point. In fact, everything was suddenly very, very complex.

We began to realize that events were careening out of our control. We had experienced glimpses in the past of an element of Divine guidance in our lives, but the events that started taking place around this time were making that concept a daily reality. It was not an altogether unpleasant sensation, as long as we refrained from constantly insisting on a celestial arm wrestle over every issue of control. But it could and did cause a great deal of frustration if ignored, which was exactly what we did in the beginning, because we had no idea what was actually going on.

Our activities started to take on a particular pattern. If Robert and I pursued things that led in the specific direction of Sanskrit and any or all of the related spiritual-based activities, we would receive an abnormal amount of support from the universe. It was as though we gently tossed a pebble into a pond, and the result was a huge splash, followed by big waves that were disproportionate to the initial action.

Conversely, if we tried to give our attention to more "regular" activities that had no obvious spiritual base, no amount of diligence would reap corresponding results. In that case, it was like throwing a boulder-sized amount of pure effort into a pond and watching it simply disappear beneath the surface, with barely a splash. This apparent mechanism of response was so consistent as to be predictable, and not at all subtle in its display.

It was due to these very real illustrations of cosmic intervention that we realized the need to adapt an attitude of complete support with regard to the girls and their pursuit of Sanskrit. In this spirit of cooperation, it was decided that I would take Sara to California, just the two of us, and we would attend a Sanskrit "Intensive" together. This was a wonderful opportunity for a little mother-daughter bonding, as well as a chance for me to try and understand the phenomenon a little further.

For three solid days we would eat, drink, and breathe Sanskrit, and my private hope was that by the end of that time, I would have a little better grasp of what was going on right under our own roof. I was hoping to find some sort of key to help in the overall explanation, and the only way I knew how to do that was to understand the subject matter a little better.

Andrea was very excited about this whole event. She desperately wanted me to understand their love of Sanskrit more than I currently did, and she thought this was an excellent opportunity for some progress on that front.

The prospect of getting away for three days was appealing, so Sara and I set off with a lightly packed car, happily anticipating our weekend retreat. Sara had always been such a mellow child, she was a lot of fun to travel with, and I loved the idea of having her all to myself for an extended weekend.

I was curious how she would feel about Sanskrit in such a strict learning environment, surrounded by a lot of adults. I had absolutely no idea what to expect from this little adventure, but I was sure it would be interesting.

The Intensive was held at a beautiful mountain retreat, and we knew we were going to have some great walks through the surrounding countryside when a deer jumped out of the way as we pulled into the drive.

After registering, we quickly found that our first day was packed full, and we had little time to ourselves. When I saw that there were no other young people in attendance, I thought that Sara might feel a little intimidated by the classes.

I should have reserved that concern for myself.

The classes were taught in an entertaining format, even though they were definitely true to the term "intensive." I had to really focus to follow each segment, but I still found myself looking over at Sara on a regular basis, trying to assess her reaction. She was quiet, but attentive. I was afraid it all might seem too academic for her, but she surprised me at dinner that night by saying that the whole thing was really "easy."

This opinion was, of course, disconcerting to me, because I did not find any aspect of it to be easy. In fact, by the end of the day, I was struggling a bit to keep up with the instructor's fast pace.

By the next day we were knee-deep in the Sanskrit alphabet and the combining of consonants and vowels, and this was where the fun (!) really started. The teacher walked around the room, and each student was expected to read some small word by combining the letters learned in the previous sessions.

Sara leaned over and asked if I knew my word.

"I think so," I answered, as I counted ahead and found the word I was expected to read. When I told her what I thought the word was, Sara looked surprised, then shook her head.

"No, Mom, that's not right. See, this is a vowel here," and moving her finger, "and also one here. So that can't be the right word. Look at it again."

I could hear the other students stumbling over their words as the teacher moved from one person to the next. I looked over at Sara again as she sat calmly waiting for her turn. It occurred to me that this weekend was not only *not* going to provide me with a greater understanding of how my kids were able to just "know" Sanskrit, I was possibly going to have even less of an idea.

One thing I did know, this language was hard! Sitting in the class, I came to the realization that any thought their dad and I had to the effect that we would be getting some kind of grasp on our lives was completely unfounded. I could feel any budding sense of true comprehension of Andrea and Sara's ability slipping quietly away. Going to this Intensive made what our daughters could do so effortlessly seem even more unbelievable to me. Having to personally confront the difficult structure of the language and realize how easy this all came to our children made the whole business just that much more unfathomable.

After three days of classes, the session was over and we packed our bags and headed home. Sara was all smiles and laughter and enthusiasm as she talked about taking the advanced version of the course.

I just had a headache.

[c h a p t e r   t w e l v e]

ABOUT FIVE YEARS AFTER SARA WAS BORN, I began to feel that now-familiar sense that it was time to have another baby. I had a very strong feeling that there was a little boy waiting to come into the world to be with our family. No amount of "reality" talks with myself about how hard it already was to take care of two young children could dissuade me from the notion that another child was knocking on our ethereal family door.

After a year or so of no success on the pregnancy front, a medical test showed that an imbalance in my thyroid gland was making it difficult for me to conceive. It seems that my thyroid, which had previously been imbalanced when I was a teenager, was once again functioning too "fast," and that fact was apparently causing an interference with the hormones necessary to sustain a pregnancy. I was given something to slow the thyroid gland down, and shortly thereafter found myself expecting.

At first everything was fine, with the exception that I had a much worse experience with morning sickness than I ever remembered having with my other pregnancies. I tried to be a trooper about it, and when the debilitating nausea finally passed, I would resume normal activities, though still feeling under-the-weather. I remember being aware that Robert was watching me more than usual, and regularly asking me how I was doing. I thought his concern unnecessary, and I brushed it off as a response to pending fatherhood, although I didn't recall him being so overly solicitous with my prior pregnancies.

One night, when I was about four months into the pregnancy, I had an amazing dream. I was standing in the middle of a huge field, with mountains off in the distance. I felt particularly wonderful and at peace, but as I stood in the field something strange suddenly began to happen. From every direction, both on the land and in the sky, animals appeared and began to come toward me. Birds of all types and sizes filled the air, until it was hard to see the sun. As I looked across the field, for as far as I could see, animals of every description were making their way toward me. I was not the least bit afraid—in fact, just the opposite. I felt a deep, universal love washing over me, and it was as though all the creatures were coming to share that love with me, in some way. As the animals continued toward me, there was some sort of deep communion taking place, almost a celebration. It was the most strangely wonderful feeling I had ever experienced.

When I awoke I felt completely refreshed and rejuvenated, as though my life had in some way been deeply renewed. And miracle of miracles, I had no nausea. I climbed out of bed, hesitant at first, but found I felt great. When Robert stirred and asked me how I was doing, I responded exuberantly that I had just had the most amazing dream, and felt the best I thought I ever had!

When I saw the way Robert looked at me then, concern washing over his features, I realized that something about the scenario was not quite right. It wasn't until my appointment at the doctor's later that afternoon, however, that my husband's behavior seemed almost prescient.

There was no fetal heartbeat, and the news was devastating. I remember driving home, blinded by a blur of painful emotions. Looking back, it seems that the only thing that kept me going that day was the residue of feelings I had from my dream the night before. Everything else just fell away, and my mind drifted through the sea of loss.

* * *

It would be a couple of years after this incident, when the girls recorded their first CD with Robert, that I would hear, for the very first time, a song called "Jenny." When the song came on the stereo, the girls and Robert looked at me uneasily, as though trying to gauge my reaction. I was slightly surprised, as I thought I had heard them rehearsing everything they recorded, and I did not recognize this particular song.

As the music continued to play and the words became clear to me, I realized what the song was actually about, and my heart ached with an intense love for my family. My husband had obviously metabolized his grief over the loss of our baby in his own inimitable way, and I did not hear about the particular direction his emotions had taken him until that moment. His anthem of love made me cry with a great releasing of emotions that day, and my memories of the special dream I had came flooding back.

* * *

A few months after my miscarriage, events conspired to make me finally question where, exactly, our dreams leave off and reality begins. And most important of all, how and why do those two worlds sometimes overlap or collide....

I had determined to put any idea of pregnancy out of my mind, as I was still reeling a bit from my miscarriage, but in my more honest moments, I would admit to still feeling like there was another child waiting to "come in." Those feelings certainly did not appear to coincide with anything real, however, and I was moving on by focusing my mind on daily life.

Whenever Robert and I talked about having another baby, I was somewhat negative in my response, expressing doubts that I would, in fact, actually get pregnant again. The doctor had said that the loss of my pregnancy was probably a result of my thyroid problems, and could possibly happen again, so I took my thoughts off the situation as completely as I could.

One night, several hours before dawn, I woke up thirsty and, rolling out of bed, stumbled sleepily to the bathroom to get a drink of water. I didn't have far to walk as it was just off the bedroom, but by the time I stood at the sink, holding my glass under the stream of water, a bizarre realization dawned. I had passed something on my way to the bathroom that was not there when I turned off the light earlier that night. Thinking I must be caught in some sort of sleep-walking episode, I shook my head a little to clear any cobwebs.

The more awake I became, however, the more startled I was at my own thoughts. I was not dreaming. In fact, I was actually pretty lucid given the time of night. I stood there, holding the glass, and felt the relative clearness of my mind. I thought, "Here I am drinking water" and "There is my face clearly reflected in the mirror."

So what in the world was it I saw sitting in the middle of my bedroom?

I quickly ducked my head around the door, and was immediately hit with the realization that something very weird was going on. I muttered the words, "There *is* something there."

And was there ever. A big, beautiful, golden cradle was sitting right in the middle of my bedroom. I stood very still and stared very hard at what had to be an amazing apparition, but I swear, there was nothing about that cradle that looked anything but completely real.

What an incredibly odd thing to have happen! I get up to go to the bathroom, and I stumble into this! A cradle!

And not just any cradle, but a huge, golden thing that was truly a sight to behold. It had a softly gleaming aspect to its surface, almost an aged golden patina, but that factor wasn't what took my breath away. (As though I needed anything else ... there was a golden cradle in my room ... Hello!)

The canopy was an amazing work of art. It was a beautiful, huge, carved snake—a cobra—and its image had been captured as though it had posed for the artisan. Its long neck was fanned out in a protective stance, and the head was slightly bowed.

What an absolutely beautiful cradle, I thought, and then I actually did that eye-rubbing motion just to make sure I wasn't seeing things. But I knew I could have rubbed all night, and the magnificent cradle would still have been standing there proudly, in the middle of my bedroom.

Finally, I realized that I desperately wanted someone else to witness this amazing sight with me, so I started to walk past the cradle to wake up Robert.

The thought "Robert is certainly going to be surprised" drifted through my head, but I was mostly intent on waking him up.

Suddenly, though, I stopped dead in my tracks and turned to stare at the cradle again. Something was beginning to dawn slowly in my awareness, and it brought me to a complete standstill.

I had not tried to touch the cradle. And as soon as I had that thought, I also instantly knew why. As real as the cradle looked to me, there was still some elusive quality about it that made it slightly different from every other object in the room. It was almost as though the cradle were standing here, in my room, but also there, someplace else, at the exact same time. It was in my room, but apart from it, as well. There was a feeling and a look to it that spoke of a difference in dimensions, and this difference could be most easily explained by stating that if our lives normally unfold in a three-dimensional world, the cradle felt like it was a part of a fourth layer that lay just beyond our everyday perceptions.

It was then that I had a very clear understanding of what this entire incident must surely be about. I had been so sad about the lost pregnancy, and had despaired over ever having the child I felt so strongly was intended to "come in" and be a part of our lives, that I had actually considered not getting pregnant again. As I looked at the lovely golden cradle, sitting in the middle of my room, I had a wonderful sense of peace wash over me that came from a very deep place inside. It flowed from that reservoir that is the origin of truth in our lives.

In a kind of intuitive seismic flash, I realized that I was going to have another child, very soon, and it was going to be a little boy.

What a lovely gift, I thought, as I stood gazing at my golden apparition with awe.

And then, because I couldn't resist the impulse, I still went over to the bed and started to frantically shake Robert! Cosmic as the whole experience was, I still wanted to know if he could see my cradle! Deeply asleep, he grumbled as I tried to drag him from his slumber, and I kept looking back over my shoulder between frantic whispers of "Wake up, wake up!"

"What? What?" He mumbled as I shook harder.

The cradle was starting to fade from my sight. It now had an almost shimmering quality to it, as though I were looking at it from a distance, and I realized, with disappointment, that no one else was going to share my experience with this magnificent cradle tonight.

Robert was still half-asleep, but he finally sat up and mumbled, "What's the matter?"

I climbed into bed beside him and, looking over at what was now just a faintly glowing outline of the golden cradle, replied, "Actually nothing is the matter. In fact, everything is going to be very all right."

* * *

One month later I was pregnant, and that pregnancy resulted in our son, Micah. I don't know if I expected everything to be completely normal, given his auspicious beginning, but I was caught off guard about eight months into my pregnancy when a couple of things happened that brought the events of both my miscarriage and the cradle back into sharp focus.

I was out for a stroll one afternoon, which, in truth, felt more like a waddle than a walk, given that Micah was a pretty big baby.

(He's a ten-pounder, for sure!) We lived in a somewhat rural area at that time, and I loved walking along and looking at the peaceful little mini-farms with their grazing horses and the sheep lounging in the sun. I was tired from the walk and feeling every bit of the eight months I'd been pregnant, when I decided to stop and rest on a rock by the side of the road. It was large enough that I could get back up once I sat down, which was a relevant issue given my current girth!

As I sat on the rock and absorbed the mild winter rays, I felt totally peaceful and time seemed to stand still. It was so quiet where I was sitting that I just mentally drifted along with the soft, cool breeze blowing gently around me.

Suddenly I had a sense that I wasn't alone, and I looked around to see if someone had come up alongside me without my realizing it. But no, there was no one there. I stood up to go, realizing the time must be getting late and I needed to get home. When I turned slightly to brush off the seat of my pants, my eye caught a flicker of movement that made me jump. Looking up, I was startled to find myself standing in front of a large group of the most quietly behaved, well-mannered cows I'd ever seen in my life.

There had to be at least fifty of them, and they were all gathered in a half-moon around the rock I'd been sitting on. They were gazing at me with their big, sweet eyes, and I just stood in absolute amazement, staring right back at them. I'd grown up on a farm, and I'd never, ever seen anything quite like this! These cows were looking at me in the most intensely familiar way I'd ever experienced, and after a moment or two, I started to laugh from the sheer absurdity of it. If anyone had seen me, this laughing, largely pregnant woman, standing in a huge sea of cows, they would have thought it a strange spectacle, indeed. *I* thought it was strange!

The cows continued to gaze at me as though at any minute I was going to do something extremely important. I had no idea how all of these cows could have gathered so close to me without making a sound, and then proceed to just stand there, waiting patiently for me to acknowledge their presence. I had seen cows at feeding time, bellowing their impatience, and there was no resemblance to this situation, whatsoever. These animals seemed as though they had something they were making a sincere cow-effort to communicate to me, but I was too bemused by the situation to do more than wave them all a smilingly baffled goodbye, and go on my way.

As I walked further down the lane, I thought about how strange what just happened seemed, and my mind turned to the dream I'd had on that night some months before when all the animals came to me across the field. The feeling I had when I turned and saw those cows standing quietly around me was reminiscent of the way I'd felt after that dream ... as though I were part of some huge, cosmic wave of love sweeping me along, and these creatures were there as part of that expression.

As I rounded the bend in the road, the *next* bizarre episode in my already strange day took place. I suddenly felt something strange underneath my foot, and the thought was incongruous given that I couldn't have stepped on anything since I had just glanced at the road a second before. I was too big and clumsy at that particular point in my pregnancy to meander carelessly along, given how uneven the road was. At the same moment I looked down, whatever was under my foot moved and, suddenly, to my horror, I realized I was standing on a snake!

I literally jumped straight up into the air, screaming, and certainly displayed more nimbleness than I could ever have dreamed possible, especially for how pregnant I was.

And then I did a kind of dance of horror. I danced and screamed and jumped all over that road, and I must have looked completely insane if anyone had happened to glance out of a window.

But appearances be damned!

I had stepped on a snake, for heaven's sake!

The poor snake, apparently uninjured by our encounter but as scared as I was, slid away into the bushes. I just stood there gasping, still doing little jumps of terror, as I tried to make sense out of what had just occurred.

I couldn't believe it! A snake under my foot! Was it poisonous? The thought crossed my mind that I had been startled enough to precipitate the onset of labor, and I cautiously felt my belly for any signs of contractions.

The longer I stood there, the more ludicrous the entire incident seemed. I had never stepped on a snake in my whole life! Why in the world would I do so now? First there were the cows! And now this! Unbelievable!

It was some time before I collected myself enough to continue on my way home. When I finally reached there, I regaled my family with my bizarre adventures, and they all looked at me in amazement. They obviously thought I had just taken the whole thing about bringing home interesting stories a little too far.

"Why would you step on a snake, Mommy?" Sara asked.

"Did you hurt it?" asked Andrea, obviously more concerned for the snake than me.

Later that night, it happened that Robert was talking to an Indian friend of ours, and he related the story of my run-in with the snake.

Apparently not the least discombobulated by what Robert just said, our Indian friend simply asked, "Which way did the snake go?"

"What? What do you mean?" Robert responded.

"When she picked up her foot, which way did the snake go?"

Robert covered the mouthpiece and, with a somewhat confused expression on his face, asked me the question. I had to think a moment, because my heart started to beat faster just remembering the incident, and it took a little effort for me to mentally reconstruct the moment when the snake slithered away.

"Left," I finally said, not at all sure why anyone would care about something like this when I'd just been scared practically to death. "He went to the left."

Robert repeated my response to his friend, and then grew quiet as he listened to what the Indian man was saying to him. I thought with no little indignation that I didn't really care what had happened to the snake, and was more than a little insulted that people seemed to care so much for its well-being!

A moment later, Robert said goodbye, and hung up the phone. He turned and looked at me but said nothing.

Feeling a little discomfited by his silence, I finally asked what our friend said.

"He said that ... you ... are going to have ... a little boy."

* * *

One month later, Micah joined our family, and his birth was accompanied by the same sound Robert and I heard when both of the girls were born. We were actually getting used to *that* phenomenon by now, but what we weren't ready for was the unique way in which our little boy greeted us and his new life.

Right after the umbilical cord was cut, the doctor picked our baby up, obviously expecting Micah to have the requisite crying response that would indicate his breathing was fine. Instead of crying, however, Micah had a completely different response from what we had ever seen before.

The doctor said to Robert, "Look at this, will you?"

I was still in a semi-reclining position, so I couldn't see the doctor that well at the end of the bed, but I could see Robert as he looked toward whatever the doctor was indicating. My husband suddenly burst out laughing.

Wondering what was so funny, I asked, "What? What are you laughing about?"

Robert took Micah in his arms and held him so I could see his face. And then I understood the reason for Robert's response.

Our brand new little boy had a look on his face that could only be described as pure, unadulterated boredom.

Still laughing as he continued to look at the exaggeratedly blasé expression on Micah's face, Robert finally managed to say, "He looks like he's thinking, 'Here I go again!', doesn't he?"

> *Here I go walkin' into paradise, eyes wide awake*
> *You would think that I'd learn . . .*
> *Do not reincarnate!*
>
> —ROBERT FORMAN
> PARADISE "THREE" ALBUM

[c h a p t e r t h i r t e e n]

BY THE TIME their little brother was old enough to attend school, the opportunity for Andrea and Sara to introduce their unique gift of Sanskrit to people other than those in their most immediate circle was rapidly approaching. As had become the norm for us, however, we didn't have the foggiest idea that anything unusual was getting ready to happen.

Robert and I were both occupied with trying to help our kids survive, and ideally even thrive, in their respective high school, middle school, and grade school environments. Robert was busy with his music career, and I was continuing to study Ayurveda, as well as teaching a series of six-week sessions for teachers, healthcare professionals, business people, etc., on stress management and healthy living from an integrated body, mind, and spirit point of view. We definitely had our hands full, which is probably why we didn't notice when circumstances started to really heat up.

It began innocuously enough. The girls would come home from school and talk about how this teacher or that one had pulled them out of a class to come and do some Sanskrit chanting for their students. Word had spread about the girls and their Sanskrit studies, and teachers called me to report how the language seemed to have a "quieting and grounding" effect on their classes.

The high school where Andrea was a freshman at this time was an extremely overcrowded public school, so I think the teachers were thrilled to find something that was entertaining, and had the added benefit of letting a little of the steam out of the pressure-cooker environment that filled the hallways and classrooms. Andrea became accustomed to being summoned from one class to accompany a teacher to a different classroom.

One of the teachers went so far as to initiate a morning meditation session, during which the students would sit quietly and "settle" themselves through quiet contemplation. She would immediately follow that up with the playing of a cassette I had made for her of the girls chanting Sanskrit. She swore that this practice had a dramatic effect on the overall attitude and attention level of her students. Parents were even commenting to her about the change in the attitudes of their children at home, once the teacher included this routine in her curriculum.

Sara was in eighth grade at this time, and keeping a low profile at her middle school. She was not relishing the idea of going from class to class chanting Sanskrit because she had already met with her own version of the peer problems that Andrea experienced. As soon as Sara's classmates heard about her Sanskrit abilities, torment-time immediately ensued. Attempting to head off the firestorm by trying to include them in what she was doing met with predictable results. During lunch break, at the request of several of the students that Sara let them hear what the Sanskrit alphabet sounded like, she gamely started illustrating the different consonants and vowels. With typical adolescent callousness, some of the kids discovered the reward of a quick laugh from the other students if they imitated Sara.

"Ah, ah, ooh, ooh," they laughed, jumping around with ape-like motions and mimicking the vowel sounds with as much exaggerated emphasis as possible. "Sara's a monkey girl!"

A couple of incidents like that and Sara just closed up and didn't discuss Sanskrit again. When a teacher would search Sara out and ask her to come chant for their class, she was less than thrilled, but always complied because the impulse to let the other students experience Sanskrit was too strong of a pull. Even if it meant there would be some meanness that followed, she didn't have the heart to decline anyone's request to hear the ancient language.

When we would talk about the conundrum she was faced with, it was clear that Sara knew the insults and cruelty were just reflections of the way kids everywhere use negative actions to try and attract attention. The unpleasant behavior of a few could not detract from the overall positive response of so many others.

It would prove interesting later on when Sara ran into some of these same classmates at various concerts. They would approach the stage sheepishly, and with eyes focusing everywhere but on Sara, ask if she remembered them. She responded, "Yes, you thought I was the monkey girl!" which she delivered with a light laugh, and when they realized she was not holding a grudge, returned her smile warmly, though with a bit of chagrin.

Around this time, we received a phone call from a good friend that seemed insignificant enough but would, in fact, have very far-reaching ramifications. The call would wind up being the launching pad for a series of events that would eventually lead to the girls doing public performances. In retrospect, it was positively magical the way each thread in our lives was beginning to wind delicately around the next connecting thread, so precisely as to seem almost eerie. But like just about every other incident that was occurring around this time, we didn't recognize this particular event as a harbinger of things to come.

The call we received concerned an evening social event/lecture with a visiting Sanskrit professor from the East Coast. Our friend knew about our daughters' interest in Sanskrit, and though she had never heard them chant, thought they might enjoy this opportunity. There was going to be a Sanskrit discussion, she told us, and because the event was taking place in her home, it would be semi-academic, but also very relaxed and enjoyable.

When I told the girls about the invitation, their response was excitement mixed with a bit of nervousness, but the full extent of their trepidation didn't really show itself until we were heading out the door to go to the event.

"What if he wants us to chant?" Andrea asked.

"Well, what if he does?" I responded. "He would probably enjoy hearing what you do."

"I would be afraid he might think we're just silly kids," she said, as we all climbed into the car.

Robert and I made some noises of disagreement, but secretly I think we were both more than a little concerned, if the truth were to be known, about what a professor of Sanskrit might think about our two little Sanskrit junkies. The girls were not formally taught, and the world of academia can be very judgmental when it comes to having to try and explain the phenomenon of knowledge that just "appears" out of nowhere. I said a silent little prayer that the evening ahead would not be an unpleasant one.

The professor was a tall, thin man, with a soft-spoken manner and a great love of his field. For the first hour, the guests all sat in a horseshoe-shaped seating arrangement around the large living room and listened to him expound on Sanskrit.

Finally, he took some questions, and that was when our friend piped in.

"Those girls over there can chant Sanskrit," she said, pointing to where our family was quietly sitting. Andrea looked over at me and nervously swallowed.

"You can?" the professor responded, looking in the girls' direction. At their nods of confirmation, his voice assumed a slightly indulgent tone.

"Well, do you girls want to do a little Sanskrit for us?"

Looking back, Andrea and Sara's response to his invitation, and the chanting that resulted, must have served as the opening of some sort of cosmic floodgate. The dramatic change in the girls' attitudes alone should have been a tip-off that there was more going on here than met the eye. Their nervousness somehow miraculously vanished, and in its place was a type of focused confidence that I hadn't even realized existed until that moment.

Closing their eyes, they settled themselves, and the professor looked on with a sort of conspiratorial smile that he shared with some of the other people seated next to him. It was that look adults affect when children are getting ready to do something "cute."

Suddenly the girls began to chant, and whatever it was that the good professor expected to hear that night, it definitely was not what he was presented with.

Andrea and Sara proceeded to chant Sanskrit for a solid ten minutes, from memory, and they recited the *Ganesh Upanishad*, the *Shri Sukta*, and the *Ganesh Stotrams*. As their sweet voices rose and fell with each line, intoning that most ancient language, the professor began to be visibly affected. The indulgent look left his face, and his smile started to fade. It was replaced first by a look of surprise, which quickly changed to one of puzzlement, and finally turned into something that most closely resembled shock.

The people seated closest to him, who seemed to be personal academic acquaintances, kept glancing at him to assess his reaction, and a vast range of reactions flickered rapidly across each person's face as the girls' chanting continued on and on.

Finally, as the last sounds of the final piece echoed softly through the room, Andrea and Sara opened their eyes and sat looking peacefully at the group. An enormous array of emotions could be palpably felt in the room, and no one even spoke for a moment or two. Members of the group kept looking quizzically at the professor, as though he would be able to shed some light of explanation on what everyone had just heard, but he seemed to be having his own difficulties with the situation, as he just sat and stared wide-eyed at the girls.

Finally, the silence was broken.

"Well," the professor began, stammering slightly, "That was ... well, it was ... where did you say you learned Sanskrit?"

Andrea and Sara both started talking then, and the sentences of their explanation danced back and forth between the two of them—how they had loved Sanskrit from a very early age, and how Robert and I obtained books for them to study. Andrea talked about the Sanskrit correspondence course she received a few years before as a Christmas gift. (This was a result of Robert's inquiries with various universities.)

What she didn't mention was how shocked her parents were when she sailed through the huge binder as though she couldn't inhale its contents fast enough, then quickly moved on to the advanced linguistic books.

The professor looked at Robert and me as though we could provide a better elaboration.

"They just studied this themselves?" he asked, incredulity and disbelief obvious in his voice.

"Yes, that's right," Robert responded, and then went on to talk about Andrea's homemade Sanskrit dictionary, and Sara's equally surprising ability to pick up the nuances of the language even faster than Andrea had.

Everyone was stunned, and questions flew around the room. The professor shifted uncomfortably and tried to answer some of the queries on Andrea and Sara's behalf. After a couple of questions concerning the probability of this particular kind of phenomenon actually happening, and his answers of "I have no idea," he finally gave up and turned the floor over to the girls.

The main theme of all the questions was the same from everyone ... "How was it possible for two little girls to become so proficient in an ancient dead language, with the only exposure to that language being that which they created on their own?"

It was my feeling that the girls' answers provided more confusion than clarification. "We just knew it" was not really very satisfying for a group of academics.

The evening ended in a sort of haze for all of us—for the group because they had just witnessed something that didn't seem to have any kind of normal explanation, and for the girls because they had their innate love of Sanskrit validated by a large group of adults.

It was pretty amazing for Robert and me, because others had become witnesses to something profoundly wonderful and strange that had, up to this point, been sort of a "family secret." Even though the kids at school, and certain parents and teachers, had heard the girls chant Sanskrit, that was not the same as having a group of people hear them who actually knew something about the language and therefore understood (sort of) how difficult and seemingly improbable all of this was.

From that moment on, there was something approaching the magnitude of a cataclysmic shift in our lives. We were clearly witnessing an amazing response to our daughters and the Sanskrit language that seemed to be a repeating pattern. People had an *experience* when they listened to the girls chant Sanskrit, and Andrea gave the phenomenon a name as we drove home that same night.

"When people hear the chanting, everything inside of them opens up, and they feel a kind of 'Sanskrit buzz'," she said. "And that's what happens when Sara and I chant it, so when we chant for other people, it's like everyone in the room is having that experience, together."

Yes, that was exactly what it was like. Robert looked at me in the semi-darkness of the car and we both knew what the meaning behind her words was. She was describing a "God thing." When the girls chanted Sanskrit, everyone shared in some kind of Divine experience.

The next invitation we received came from a completely unexpected source. In the spring of 1995, a professor of Sanskrit at the University of California at Berkeley called with an exciting proposal. He had heard about what the girls were doing, and was wondering if they could come and chant for the post-graduate Sanskrit class at the university, as well as meet an esteemed guest from India.

We were all a little taken aback by the invitation, but there was a growing compulsion for us, as a family, to go toward that which, with increasing regularity, seemed to beckon, and this phone call was a clear pull in an entirely new direction. It had not occurred to us to actively seek out an academic environment for the girls to demonstrate their great love of Sanskrit in, but now that the invitation had been sent, we knew the response that was required.

We packed into the car and drove the four hours to the Bay Area. Arriving in Berkeley, we followed the clear directions the professor had provided. Once we reached the university and found parking, the girls were fascinated by the large campus as well as the subdued sense of purpose as students hurried to and from their classes. But the longer we walked through the vast campus, the more intimidating the surroundings became. After several wrong turns and much backtracking, we finally found the appropriate building, but by this time, everyone was pretty tired. As the girls walked up the stairs to the classroom it was obvious they were feeling more than a bit anxious.

The professor offered a warm welcome and invited us into his classroom, where he introduced our family to his students and then, turning, presented his guest from India. The gentleman who stepped forward with outstretched hand proved to be none other than the Representative of Sanskrit for all of India!

If the girls were feeling intimidated before, this newest development catapulted them right over the top. To actually have to chant Sanskrit for a group of students at the University of California-Berkeley was difficult enough. But the Representative of Sanskrit from India?!

What would this scholarly man think about two self-taught little girls from the West, chanting India's most sacred language? Andrea and Sara looked like they were being led to the gallows when they stepped forward to sit in the chairs the professor motioned them toward.

Fortunately, the blessings of Sanskrit seemed to once again carry the day. As soon as they started chanting, both girls' faces relaxed and the language seemed to support them from within. Their voices grew stronger and more confident with each line, and the classroom was completely silent except for the two of them.

When they finished chanting, they met with an appreciative and surprised hush, which was immediately followed by warm applause. The gentleman from the East looked at the girls with great affection and approval, and then referenced the ancient Indian text, *The Ramayana.*

"As Sita said to Lord Rama, after he recited the thousand names of Vishnu, 'You did it perfectly'."

His response could not have been more encouraging, and, once again, Robert and I breathed a heartfelt sigh of relief on our daughters' behalf that their efforts had been so kindly received.

[c h a p t e r   f o u r t e e n]

SEVERAL MONTHS LATER, we found ourselves again engaging the academic world. This time the invitation came from a university in Iowa called Maharishi International University. This particular school, started by the founder of the Transcendental Meditation movement, Maharishi Mahesh Yogi, had a Sanskrit department that was very interested in what the girls were doing.

Andrea and Sara were invited to come and spend ten days at the university, where they would be given an opportunity to sit in on the Sanskrit classes and also chant for the Indian pundits who were a part of the faculty. This would be a big adventure for the girls because it was the longest time they had ever been so far from home, on their own, and Robert and I exchanged many lengthy phone calls with the school regarding the details of the visit. They were to stay with a family who lived near the campus and had children of similar ages as Andrea and Sara.

There was quite a bit of excitement on the girls' part about taking such a big trip by themselves, not to mention the anticipation of so much Sanskrit interaction. Robert and I thought it would be a great opportunity for them to experience a little taste of independence, within a protected atmosphere, and it seemed like a great way to begin their summer.

The first calls we received after they arrived in Iowa were filled with bubbly excitement and stories about all the new people they met, and how nice everyone was. But after a few days the calls took on a tone that was slightly more strained.

Andrea and Sara had been introduced to the Indian pundits, and apparently all had not gone as well as they might have hoped. I recall one conversation in particular was filled with teary voices as first one daughter, then the other, took the phone. They described how when they chanted Sanskrit for the Indian pundits, both of whom were male teachers, they laughed at the girls' efforts. One had even asked, in a not particularly respectful tone of voice, "What do you intend to do with this knowledge?"

One of the most difficult things for a Westerner to comprehend about Eastern cultures is how little regard some people can have for women. These male pundits heard Andrea and Sara—young American females—chanting a language that had been passed down from father to son for as many generations as existed in their families, and their response was reflexive.

Even though, early in the history of Vedic Culture, women *and* men cognized the *Vedas* and chanted Sanskrit, eventually the chanting of Sanskrit became an honor reserved only for the Brahmin (highest caste) males of the culture, presumably because women were occupied with the children and the home, and the study of Sanskrit required the devotion of all one's time and energy. Sanskrit pre-dates any written language, so it was kept intact through the verbal efforts of scholars over thousands of years, until the development of the Devanagari script.

> *The Rishi is Ghosha, daughter of Kakshivat, a Brahmavadini;*
> *the metre of the last verse is Trishtubh, of the rest Jagati.*
>
> —The Vedas
> Tenth Mandala
> Shloka Three, Verse Ten

But old habits die hard, and the tradition of allowing only males to chant Sanskrit is still very much imbedded in the psyches of Indians around the world. To hear these young girls chant this extremely ancient and sacred language was, no doubt, something of a cultural insult for the pundits.

After listening to the difficulties the girls were encountering at the university, a rousing four-way discussion took place over the phone in which their dad and I admonished them not to apologize or feel intimidated. It broke our hearts to hear the sniffling on the other end of the line as they hung up the phone to go to bed.

A day or so later, we were relieved to receive another call that had a very different tone. Apparently, after another chanting session, the girls made sure they were given time to demonstrate the fact that they were not just mindlessly chanting ancient scriptures. When they tried to clarify their abilities to read, write, and translate Devanagari, and their desire to do so with the utmost respect for tradition, an attempt was made by the pundits to cut them off and not even hear them out. Andrea and Sara, drawing on some deep reserves of determination, ignored the disrespect and insisted on finishing their explanation. They forged ahead and demonstrated their obvious intention to revere and honor the sacredness of the ancient knowledge. Eventually there must have been something about their passion that served to break down some of the Indians' prejudicial attitudes, because there was a sea change in the way the girls were treated.

Both of the Indian teachers became more considerate and polite toward the girls, and in fact, in a gesture that spoke of great acceptance, one of the pundits' mothers, after hearing the girls chant a particularly beautiful Sanskrit piece, approached them and put two lovely floral garlands around their necks. The mother, through a translator, told Andrea and Sara of her great admiration for them and their ability to chant Sanskrit. It was a very moving experience for the girls to have an Indian woman honor their efforts with such respectful sincerity.

Suddenly their visit had become an enriching cultural exchange in which the teachers even agreed to answer some questions about Sanskrit that the girls had been dying to ask all week. Some type of cultural truce had been reached, and the phone calls home reflected their elation at the dramatic change in the attitudes and cooperation of the pundits.

* * *

Ten days after their arrival in Iowa, it was time to pack their bags and bid their new friends farewell. It had been a wonderfully enriching experience, but both girls were eager to get home. It was a long drive to the airport—several hours, in fact—and the school had arranged for two of their alumni to drive them. It seemed the elected drivers, two young women who were heading into the city anyway, did not mind the extra passengers.

Everything about the plan seemed fine, except, as she noted later, Andrea was a little concerned when she saw the age of the car in which they were to drive that long distance. The women were exceedingly nice, though, and both girls decided it would have been the epitome of rudeness to say anything other than "thank you" when the ride was offered. Andrea and Sara wanted the entire experience to end on a high note, so they piled into the car with all their belongings and settled in for the long drive.

The first couple of hours went well, and everyone had something interesting to talk about to pass the time, but our girls were nervously checking their watches as the old car chugged along, traveling at a slower pace than they certainly would have wished, given the departure time of their flight. The women seemed oblivious to the problem, however, and just merrily chatted away as the miles rolled slowly by.

Once or twice, one or the other of the girls tried to broach what they felt to be a growing concern.

"Well, I hope we don't have any problem making our flight, because we sure do need to get home tonight," Andrea broadly hinted, hoping the driver would push the car a little harder. She and Sara had no desire to spend that night sleeping in chairs at the airport, waiting for another flight.

"Oh, no, we'll be fine," one of the women responded, with no trace of concern. "We make this drive all the time." And then, a little humorous sarcasm edged into her voice, "Besides, I thought you did a Sanskrit prayer to Ganesh when you were chanting last night, so why are you worried?"

The woman was referring to Andrea's explanation of the Sanskrit pieces they were chanting to the group that had gathered on the girls' last evening. Andrea talked about an ancient Vedic piece called the *Ganesh Upanishad,* which is offered to the aspect of God that removes obstacles from our path so we can more easily obtain our desired goals. This woman was obviously referencing that prayer as a reason why they shouldn't worry about missing their flight, though she was doing so with a very apparent tongue-in-cheek attitude.

Her comment brought another thought to Andrea's mind, though. The girls had two tiny golden statuettes of Ganesh that they always took with them when performing, placing them on their laps as small, silent guests while they chanted. They did this now out of habit, and the statues (loving gifts from a group of East Indian friends) had become very dear to them. They were guardians at every performance. Having the miniature representatives of Ganesh so near whenever Andrea and Sara were chanting served as a wonderful reminder of the benefits of removing obstacles from their minds, which would be distractions to the goal of sharing Sanskrit in the best possible way.

It was this train of thought that made Andrea start to check and make sure they'd remembered to pack their statues after the performance the night before. She remembered then that she'd put the case containing the statues into the trunk, so any checking would have to wait until they reached the airport.

"Yes, that's true," Andrea responded to the woman's comment about the prayer, glancing at her watch for the umpteenth time. Calculating the remaining miles, Andrea realized there was no possible way they would get to the airport to catch their flight. Traveling at their current speed of about twenty miles an hour under the speed limit, they would be lucky to arrive by dinnertime. "But there's that expression that 'God helps those who help themselves' . . . so maybe if we could go just a bit faster. . . ?"

She wasn't able to finish the sentence before all hell broke loose.

It started with a loud sound that seemed to emanate from the trunk. As they related to us later, both girls turned then, simultaneously, to look behind them, because they each thought of their Ganesh statues at this particular moment. As they realized later, for some unfathomable reason an image of Ganesh popped into both of their minds, and it was as clear as though they were looking at the statue itself, only the vision in their heads was much larger in size.

Then the sound started to change and become louder, and their attention was riveted on the way the road seemed to be coming apart underneath them. Suddenly there was a terrible roaring sound and the car started to shake violently. No one knew what was happening, but it felt as though the car was surely going to fall to pieces. The noise grew louder and louder, and then, Scrreech! Scrrreeeach! BAM! A series of sounds so loud it actually hurt their ears, and as the car came to a shaky halt by the side of the road, both girls turned around in time to watch as one-half of the back end of the car . . . just . . . fell . . . off!

Everyone sat in the car for a long moment, too shaken to move, and then gradually each person stirred. As though in a state of shock, one by one, they climbed out of the car to see exactly what had happened. As they all stood looking on in fascinated horror, the remaining back half of the car fell to the asphalt with a loud crash, where it lay like a large amputated body-part.

The girls' eyes were stinging with tears as they realized they wouldn't be reaching home any time that day, that night, or even possibly anytime in the foreseeable future, at least at the rate things were going. Andrea and Sara looked at the two women, who, in turn, looked back at them with expressions of complete stupefaction.

No one spoke.

Then, finally, the driver, in an obvious attempt to take charge of a rapidly disintegrating situation, stated that they could probably still drive the car if the back tire could just be fixed. When the back end of the car fell off, the sharp metal gouged a big hole in the rubber, and the tire was now sitting on its rim, as flat as the girls' hopes of making their flight on time.

As the women made motions of trying to find the spare tire and the jack, the situation started to become almost comical in a dark, perverse sort of way, and both girls began to feel a little hysterical from the combined experiences of the past ten days. First, there was the trip itself, so far away from home, for the first time by themselves. Then there was the pressure of chanting Sanskrit for those initially difficult Indian pundits. And now this! A bizarre trip to the airport that deserved, at the very least, a chapter in a book of "A Traveler's Worst Nightmares!"

As far as they could see, in all directions, there did not seem to be another living being. Not a house to hike to, not a car to flag down, not an emergency phone to run to. Nothing. To make matters even worse, it was a miserably hot and humid day, and the women were dressed nicely for a day of shopping. Andrea and Sara found that watching the two of them totter about in their high heels and nice dresses on the hot, sticky asphalt as they tried to figure out what to do next was, simply, too much. Tears and laughter fought for first place as the minutes clicked by and the girls looked at each other for some brilliant solution.

The women continued to fuss about, while the car just sat on the road, groaning and heaving like a tired old horse that had just gone its last mile.

Finally, the situation reached the point of imminent meltdown. The same woman who made the comment in the car to Andrea about not worrying about the time now turned to both girls with a frustrated, strained look on her face.

"Where's your Ganesh now, girls? I thought he was supposed to protect you from obstacles! Well? What do you call this?"

The woman was shaking with frustration and her efforts to keep from crying, as the situation seemed increasingly insurmountable. As the story was told later on, both women had received a stern lecture from the concerned host parents that the traveling aspects of the trip be handled smoothly. This episode would definitely fall into the "not smooth" category, and I'm sure these two women were more than a little apprehensive about the repercussions once they finally made it back to the university.

The next thing that happened was so bizarre as to seem fictional. No sooner had the woman said, "Where's your Ganesh now, girls?" than a huge truck suddenly appeared over the horizon, barreling down on them like an impatient answer to a prayer. Where it appeared from wasn't clear, because none of them saw any sign of a vehicle, much less something as large as this truck, when they scanned the road seconds before in both directions. But appear it certainly did, and as the driver spotted the four of them standing dejectedly on the side of the road by the broken car, he applied his brakes and coasted slowly to a stop.

Stepping down out of his cab, that truck driver must have looked like John Wayne, Clint Eastwood, Robert Redford, and Tom Cruise all rolled into one, and it's a good bet that those four women, without exception, had never been so glad to see a big, strong man in their whole lives. Had it been a little earlier in history, there might have even been a little swooning going on, but reserved sounds of delighted relief would have to do for this particular group.

"Need some help, I see," the truck driver drawled, in a comfortingly casual understatement of the situation.

Even though there was a feeling of huge relief at the turn in the group's luck, Andrea and Sara still knew they weren't home free. The truck driver listened patiently as, first, the older women tried to explain what happened to the car, and then as the girls told him about their scheduled flight. He finally shook his head with dismay when they related how little time they had before their departure.

"Well, I can change that tire for you, but the rim's bent a bit, so you're going to have to go really slow. No way you're gonna be able to get to that airport on time."

With those grim words, the truck driver must have decided "talking time" was over, because he rolled up his sleeves and set to work. The older women both looked at Andrea and Sara, and the one who'd been driving the car shrugged her shoulders as though to say, "Well, that's that."

But apparently she was wrong. Just then, another (!) vehicle appeared on the previously deserted stretch of highway, this driver also taking in the whole scene at the side of the road. The car slowed down and pulled up behind the truck. As the car door opened, an individual stepped out that both girls would later laughingly describe as the one "perfect person your children could get into a strange car with, and there would be no need to worry"!

She was a quintessential midwestern, grandmotherly figure, with a lively step and an air of quick competence that contradicted her apparent age. She walked over to where the four women were all standing around the car and watching as the truck driver worked to remove the ruined tire.

"Is there something I can do to help?" the woman asked, immediately assessing the situation. "I'm on my way to town with my granddaughter, and I saw you all had broke down."

Before the two older women could even reply to the grandmother's inquiry, Andrea and Sara had taken one good hard look at her, and another at her granddaughter, waiting in the nice, comfortable, WORKING car. Then they looked back at each other. This surely qualified as an emergency, and they knew the decision they'd just simultaneously made was a good one, under the circumstances.

There was also the fact that this nice lady's car certainly looked a lot safer than the old heap currently lying on the side of the road.

The girls quickly explained their dilemma, and before the other two women could intervene, the grandmother agreed to their plan with brisk enthusiasm, immediately grasping the urgency of the situation.

"Well, you just grab your things right now!" She was already turning, and heading back to her car. "I can get you to that airport on time."

Her confident attitude left no doubt that she would certainly give it a good try, and without another word, she climbed into her car, popped open the trunk, and revved the engine in anticipation of the challenge ahead.

The girls grabbed their bags and gave a quick hug to the other two women who were standing, mouths slightly agape, as the whole conversation transpired. The truck driver, from his kneeling position, nodded his agreement with their plan, and Andrea and Sara knew the two women they were leaving behind were in good hands, especially since the tire could now be fixed properly because the urgency had been removed from the situation.

The same woman who made the comment about Ganesh right before this whole mess began now looked somewhat sheepishly at Andrea. Glancing from her, to the truck driver intent on his work, to the grandmother already waiting in her car, the woman shook her head in disbelief and mouthed the word, "Wow."

Andrea knew exactly what she meant by that exclamation, and smiling at her, said, "Amazing, huh?"

With that she turned and followed Sara to the waiting car, where they threw their bags into the open trunk and hopped in.

As Andrea later described this incident, I thought to myself that that poor woman would undoubtedly think twice before being so cavalier about the possibility of Divine intervention again.

This grandmother was not only a life-saver, she must have also been a superb driver, as well as a competent story-teller, because the miles just flew by as she regaled Andrea and Sara with amusing tales about her family's "quiet" midwestern life. Had they searched far and wide, the girls could not have found a better representation of the finer side of human nature. This wonderful woman and her charming granddaughter will forever be "friends" to us, in their unassuming roles as the true and loving embodiment of "good people."

They arrived at the airport just in time. With a flurry of hugs and promises to write, the girls grabbed their bags and ran into the terminal.

After checking in, with a minute or so to spare, they decided to quickly call home before the plane boarded. At that particular point, the actual impact of the whole adventure must have finally been felt by them, because when I picked up the phone I heard massive confusion on the line, with both girls talking at once and crying as they tried to relate their trial by fire. I could barely understand them, and through my own concern at the sound of their tearful voices, finally got them to say that everything was fine, and they were getting on the plane.

It was agreed that they would wait to tell me all about their adventure when they arrived home. At least that was what I thought I heard through all the commotion. Adding to the confusion, and making it increasingly difficult for me to make any sense at all of the phone call, was the fact that they seemed also to be talking to other people while on the line with me.

"Oh, no, thank you."

"Oh, yes, we're all right."

"Oh, no, thank you, we have money."

To my questions of "What? What is going on?" I could hear them both starting to giggle helplessly, and then, as their flight was called over the intercom, a quick goodbye and a promise to tell me all about it in a few hours.

When Robert, Micah, and I went to pick up the travelers at the airport that night, we found two dirty, disheveled girls standing at the gate, wearing huge grins of relief. We decided to immediately go where we could get something to eat, because both of them looked like they were starving, as well as bursting to tell us what happened.

As we sat around the table at a small restaurant just down the street from the airport, and after the contents of the large milkshakes had been considerably reduced, the story came tumbling out. We heard all about what happened, from the time they left the school, and how one event unfolded into another. Their dad and I must have looked concerned when they talked about having to take a ride from a stranger, in the middle of nowhere, but as the story continued, we understood the rationale of their decision.

One sister would pick up, mid-sentence, and finish a thought for the other, and so they would go, back and forth, back and forth, until we'd heard about the entire adventure. Right after they recounted the details of their timely arrival at the airport, I asked who it was they were talking to in the airport while they'd been on the phone with me.

"Oh, those were just people walking by," Sara said, between sips on her straw.

"They were trying to give us tissues, because they saw us crying," Andrea said.

"And then other people were trying to help us," Sara supplied.

"They were giving us money," Andrea said.

"Money?" Robert said.

"Why were they trying to give you money?" I asked.

"I don't know," Sara answered, shrugging her shoulders. "I guess they were just trying to help, but we had to keep handing back the money they were stuffing into our hands."

"This one lady even started crying with us!"

Hearing how the events had unfolded was both amazing and a little unsettling. Robert and I must have had stunned looks on our faces, because Sara finally said, "Mom, you guys don't need to worry. We were totally being taken care of."

It was then that I realized the depth of the truth she had just spoken. Robert and I certainly could not have designed any events, after the initial problem with the car, that would have been any more protective or supportive of them if we'd tried. The description of the final scene at the airport, with all the kind people pressing help on these two young girls, so far from home, was really just too much to take in, on top of everything else that had already happened.

We sat around the restaurant table for a long time that night, listening to all their experiences, and reveling in the wonderful and mysterious ways that life can choose to unfold its magic.

[c h a p t e r   f i f t e e n]

"WE JUST LOVE YOUR TAPE! When are you going to be recording another one?"

Normally, comments of this type would cause an artist's heart to beat rapidly with delight, but given the fact that we had not formally recorded anything the girls were doing up to that point, we experienced some heart symptoms, but they were hardly palpitations of joy. We realized that a recording of the girls was circulating, obviously made during one of their various performances. Since the only way the recording could have been done was on a small, hand-held recorder, in a living room or some other acoustically challenged environment, it was a pretty scary discovery! We had a fairly good idea what the quality of the recording had to be, not to mention that additional copies were being made off the original, and as anyone can attest who has ever heard a copy of a copy of a copy, the quality is so diminished from the original as to be almost unrecognizable. Whatever was being passed around as a recording could not possibly do justice to Andrea and Sara's chanting, or capture the true essence of the glories of the Sanskrit language they so loved.

There was also the added and very real concern that if any pundits or Sanskrit teachers heard a distorted recording of the girls, they might be alarmed that Sanskrit was being represented in such a manner. We realized that we had to do something.

In a tradition that is the equivalent of Murphy's Law and the observed phenomenon of things that can go wrong, there is a corresponding, opposite impulse in nature that seems to endow certain circumstances with the ability to, somehow, fix themselves. We call this particular phenomenon Robert's Law, because the members of our family fully understand that my husband simply *has* to be receiving some Divine intervention when it comes to the way things tend to work themselves out for him. For us, it is an accepted premise that *something's* going on, because there's no possible way he could come up with the miraculous "fixes" that seem to just magically occur for him.

The need to address the recording problem, and the resulting situations that grew out of that need, are the things of which good stories are made. And they're also a good illustration of Robert's Law.

Since Robert had such broad experience in music and studio recording, it was decided that he would do a professional recording of the girls that could be turned into a commemorative CD. Our thinking was that when the girls were all grown up, with families of their own, they would be able to listen to what they had done at such tender ages and be amazed at their own accomplishments. (Of course, at this time, it never really occurred to us that they would still be doing exactly the same thing when they were older, so the nostalgia thing wouldn't have quite the same impact as we'd originally thought!)

Anyway, we were also starting to deal with regular requests for a tape or CD, from people in the various groups the girls would chant for, which is how the recording that we'd just heard about started circulating in the first place!

I don't know if I'd say that members of our family tend to be oblivious of the obvious, or if we're just too preoccupied most of the time to clearly see what is right under our noses, but it does seem as though things have to be practically shoved in our faces for us to notice them! Not to mention the added conundrum of us finally figuring out how we're supposed to respond to these situations with some sort of correct activity.

Now that we took a moment to think about it, we realized that people had, in fact, been asking for months if we could record something with the girls, but it didn't really penetrate our awareness as a problem until the renegade "bad" recording came to our attention. If we thought about it at all, I believe we just felt people were being polite in asking, not that they actually wanted a recording!

Now that we finally recognized there was a problem, we also had to figure out how to address it. Our biggest concern seemed to center on how we could overcome the specific dilemma of capturing the "magic" that people experienced when they heard the girls chant Sanskrit in person, and translating that to a very impersonal plastic disc. That obstacle was one of the reasons we had not gone skipping with excitement into the recording studio earlier. It seemed a formidable task.

Robert started recording the girls chanting Sanskrit, and, through trial and error, found a way to capture as much of the "live" feeling of chanting as possible. The girls practiced the pieces that they wanted to record so many times, they were practically chanting Sanskrit in their sleep (this actually does start occurring later!) before the recording had even begun, and Robert worked with the sound engineer for weeks to achieve the clearest possible recorded replication of the chanting.

*   *   *

Somewhere during this time, the thought occurred to us that if there was, in fact, going to be an album, there also had to be a name. We couldn't just call the finished product "Girls Chanting Sanskrit" or "Andrea, Sara, and the *Vedas!*" We needed to think of a name for them that captured the energy behind what they were doing.

"What do we call ourselves, Mom?" Andrea asked me one day while I was standing at the kitchen sink, washing dishes.

One word popped immediately into my mind.

"How do you say 'peace' in Sanskrit?" I asked her, drying off my hands.

"Shanti," she replied.

"Then, you are 'Shanti Shanti,'" I said, and from her look of complete elation, I knew we had just found their name.

*　*　*

One day, several weeks after they'd started recording, Robert was in the recording booth listening to them chant, and the melody to a song started drifting through his mind in perfect rhythm with the ancient Vedic lines Andrea and Sara were reciting. During a break, he picked up his guitar and worked out the melody he'd heard in his head, and then later on that day, he put English lyrics to the tune. By the time he played the partially written song for the girls, they all were able to hear something that moved them with its potential, and Andrea and Sara immediately started adding their own Sanskrit lyrics.

Before the day was over, the first Shanti Shanti English/Sanskrit pop song had been written, in its rough form, and one more step had been inadvertently taken along a strange and winding path.

The more Robert and the girls worked with the new music and Sanskrit integration, the more they realized how appealing the combination was to them. To hear the Sanskrit so artfully intertwined into a pop music format was extremely exciting, because they all knew what the potential was. It was the opportunity to appeal to a very broad audience and give people, who might otherwise never have it, the chance to experience Sanskrit. By using the original songs their dad was writing, the girls felt like they were opening the door to a much larger possibility of exposure, and providing the opportunity for Sanskrit to make its subtle and powerful statement of the ages *during this age*. Ideally, that initial exposure would stir the listener's desire to hear more of the enchanting quality that is the essence of this most ancient language.

The three of them started performing the new songs every chance they had, and the responses from audiences were extremely encouraging. Teenagers, younger children, and adults loved the music and songs, and raved about the way the Sanskrit was interwoven into the whole musical expression. The girls also continued with the pure Sanskrit chanting, and it all seemed to be a dynamic combination.

Trying to finish up the actual recording so it could be turned into a CD proved to be much more of a challenge, however. Every free minute was spent practicing, or recording, or preparing new material. The girls were also constantly learning new Sanskrit pieces, as well as having to address the problem of staying caught up at school as full-time students.

Plus, now that the concept of combining Western pop music and ancient Sanskrit had proved to be such a hit, Robert had to write more songs!

One day, after a particularly exasperating and exhausting session spent recording, an invitation came for the family to go to San Diego and have the girls appear at a large function for a Shanti Shanti performance. It was a wonderful opportunity, but we knew there was no way to get the CD finished and manufactured in time for the appearance. Even though we would have liked to take the completed CD with us, Robert didn't feel overly stressed about us not being able to do so. It was decided that the girls could tell the audience there would be a CD available sometime in the near future, if anyone expressed interest. A friend suggested that we put an order form by the front door, which sounded like a good solution.

When we reached San Diego, we located the venue for the event and made arrangements for a sound check so that microphones and equipment could all be set up ahead of time. The room in which the performance was to take place was large, and we saw that seating arrangements had been made for a crowd of at least three hundred. This would be the largest audience the girls had performed for so far.

When we arrived that evening, Andrea and Sara had typical butterfly jitters, which increased when they saw the actual number of people seated and waiting for Shanti Shanti. It's one thing to picture hundreds of people anticipating your performance; it's quite another to actually peek through the door and have all those eager faces looking back at you!

When Shanti Shanti was introduced, the girls went up and stood center stage, and Robert moved to the side where his instruments were set up. They opened with a particularly melodic Sanskrit piece, and after the first two or three minutes, the Sanskrit had exerted a firm hold on the audience. The crowd was warm and responsive, erupting with quick laughter at the girls' quips and applauding eagerly after each piece.

Everyone seemed to enjoy the performance wholeheartedly, and as the evening progressed, it became obvious that the audience was having a very special time. Close to the end of their presentation, the girls had Micah join them for several songs, and the crowd was extremely warm in their response to the presence of the three of them on stage. When they announced their final song, an audible sigh rippled through the room as though the crowd was sorry to have the night end.

It was after the last song was finished and the applause had started to die away that a gentleman who had, up to this point, been sitting discreetly in the back, suddenly stood, and gestured for the audience's attention. He was a very commanding figure, dark and tall, with silver hair, and dressed in garb that was very striking and elegant. (I later learned that he was, in fact, an Indian Sikh, and also a prince, and his stately white attire was a reflection of his royal status.) He was quite dignified, and when he finally spoke, it was in perfect English, with just the barest hint of an accent.

The whole room grew still as the crowd waited to hear what the gentleman had to say, and when all noise had ceased to the point one could have heard a pin drop, the prince lifted his arms as though to encompass everyone in the room and began to speak.

"Do you have any idea what you have just heard?" he asked, his voice carrying to every corner of the room. I was surprised that, from my seat all the way across the room, I could see the emotion flaming in his dark eyes.

And then he continued, as though to emphasize his point, "Do you realize how extraordinary these children are?"

As he spoke, his eyes scanned the room, gazing intensely at those who met his look, as though to give personal significance to his words. The people in the audience nodded their heads in acknowledgement and smiled at him warmly, as though somehow pleased that this man was expressing their own sentiments.

Continuing to speak, his words thickened slightly with emotion, "This is truly a gift, and we are all witnessing a phenomenon."

He then made motions that the entire room should stand with him, and as everyone stood, the applause began. The sound of appreciation became a soft roar as it went on and on, only increasing in enthusiasm as the girls took hold of their little brother's hands, and they all bowed in unison. Then, all three of them lifted their hands, prayer-like, in front of their faces, in the traditional Eastern gesture of thanks and respect.

Andrea and Sara, as well as Micah, all looked a bit overwhelmed by the depth of the audience's response. Leading the applause with great heart-felt exuberance was the prince from the East, and Robert and I were greatly moved by the attitude of extremely warm generosity that pervaded the room.

Finally, after the evening wound down and everybody headed home for the night, with the exception of the employees of the hotel who were starting the long process of cleaning up, we began to pack up the equipment for the trip home the next day. As we worked, we softly discussed the events of the evening, and we were all muted in our responses. It was obvious that the evening had been so strongly emotional as to leave us all feeling a bit dazed by the outpouring of affection.

We were still talking quietly while we put the final instruments and cords away when a waitress walked up carrying a basket and asked us what she should do with it. None of us recognized the basket as belonging to us, and we must have looked a bit perplexed at her question, because she then tipped it forward and revealed that the basket was stuffed full of the CD order forms that we'd casually left by the front door hours earlier.

We all looked at Robert with surprise, because he was the one who had maintained, convincingly, that there was no urgent need to finish the CD since we weren't even sure it was something people were going to want!

He reached into the basket and picked up, literally, hundreds of orders. Clearing his throat, he made the understatement of the evening, with his astonished pronouncement, "I guess this means we've got to finish the CD."

[c h a p t e r s i x t e e n]

AROUND THIS SAME PERIOD OF TIME, an opportunity arose for the girls to take on a very unusual "summer job." From out of the blue, we received a call from Mike Love of the Beach Boys, and it seemed he and his wife had heard of Andrea and Sara's Sanskrit chanting. They wanted to know if the girls would be interested in coming up to their house at Lake Tahoe, a couple of times a week, to tutor their two children. Apparently, the Loves were interested in Eastern studies and liked the idea of their children learning Sanskrit!

The whole family was invited for a "getting-to-know-you" visit to Mike Love's house, and we carefully followed the directions to his estate. Several days earlier, we'd been told by a mutual friend that we couldn't miss the house because it was so large and beautiful, so we weren't that concerned about specific house numbers once we found the actual street.

We spotted the large rock façade that had been described and pulled into the drive. As we all piled out of the car, we were so busy enjoying the always-gorgeous spectacle of the lake and the surrounding mountains that it took us a moment to focus our attention on the grand house.

Our friend was right. It was really big! We didn't see anyone as we looked around the outside of the home, so Robert walked up to the door and knocked while we all waited patiently, admiring the scenery. What a great summer job this was going to be for the girls!

To our surprise, no one seemed to be at home. Robert knocked again, and even tried ringing the bell—a big, clanging thing—but no one answered. As we stood looking around the apparently empty estate, everyone started to worry a little. It occurred to us that maybe we'd missed the time.

Andrea looked in her date book, but no, this was the right day, and we were definitely supposed to arrive for lunch. Well, this was certainly odd. We wondered aloud what we should do. Should we just get back in the car and drive home to Reno?

Finally Robert decided to walk a little further up the hill to get a different vantage point. He definitely must have managed to get a better perspective, because whatever he saw caused him to erupt with a loud, derisive snort.

"Everybody, get back in the car."

"Why? Why do we have to get back in the car, Dad?" Sara asked, confused at the sudden change in her dad's attitude, but trailing behind him as he stomped down the hill to the car. "Maybe they just aren't hearing the doorbell."

"No, and I don't think they will," he stated, surprisingly emphatic. "Especially since this is the *guard house*, and not the actual house."

His pronouncement caused us to all stop and look around again, and sure enough, the situation became clear. We'd been knocking on the guard house door and, in fact, still had to drive down the private lane a little further before reaching the actual estate, which we could see, looming hugely, in the near distance.

Back in the car we recovered from our initial embarrassment, and the thought of how we must have looked, admiring the astonishing beauty of the *guard house*, struck us as unbearably funny. Once we started laughing, we couldn't stop, and it was with great difficulty that we finally managed to settle ourselves down and assume a reasonable demeanor before getting out of the car and trooping up the (real!) front steps.

When Mike Love came to the door, I have no idea what he must have thought, looking out and seeing the red-faced Forman family standing on his porch, still struggling to suppress sudden explosions of giggles, but we were politely and warmly welcomed inside his home, where we proceeded to spend a lovely afternoon.

Andrea and Sara wound up taking the job that was proffered, and they spent their summer commuting back and forth to Mike Love's house to teach his two young children the Sanskrit alphabet and the beginning steps of language structure. It proved to be a fruitful experience for the girls as much as it did for their charges, because through this process, Andrea and Sara realized how much they liked teaching the joys of Sanskrit to kids. They found it extremely rewarding to watch how children, with the gift of youthful, flexible nervous systems, could be so immediately responsive to the "Sanskrit buzz."

After the summer was over, the girls began to seek out every opportunity to do performances for children, and they also started giving simplified talks on the origins of language that adults and kids alike could enjoy. Andrea and Sara constantly commented on how particularly fulfilling it was to walk into a classroom of young children and watch their faces literally light up after hearing just a few minutes of Sanskrit. The kids would then follow the girls outside to ask where they could get the CD, because they loved the way "that language" made them feel.

Micah's school became a sort of testing ground for new material. After the girls were invited to do a performance for a holiday celebration, the children all wanted them to come back as often as possible. It was inspiring to observe how eager the kids were to hear the Sanskrit, and how completely enraptured they would be as soon as the first few words of an ancient *schloka* drifted softly through their classroom.

These types of experiences became an amazing testimony to the effects of Sanskrit, because the kids definitely seemed so much more peaceful and happy after listening to it. The girls were prompted to start developing a Sanskrit workbook that would be user-friendly for adults as well as children. The day a neighbor child showed up at our door, holding a practice sheet of Sanskrit letters that he received from his teacher at his charter school, was a real turning point for the girls to fully understand the educational possibilities waiting to be realized. The little boy was excited to show us that he was learning some of the Sanskrit alphabet, and we were amazed at this clear indication of an educational shift going on, from a societal standpoint. I could almost hear Bob Dylan's voice intoning, "the times they are a-changing." Yes, they certainly were.

These thoughts became even more pronounced after an episode at an elementary school where the girls thought it would be fun to let the children try and chant a little Sanskrit along with them. These were very young children, six or seven years old, and their desire to vocally express their enjoyment of Sanskrit was incredibly sweet. Because they were still so young, they were not yet inhibited by self-awareness, and therefore not "embarrassed" to participate fully in the exercises. Once the children began repeating the Sanskrit phrases after Andrea and Sara, they quickly got the hang of it, and then there was no stopping them! Their desire and pleasure were clearly evident, and it was obvious they were able to really "feel" the Sanskrit.

The experience was profound to witness. The girls later described the poignancy of hearing those children's sweet voices so engaged in the effort of chanting the ancient words, making it almost difficult for Andrea and Sara to continue. Andrea said it was like having their hearts so deeply touched that it was actually difficult to keep chanting.

Another testimony to the amazing effects of Sanskrit came from the host of a local PBS talk show who purchased a Shanti Shanti CD and used it to get the attention of a group of inner-city kids he was working with. He put the CD on to play, and to his amazement the room gradually grew quieter and quieter until the only sound was the Sanskrit chanting. He spoke about his total surprise at the change in the atmosphere of the room after just a few minutes of playing the CD.

As far as Andrea and Sara were concerned, their goals were solidifying. They felt that giving parents and teachers the ability to expose children to the effects of Sanskrit was absolutely the most important thing they could wish to accomplish. Their own school experiences made them acutely aware of how much some sort of positive intervention was needed.

With all of the publicity addressing the bad effects of smoking, drinking, doing drugs, and engaging in promiscuous sex, there has actually been very little decrease in the number of children and young adults pursuing such damaging behaviors. It is obvious that what is needed is not a negative reason to **not** do something destructive, but rather a positive reason to do something good. The key seems to lie within the experience itself, since words alone seem to have little impact. And since the forbidden has always held a strong allure, it requires a formidable challenge ... when a child has the life-altering experience of the Divine within, it can be the strongest weapon against decay in any society's arsenal.

Helping children to see, and feel, their own true natures ameliorates the impulse to be self-destructive. What hold can a drink or a drug exert over us when God is beckoning?

chapter seventeen

OF THE MANY AMAZING THINGS that can happen in the presence of Sanskrit chanting, one of the most obvious is the dramatic effect it can have on our environment. The sound waves produced by the ancient language are so pure as to produce a variety of fascinating repercussions.

I had not noticed any difference, for example, in our yard until two years or so after we'd first moved in, and a number of people commented on how different the trees and shrubs around our house seemed compared to the other houses on our street. When I took a good look to see what it was they were referring to, sure enough, everything we planted when we moved in was at least a third larger, or more, than would have been expected under ordinary growing circumstances. People regularly commented on how fast everything we planted seemed to grow, making it seem as though we were in possession of the proverbial "green thumb." But the reality was that we barely had time to water, let alone fertilize, so we couldn't take much credit. In the same way it has been observed that plants, when spoken to, can respond to the vibrations of the human voice with better growth and health, so too do living things respond to the pure tones of Sanskrit chanting, only more dramatically.

Then there are the animals. Another fun result of having Sanskrit reverberating through our house at all hours, each and every day, is the reaction it seems to cause in our pets. Our two shelties love to lie by the girls as they chant, and before long their little doggy voices are croaking and growl/singing along in a comical attempt to participate. Their faces are earnest with effort as they try their best at vocalizing, but this anomaly is something reserved only for accompanying the girls at Sanskrit practice. Other oral expressions in the house can easily elicit howls of disapproval from the canine forces.

As amusing as these types of responses to Sanskrit can be, there is nothing humorous about the amazing reactions that people can have. The numerous effects that can be brought about through exposure to the sound waves of Sanskrit are both intense and diverse. It is a profound thing to witness, and the human nervous system offers the best examples of the Sanskrit phenomenon.

One particularly memorable episode occurred when the girls were giving a concert and, at the last minute, a number of "rough" boys from their school showed up. They epitomized belligerence and macho attitude as they strode into the room, and everyone's attention was immediately drawn to their presence.

Andrea and Sara saw them come in and were less than thrilled, because this particular group had a reputation for being rude and unpleasant. Other people in the crowd looked around apprehensively as the boys made their disruptive way through the chairs to finally sit down, all the while talking loudly and obnoxiously. People were obviously concerned that their enjoyable evening was going to be ruined, and their eyes kept shifting over to where the teenagers were continuing with their annoying behavior. The boys, either oblivious to the discomfort they were causing or perhaps enjoying it, continued to talk and gesture as though they were the only ones in the room.

When the concert started, the unruly teenagers stared at the girls with arrogant and contemptuous expressions, made faces at each other and burst out laughing. Andrea and Sara just forged ahead, performing their Sanskrit pieces, and then, with their dad acting as support (musical and otherwise), moved on to do their original songs as well. All the while they steadfastly ignored the troublemakers.

The girls kept expecting the rowdy group to get up and make a big thing out of leaving, as an expression of their disdain, but surprisingly, the boys continued to sit and, at some point, actually seemed to start listening. In fact, after a time, they even stopped talking to each other and gave their full attention to the stage. As the performance progressed, everyone in the audience forgot about the teenagers and just relaxed into the pleasure of the evening.

The concert passed uneventfully, except for the wonderful response from the audience that grew more enthusiastic with each number. By the time Andrea and Sara started into the last song, with Robert playing acoustical accompaniment, all potential problems had been long forgotten. The whole room was part of the reflected joy of Sanskrit.

After the bows were over, people started making their way to the stage to express their delight with the concert and to have their CDs autographed. The room was buzzing with the post-performance excitement that always accompanies a Shanti Shanti concert, so Sara was caught somewhat off-guard when she looked up after signing her name to find the teenagers from school standing right in front of her.

She felt a trifle uneasy now, as she realized that she and Andrea had completely forgotten about the boys' presence, because they had ceased to be disruptive. She had no idea what they wanted, and was a little hesitant as she smiled at them.

To her amazement they all smiled back, huge grins of delight smeared across their faces.

"That was totally cool. We really like what you do," one of the boys said, startling Sara with his enthusiastic response. What had happened to the surly teenagers who came swaggering in, just ninety minutes earlier?

"Yeah," one of the other boys piped up. "It was cool. That stuff is amazing. It makes you feel weird."

Sara, completely taken aback by their changed attitudes, stammered a reply and remembered to thank them for coming. She was having a hard time adjusting to the about-face in the boy's personalities. They were behaving so ... nice! Who could have guessed this would happen?

After purchasing some CDs, the boys again walked by the stage and waved and smiled at Andrea and Sara, then made their way politely to the door. People in the audience who witnessed the surprising exchange with Sara looked at the door through which the teenagers had just passed, and then back to where the girls were standing.

"What in the world was that about?" one person asked. "How did that happen?"

"It's the Sanskrit," Sara answered for both of them. Even though the girls were well aware, first-hand, of the amazing qualities Sanskrit can evoke in the listener, it was still a moving experience for them to watch such a dramatic metamorphosis take place.

Just then, another person who was standing close by expressed her own reaction.

"You're telling me that Sanskrit can have that dramatic an effect on people? You should bottle it and sell it to the high schools across the country!"

Everyone laughed, but the amazement at what had just transpired was eclipsing the evening. No one could believe the transformation in those boys after they were exposed to the concert, and everyone wanted to talk about it. The change was dramatic and obvious. They walked in with one attitude, but clearly walked out with a completely different one, and people seemed almost startled to witness such a marvelously positive mood adjustment.

This was not the first time Andrea and Sara had witnessed an audience experiencing this phenomenon, and it certainly wouldn't be the last. This episode was, rather, one incident in a long string of events that would eventually give rise to the realization that it would be an outstanding "life-goal" for them to try and expose as many people as possible to the wonders of the ancient sounds of Sanskrit.

Andrea half-jokingly refers to this experience as the "Sanskrit buzz" when asked about it while on stage, but the girls' realization that they were dealing with something very profound motivated them to begin the process of studying exactly what it is that causes the amazing reaction.

Here is an encapsulation of what many years of study and practice eventually revealed.

The word *Sanskrit* means "the perfected," and the Sanskrit language itself has been dated using archeological, geological, and literary methods to narrow the very broad spectrum of the possible date of origin, which has been the subject of many debates for centuries. By the most conservative accounts, Sanskrit has been in constant use since 1500 B.C., and by the more liberal interpretations, it was used before 6000 B.C. It is, in fact, the oldest and most continually used language in the world and may represent the "oldest and most original form of language" (Frawley 1995).

The Sanskrit language originated with the Indus Valley Civilization, also known as the Saraswati Culture, located in modern Northwest India. According to scholars, this society was more advanced and grandiose than the Roman Empire, and based on current studies, the various facets of human society were first established in the Indus Valley and then later adopted and modified by the Persian, Greek, and Roman civilizations. According to what remains of archeological records, the Indus Valley was an advanced society that not only contained many "well-planned cities," but also provided a massive collection of literary works that have stood the test of time. These literary works were composed in Sanskrit, and the initial and perhaps most notable of these are the *Vedas*, or the "books of knowledge." While India has many, many monumental scriptures that were composed later on in its history, they all sprang from the initial Rishis, or "seers of knowledge," who cognized these ancient texts which came to be known as the *Vedas*.

The *Vedas* consist of four books: *Rig Veda, Sama Veda, Yajur Veda,* and *Atharva Veda.* They established the religious basis for the Indian culture as well as set up a linguistic foundation. These scriptures are sacred to the Hindus, Jains, Sikhs, and Buddhists, but they contain the universal philosophy that has directly or indirectly been a part of the teachings for all of the major religions of the world today.

Sanskrit is the probable root for the Indo-European branch of languages. That would mean that Sanskrit is the basis for not only the languages of India, but is also the root language for Europe. Through observation of the various languages that stem from Greek and Latin (e.g. French, Italian, German, etc.), scholars have found that the base grammatical concepts and some root vocabulary can indeed be traced back to Sanskrit. This is, in and of itself, a rather controversial topic. The renowned nineteenth-century scholar Max Mueller stated: "It is not very long ago that all the Greek and Latin scholars of Europe shook their heads at the idea of tracing the roots of the classical languages back to Sanskrit, and even at the present moment there are still many persons who can not realize the fact that, at a very remote, but very real period in the history of the world, the ancestors of the Homeric poets and of the poets of the *Vedas* must have lived together as members of one and the same race, as speakers of one and the same Idiom" (Mueller 1874).

If one considers that Sanskrit is the distant relative of the languages spoken today, then that would mean that when we are speaking English, for example, we are just speaking a very watered-down version of Sanskrit. Actually, one can trace numerous words back to the Sanskrit language. The word "three" comes from the Sanskrit word, *tri*. The words "stay, stand, stale," etc., can all be traced to the Sanskrit root *sta*, meaning "to remain." This is not to mention all of the recently imported words from Sanskrit such as guru, pundit, yoga, etc. Due to the intense spiritualization of pop culture, Sanskrit words are popping up in English as well as in other languages.

While the history of Sanskrit is fascinating, it is because modern culture has rediscovered the transcendental qualities of this ancient spiritual language that there is such a resurgence of interest by layman and scholar alike. Anyone exposed to the sounds of Sanskrit has probably noticed its profound effects on the entire physiology, not to mention the ways in which it can increase the ability of the individual to enjoy heightened spiritual experiences. During ancient times Sanskrit was referred to as the "Language of the Gods." There are many theories as to why Sanskrit was given this impressive title. Perhaps it is because every word in Sanskrit is a prayer to God. Or perhaps it is because Sanskrit is believed to be the language used during ancient times to communicate with God, "because it was capable of producing God-like thoughts and profound spiritual subtleties" (Tyberg 1943).

The professor of Sanskrit for the University of California at Berkeley eloquently touched on Sanskrit's uniqueness. He states that "Sanskrit has the distinction of being perhaps the only language in the world that is neither 'dead' nor 'alive.' It is a special, timeless language...."

—ANDREA AND SARA FORMAN
The Shanti Shanti Sanskrit Workbook

The pure, coherent sound waves created during Sanskrit chanting produce an effect on the brain, and the actual formula for chanting the *Vedas*, where perfect pronunciation and proper meter are emphasized, is done to specifically enhance this effect.

Scientific and many spiritual writings, including the *Vedas*, state that we are made up of sound, then of light. Throughout Vedic writings, sound is described as the modality of creation. By accessing the most fundamental aspect of creation, namely sound, Sanskrit is the closest thing to the sound of creation. It is the oldest intact language in the world, with a special tonal purity. Just like the loss of sonic integrity that is experienced when we take a cassette and begin making copies, and the way each copy is less clear and precise than the one before, so it is with the languages that developed out of Sanskrit. The older and closer to the source the language is, the clearer its association.

Sara has a wonderful way of describing how language unfolds through Sanskrit:

> The entire Sanskrit language emerges from the sound "Aum" and unfolds like the petals of a lotus flower. The intricate layers are profound expressions of individual manifestations of communication that emerge as the Sanskrit language, and thus into all other forms of communication.

If we follow the path of just that specific word, "Aum," we find that it reaches into modern language through all Christian, Judeo, and Islamic uses of the word "Amen." When we read the following words from the New Testament, in the Gospel of John, "In the beginning was the word ... and the word was God," we see the importance of, and spiritual connection to, the Divine Word.

Aum, the creative vibration that externalizes all creation.

—PARAMAHANSA YOGANANDA, 1946

There are many examples of the profound experiences that Sanskrit can produce and our family has certainly received its share through letters, phone calls, or even in person when someone waits until after a performance to share a particularly meaningful episode. One of the most common experiences that tends to pop up repeatedly is that of an overwhelming feeling of the "opening" of the heart. A woman tearfully told us how her husband, who hated even the idea of stepping through the doors of a church, had come to hear a Shanti Shanti concert and wound up talking for days about a deeply religious experience he'd had, which he felt was the direct result of listening to the Sanskrit. He shocked his wife even further by informing her that he wanted to start attending church with her every week.

The miracle of Sanskrit seems to reside in its ability to release within the individual a personalized, unique experience of God. Mormon teenagers have spoken to the girls of really "feeling" their religion, sometimes for the first time. A young Jewish man related how, after attending a Shanti Shanti performance, he felt an overwhelming desire to study Hebrew, something his parents had been begging him to do his whole life. He said that suddenly during the concert he experienced a moment of pure inspiration, and understood why they had been so insistent upon him doing so. He couldn't wait to begin exploring the depth of his own Jewish tradition.

One of the most moving experiences of the girls' performing history occurred after they completed the taping of a TV interview for a local public broadcast station. There was a live audience seated in the television studio, and Andrea and Sara did a "mini" concert at the request of the show's host. After the cameras had been shut off and people were milling around, talking and buying Shanti Shanti CDs, Sara happened to look over to the table where the CDs were being displayed and noticed a young man standing at the table, using sign language to communicate with his father. She was aware of their relationship because the man was also the show's host, and at the beginning of the taping had pointed his son out to the girls. It was obvious from the gestures now flying back and forth between father and son that the younger man was telling his father he wanted to purchase one of the girls' CDs.

Sara asked one of the station's employees if the host's son was partially deaf, and would therefore be able to hear at least some of the recorded music. To her surprise, the father, who had just walked over and picked up the tail end of her question, turned toward Sara and smiled as he provided a most unexpected answer.

"No," he replied, "He's completely deaf."

Addressing the quizzical looks from everyone in the near vicinity who had heard the exchange, the father went on to explain.

"He says he likes the way the Sanskrit makes him feel."

To the uninitiated, this declaration would be confusing at best, but to lovers of this most ancient language, it is completely understandable. Sanskrit affects the physiology on all levels. The vibrations that are produced when Sanskrit is chanted properly are so coherent that the sound waves actually create an effect, whether the sounds are "heard" or not. The body hears and feels things on its own level, just like when we are very angry or very happy, those thought waves can produce a particular response in us. Negative, angry thoughts can elevate our blood pressure as well as give us irregular heartbeats, and even cause a drop in our immune system. If one just walks into a room where people have been fighting, it is easy to sense the tension in the air. What we are actually experiencing are the residual "waves" of anger still present in the room. When someone shouts angrily at us, we can actually feel their anger penetrate our body, and not just through our ears. Under certain circumstances, it can feel as though our whole body has been physically assaulted, just through the negative use of sound.

Conversely pleasant thoughts can lower our blood pressure, slow the heart rate, and increase the body's ability to fight disease. Thoughts and sounds both produce a type of "vibrational wave," albeit at different frequencies, and with different molecular densities. The pure, coherent nature of Sanskrit envelops the listener's entire being in the effects of that ancient, primordial expression. The son of the TV host could not "hear" Sanskrit, but he could feel its extraordinary effects.

Story after remarkable story has rolled in as the years have passed, and each one holds its own special dramatic meaning for the person who related it. A man wrote about his uncle, who lay in the hospital in a near coma for weeks. When the girls' CD was played over headphones placed on the patient's ears, his uncle actually opened his eyes and responded to what he was listening to for the first time in weeks. His recovery, according to his nephew, began at that moment.

Andrea and Sara speak of their own amazing experiences surrounding Sanskrit, and there have certainly been many. One incident specifically recurs while they are studying Sanskrit. When having to repeat a word over and over again in an effort to perfect the pronunciation, the girls find that a specific manifestation takes place.

This phenomenon seems to occur most often when they have been chanting for long periods and have spontaneously "dropped into" that clear experience of the deeper Self.

In one specific incident, they were repeating a Sanskrit word that would most closely translate as "to move." Suddenly, the glass candleholder on Andrea's trunk-top moved several inches. Both girls heard the sound of the glass holder sliding, and they stopped what they were doing and just stared at the candle. They wondered if they had missed an earthquake or some other thing that would explain the movement. When nothing else happened, they resumed their practice.

Again, the candle responded, only this time it moved all the way across the trunk. Repeated results were obtained every time they said that particular Sanskrit word.

This phenomenon encouraged the girls to begin studying the relationship between sound and movement, and they have found many interesting references to what they themselves have been clear witnesses to. Books on sound therapy abound in research libraries everywhere, and time and time again, studies reveal that there is an indisputable relationship between sound and its ability to affect matter.

And this is where it starts to get really interesting. Matter can refer to things other than candles on a trunk. It can also take the form of physiological or psychological manifestations, as in the case of illness, and in those particular instances, the use of sound as a non-invasive form of treatment is just beginning to be explored.

> *Studies illustrate that sound waves cause material objects to move and cluster in different shapes and patterns, depending on the tone being produced.*
>
> —DR. HANS JENNY

I could go on and on with regard to this subject, but the point here requires very little additional elaboration. Exposure to Sanskrit seems to create the ability for an individual to experience his or her own connection with the Divine. It is for this reason that the Vedic Civilization of so many thousands of years ago called Sanskrit "The Language of the Gods."

[c h a p t e r   e i g h t e e n]

THE TIME HAD COME for us to actually sit down and take a good, hard look at what was happening in our family. The lengths to which we had to go to try and "explain away" things that we ourselves could barely understand, let alone help someone else grasp, were beginning to wear a little thin. There had been too many unusual "coincidences" and "extraordinary events" to be jauntily dismissed as some sort of strange examples of happenstance. We finally had to stop and ask ourselves some very honest questions, and not be afraid of the answers we might receive.

These were some of the issues that were weighing heavily on our minds:

1. What exactly was it we were being asked to observe as, time and time again, things occurred that seemed to have no basis in logic?

2. What was the "lesson" that we were being force-fed through constantly being the clear recipients of some sort of "cosmic" support for specific types of activities? If we engaged in anything that was off the path, by even a few degrees, the support disappeared, and whatever we were engaged in became increasingly difficult.

3. What exactly was it that we were experiencing, when it seemed that there was some Presence in our lives exerting a very powerful influence over everything we attempted to do, or were already doing? And how was it we were able to so clearly feel the "Divine" in prac-

tically every aspect of our existence, but most acutely in those areas that were consistent with "our path?"

In other words ... WHAT IN THE WORLD WAS GOING ON?!

To understand a little about the unusual dynamics we were all experiencing, we tried to stand back and take a look at the sequence of events that had brought us to this point where we could even think to ask the question to begin with. We had been bombarded by so many extraordinary events that it was becoming harder to ignore the obvious than to just accept it. It was definitely feeling as though some underlying message was trying to penetrate our understanding, and frankly we were tired of pretending that we didn't hear the insistent rapping on the door of our collective family consciousness!

As we sat together over many days and weeks, having long conversations and contemplating the events of the past years, it wasn't difficult to find some common threads that had woven themselves into a pattern. When looked at through the perspective of so much time and the experience of so many different events, that pattern proved helpful in providing insight into just what it was that might be happening. It really all seemed to boil down to the act of accepting and understanding a very simple truth.

Life is full of magic.

That was it. That was the answer and the solution, all in one short sentence.

The phrase "it's a God thing" that Robert and I had always used to categorize the intellectually unexplainable was really just an acknowledgement of the repeated manifestation of "magic."

We as human beings tend to run into problems because most of us have a hard time perceiving the magic in our lives, except possibly during brief experiences when we might have felt that something special or extraordinary was taking place. But in the normal course of events, we inevitably decide it probably wasn't anything more than our imaginations, and we resume our lives, devoid of any concept of the presence of something magical. We are all too busy, too tired, too disillusioned, too bitter, to accept the "God thing" as a constant in our lives, and so we are filled with disappointment and suffering.

We look at mountains and see only obstacles; we look at the ocean and feel alone; we look at the heavens and feel insignificant. We look everywhere, and see nothing, because that is what we expect to see. The problem is, that very limitation of vision is what restricts our lives.

As a result of the extensive contemplation of our family's own bizarre experiences, combined with the unique perspective brought about by the observation of my Ayurvedic patients, as well as the many stories people related to us over the years, some specific realizations began to unfold.

It became increasingly obvious that there are some amazing and constant dynamics present in each and every one of our lives, but most of the time we are unaware of these influences. The tendency is to be so distracted by the fleeting impressions of daily life that there is little room for us to perceive that anything truly profound could be taking place.

This experience can make us feel as though we are caught on a treadmill of frustration. Most of us have a running dialog in our heads, and it can take the form of a basic series of questions that are just repeated over and over. The conversation might sound something like this: "Why do I have to try so hard? Why can't I be happy in my job? Why don't people appreciate all that I do for them? Why can't he/she understand how unhappy I feel? Why does everyone else get all the breaks? Isn't there supposed to be more to life? Why is it so hard for me to do things that are good for me, but so easy to do things that are bad?"

We ask ourselves these types of questions, in different forms, on a fairly ongoing basis. Even if we don't ask someone else for the answers, the questions still reverberate quietly in our own consciousness as we go about our days. If I were to add up all the various complaints of people who came to see me in my practice, and then divide it by the common denominator of the most unasked, underlying question, the answer would consist of one simple sentence. "Why can't I find my peace?"

Whether we're aware of it or not, we are always engaged in this "search," this endless quest for that special something that will quiet our persistently seeking natures. The irony is that we so badly want access to a feeling of peace, which is an expression of the infinite cosmic joy of creation, that we'll try almost anything to achieve it. But that is where we run into problems.

It is within the vast scope of infinite choice that we experience the mixed blessings of free will. We try so hard to attain that seemingly unattainable "something"—that special, missing ingredient that will make our life as wonderful as we inherently know it can be—that we overshoot the mark. It is easy when we have so much freedom to find ourselves overwhelmed by the quagmire of being given such an abundance to choose from. It is a similar experience to what we feel when we walk into a huge mall to buy one simple thing, and find ourselves walking out, empty-handed, hours later. Too much choice is overwhelming, and we lose our focus.

Most of our feelings of frustration and occasional despondency can be traced to the elusive quality of any perceived solution, given the scope of choices we can pursue. We exhaust ourselves looking for that evasive, enigmatic "thing" that will, once and for all, give us the feeling that we can finally stop the search, and start the delayed process of enjoying our lives. We all know that's how it's supposed to work, because modern life is one massive commercial telling us what we have to do. TV shows, self-help books, and magazine articles all offer the same respite from our woes: if we just do this or that *one thing*, our lives will suddenly come into perfect alignment. We will finally attune ourselves to some wonderful cosmic rhythm and attain a true understanding of that which always seems to lie just a fraction of an inch out of our spiritual reach.

And when we find "it," we know we'll be done. Over. *Fini*. That will be all we have to do, because once we've attained "it," "it" will be ours for the rest of our lives. In other words, our entire existence is caught in a perpetual holding pattern until we figure out the magical formula to finally making ourselves really, truly, forever, happy.

The ironic thing about most absurdities in life, and this is certainly no exception, is that there's just enough truth present in them to lure us in, and then keep us coming back for more. For example, that Supreme Life Truth that we're all seeking really is, as we always suspected, very close to us. But it actually lies just within our reach, not beyond it, as we've come to expect. And the reason we continue to feel that we should have the opportunity to live our lives more fully and wonderfully is because, somewhere deep within ourselves, we know that to be a very real state to aspire to.

So, we find ourselves in a constant dilemma. We want to be happier, we want to be more fulfilled, we want to attain a greater peace, and we want to do it all as quickly as possible, so we don't have to spend the rest of our days engaged in this seemingly endless search! What are we to do? One of the most common responses we have to this on-going problem is to try everything possible to bring about a change in our lives, and then when those efforts don't work, try a brand new set of answers, and so on, and so on! Our lives start to look like a bad TV infomercial, advertising potential life-changing possibilities. New husbands, new wives, new jobs, new homes, new towns, new cars, new religions, new drugs, new weight, new therapists, new whatever it takes, until we finally find something that makes us happy and fulfilled!

If we just keep trying new things, we will eventually, or so the thinking seems to go, find that special something we've been missing all along. The obvious problem here is that the harder we pursue our happiness, the more elusive it appears to become, but as strong testimony to the resiliency of the human spirit, that fact doesn't seem to deter us. We just keep chugging along.

We cannot say, for obvious reasons, that change is not a positive action to take in our lives. We know that it is the catalyst to new experiences, so we embrace it enthusiastically. Change is a powerful tool when we are using it for a direct purpose and not, as so often happens, a solution in and of itself. In other words, just because we change something, we haven't necessarily made it better. That distinction can be frustrating since it sometimes conflicts with the feeling that to change something satisfies the urge to affect the status quo. If we're always changing, we can remain in constant motion and never really feel what is making us so very uncomfortable.

We can also take this same pattern and go in the opposite direction. We can strive to reach that state where we have finally denounced all the hindrances in our lives that we perceive to be the obstacles holding us back from our own fulfillment. We can experience the full spectrum life has to offer in the direction of less and less, until we reach the exalted state of "no." No wife or no husband, no car, no house, no obligations, no problems, no, no, no. But what about finding our infinite joy? No!

We can repeat this cycle many times, until finally, as I saw over and over again in my practice, we exhaust our capacity for renewal and reach a point where we just burn out. We can become so tired of trying to obtain such an elusive goal that we finally just sit down in the nearest comfy chair, pick up a tall, cold beer, and turn on the wrestling channel. In other words, after all that effort, life really didn't change in the way we wanted it to and, in fact, the problems just seemed to get bigger.

And the solutions? Well, they appeared to move further and further out of our reach.

Life, no matter how trying it can be at times, is always attempting to encourage us to move in a particular direction. We might fight and kick and yell about the unfairness of it all, but in the end, if we don't find the courage to trust our true nature, our essential Self, we can lose our way altogether. The question we all ultimately have to answer is "in which direction does my peace reside?" And this can be where things get exciting.

Life often presents us with an interesting anomaly. Those actions that seem easiest in the short term invariably cause us the most pain in the long run, and conversely, that which is most difficult at the outset can, over time, prove to be our greatest joy.

There is a scene in one of the Indiana Jones movies where Harrison Ford is standing at the edge of a huge, dark precipice, and he knows he has to get across to the other side. The problem is the gap is too wide to cross, with no obvious places for him to step. Just thin air lies between him and certain doom. At the last possible second, though, Indiana Jones remembers that he has to have true faith, true trust, to accomplish his ultimate goal, and with that thought as his mantra, he tries to step out. He is hesitant at first, as he "tests the air" to see if he'll be kept from falling thousands of feet into the enormous chasm. But no rock or ledge manifests to support him in his journey across the abyss. Because he would not step off the precipice until he was sure he would, in fact, be saved from peril, he receives no assistance at all. Finally realization strikes, and Indiana Jones understands that the key to his safety lies in the fact that he has to fully commit to his faith and trust.

Armed with just his belief, Indiana steps out into what appears to be absolute nothingness. As the audience gasps with fear that he will fall to his certain death, a stone suddenly materializes under his foot, and as his weight comes down upon it, he is safely held aloft. With his next step, another stone appears, and another, until Indiana Jones is safely on the other side of his terrifying obstacle. He had to *believe* the stones were there, even though he could not *see* them.

This is really a wonderful parable for our own lives. We have to believe. We have to cultivate our relationship with God to the point that we cease to be surprised when stones manifest out of thin air and keep us from falling. Most important of all, we must have faith in something outside of ourselves.

The gift our family has been blessed to experience sprang from the acceptance of the phenomenon that was unfolding around us. We finally just had to accept it as the Grace we needed to truly "live" our journey. To find our peace, we simply had to open our eyes and experience that which was surrounding us at every single moment of each one of our days.

And that's the huge secret. Nothing that any of us needs is ever being kept from us. It's always right here.

But as we go about our daily lives, fighting to keep up with the current that seems to tug at us with every stroke, we are pulled further and further away from that quiet truth. If there's any real mystery, it's how to claim our true birthright, which is our Divine Right to believe and have faith. We have to rediscover that our peace lies in the acceptance of the knowledge that life really, truly contains all the magic we used to believe was possible when we were children. We've just forgotten to look.

Notice I didn't say "where to look" or "how to look," but simply "*to* look." We don't look because we're afraid that there actually is something beyond what we can readily see and touch, and we don't want to be disappointed if we don't see it. If we never ask the question, we won't dislike the answer. So, we don't actually see the Divine Magic that is at play all around us, all the days of our lives. We are terrified of stepping onto those invisible stones, and by not choosing to live with faith we are only living a portion of our lives. We just keep trying a multitude of other choices, none of which work for any prolonged period, because the more difficult, immediate decision seems too hard.

We opt for what appears to be easier, which is to lose ourselves in the endless distractions of daily life, never stopping long enough to actually see what we have right at hand.

And our peace, it seems, is forever waiting for us on the other side of the abyss.

[c h a p t e r   n i n e t e e n]

LITTLE DID WE REALIZE IT, but a definite increase in tension between ancient traditions and modern manifestations was about to occur. It started innocently enough, in the form of an invitation for the girls, who were sixteen and fourteen at the time, to travel to Pennsylvania and New York to study with a group of Indian pundits and priests. There was a flurry of phone calls to start with, during which a brief introduction, in a thick East Indian male voice, would identify the caller as a Vedic pundit. Once the caller had established that he had either Andrea or Sara on the phone, the voice would then command, with the utmost brevity, "Show me what you do." This was interpreted by the girls as a request for them to chant Sanskrit.

Holding the phone between them, Andrea and Sara would proceed to chant some Vedic scripture, at the end of which the pundit, again not particularly talkative, would usually gruffly request, by a specific name, some additional Sanskrit piece. They would comply if they knew it, and this would generally be followed by silence. Then, abruptly, "OK." And click.

This went on for some time, until Robert one day picked up the phone to hear a polite but thickly accented voice inquiring if we would let the girls come to a particular holy place, or ashram, in Pennsylvania, to meet with some pundits. There was also the suggestion that there would be some pundits in the New York area that our daughters might be interested in visiting. When Robert asked how they knew about Andrea and Sara, the response was as brief as everything else had been.

"CD."

"CD?" I repeated later on that night, as we discussed the curious phone call. "That's it? They want us to have the girls travel all the way across the U.S., just based on them hearing the CD?"

"Apparently," Robert replied, obviously at a loss for more of an explanation given the pithy nature of the phone call. "They just want them to come, and that's that."

At first it seemed like a ridiculous idea, but then a seminal change somehow occurred as the days passed and the concept began to foment in our minds. The girls were thrilled at the thought of such a long trip to an area of the country they'd never seen, and the opportunity to chant Sanskrit for a group of pundits became as exciting a prospect for them as it was a terrifying one for me!

Almost before we realized that we were, in fact, acting on their request, Robert found himself inquiring about a meditation retreat in close proximity to the location of the ashram that the pundit asked the girls to visit.

It was decided that Robert could use a much-needed break from work, so he could escort the girls back east, and then, while they were spending time at the ashram, immerse himself in a meditation course. I opted to stay home with Micah so he would not miss school, thereby also keeping some semblance of our normal business routine going for the ten days or so they would be gone. As bizarre as the concept seemed when we first received the request from the pundit, by the time the three of them departed there was nothing but excitement and anticipation, and no one could quite remember when the idea actually transformed itself from absurd to brilliant.

The first few calls home were full of descriptions as to how beautiful the surroundings were in Pennsylvania. Andrea and Sara had been welcomed to the ashram with a warm hospitality, and Robert met the various people who were instrumental in arranging the trip.

From the attitudes of the people who greeted them on their arrival, it was obvious that the girls' visit had been happily anticipated.

After talking with the various coordinators to make sure that everything was copacetic, Robert left for his own retreat into the peace and quiet of the beautiful Catskill Mountains, with the assurance to the girls that he was just a phone call away and would check in with them regularly.

The girls encountered their first glimpse of the only other females present at the ashram in the form of secretaries and assistants. Everyone else was male, and there was a definite hierarchy of priests and pundits that would soon become familiar to Andrea and Sara. They had pretty much expected this scenario, given the history of the traditions through which Sanskrit was preserved through the ages. As mentioned, this language was considered to be the domain of Brahmin males, even though ancient texts reveal the fact that Sanskrit was cognized and spoken by both males and females during the earliest times of the Vedic Civilization. But as that civilization declined and various religions evolved, the Hindu priests, who were male, were the ones charged with the guardianship of this ancient language. Eventually, in an effort to preserve the purity of the *Vedas* against the ravages of time, they were recorded in written script. There was a script that predated Devanagari, but Devanagari was the first script to survive, intact, to the current time. This was the origin of the tradition of the *Vedas* being passed from father to son, generation after generation, and this is what has continued pretty much to this day.

Even though the girls were familiar with the tradition regarding males and the *Vedas*, they were still taken aback when, upon being introduced to the various priests and pundits at the ashram, their reception was considerably less warm than expected, given that they had been *invited* to the ashram in the first place. Before the first day ended, in fact, the girls were both asking themselves why they had been asked to come at all.

Finally, one young priest must have sensed their discomfort and taken pity on them, because he kindly invited them to come chant Sanskrit for him so he could review their progress in the language. At first he was a little stiff and remote as they began to chant the *Vedas*, obviously influenced by the tradition in which he was raised. After all, these girls were not just females, they were Western females, and they were sitting in his ashram, chanting the *Vedas!*

His initial reserve began to diminish, however, the longer they chanted, and as he began to realize the depth of their understanding of Sanskrit. He opened up and was soon exchanging thoughts and ideas with them in a very generous manner. The girls were thrilled to have found a friend, and they relaxed a little under his warm and respectful tutelage. The best part of this relationship, from Andrea and Sara's vantage point, was that this priest, whose name was Ravi, could show the girls some of the ancient ceremonies and traditions, the learning of which was almost always reserved for males. Within a few days, thanks to Ravi, the girls were enjoying being the recipients of some very special aspects of Sanskrit knowledge.

Not every experience was that rewarding, however, if Andrea or Sara ventured to speak with any of the other pundits and priests at the ashram. One fellow in particular could barely contain his disdain of the girls, and at every opportunity he expressed his displeasure at the fact that they were chanting Sanskrit at all, much less the *Vedas*. He would barely listen to them before starting to criticize, harshly, their audacity at attempting such a revered language. He succeeded in making them cringe every time he entered a room they happened to be in.

As the days passed, this particular priest grew more critical and severe with the girls until they found themselves counting the days until they could leave. In spite of Ravi's increasingly warm friendship, Andrea and Sara still felt themselves to be functioning more at the fringe of the male-dominated ashram, as opposed to being an actual part of its routine. The lack of open acceptance was understandable to the girls, even if they did feel a little piqued by the obvious prejudice surrounding their involvement in Sanskrit.

Their dad had come to visit them several times during their stay, and his advice had been "try not to be defensive" about any perceived slights. He pointed out, correctly, that it was a high honor for two Western females to be invited into an all-male enclave like the ashram to begin with. The only exceptions to this standard were the few females who functioned in some sort of clerical capacity. Therefore, as their dad optimistically pointed out, the girls' invitation could only be considered a giant step forward within the boundaries of such a well-established tradition. He reminded them that the point of the visit was to expand their knowledge of Sanskrit, and it had been a huge success from that perspective!

Toward the very end of their stay, an invitation arrived for Andrea and Sara to attend a gathering at which the head priest, whom the girls had not yet met, was to be in attendance. As a gesture of respect, they decided to wear outfits of traditional Eastern garb to the event. Their daily wear at the ashram had also been consistent with the general atmosphere. No shorts or skimpy shirts, as they knew that type of dress would only add to the latent hostility that was already so prevalent.

As the girls walked into the large room where the event was to take place, they looked around for the least conspicuous seats. The last few days of their visit had gone pretty well, and since their desire was to wind everything up on a high note, they wanted to cause as little friction as possible. The girls sat down and casually looked around at the other guests. They noticed a gentleman seated at the center table who was generating a large amount of attention from the priests and pundits, so they assumed he was the head priest and, therefore, also the person responsible for their invitation. He looked up and quietly acknowledged the girls' attendance with a brief nod of his head, and then his attention was drawn away by one of the other attendees who approached his table.

The evening progressed uneventfully, except for the guarded looks the girls periodically received from one male pundit or another. They were the only females in the room, and that fact added to the tension they felt when the same priest who had been less than gracious to them from the beginning of their visit scowled in their direction.

The head priest looked up and indicated that he had something he wished to say, and all attention in the room shifted toward the front table. He spoke eloquently about some chosen spiritual topic, and the girls thought he seemed every bit the wise and kind patriarch of this large group of holy men.

When the head priest finished with what he was saying, he suddenly and unexpectedly looked directly at the girls and asked if they would like to chant Sanskrit for the entire gathering!

Obviously, this caused tremendous consternation on the girls' part, but there was also a stirring of disapproval by some of the men in the room. It was a muted response, given the fact that this highly regarded man had issued the request. After a moment's pause to control the rising sense of trepidation they were both feeling in response to his invitation, Sara and Andrea rose from their seats, a little hesitantly, and moved to a more central location in the room, as an attendant indicated they should do.

To say the girls were nervous at this point would certainly be an understatement, given the surroundings in which they were being asked to chant. There was an underlying hostility present in the room, and it took all the courage they could muster to do as the head priest requested. Ravi, of course, was smiling at them encouragingly, but the priest who had been so aggravated by them since their first day at the ashram glanced disdainfully in their direction. Then, in an obvious show of disapproval, he removed his attention from them completely by turning his head and speaking with the person seated next to him.

Andrea and Sara sat silent for a moment, trying to center themselves and form the connection with that special, inner quiet that they both have always believed must be established before they chant, in order for the Sanskrit to work its magic. As soon as they felt themselves "drop" into that transcendental space, their voices rose together to begin the Sanskrit piece.

They chanted for several minutes, and the more the Sanskrit reverberated through the room, the easier it all became. Before they knew it, they had moved seamlessly from one ancient piece to another, and the room was hushed except for the melodious rise and fall of their voices. As the last Sanskrit words trailed away, the room sat in rapt but surprised response, no one moving or speaking. Finally the head priest looked at the girls and smiled, and as they related to me later, it was the most beautiful smile, reflecting pure, loving kindness.

He then began to speak, and what followed was a remarkable validation of the goal Andrea and Sara had been pursuing since they were very young, as well as an enormous stamp of approval for all of their efforts. The fact that it was coming from the head priest of an all-male ashram made it truly astounding.

He began by looking out at all the men sitting quietly in the room, and then he opened his arms toward the girls as though embracing them from across the room.

"It is no accident," he began, looking around the room at the faces of all the men, "that these two, seated here before us, are female. It is also no accident that they are from the West. They are doing something extremely special, and they are trying to share it with the world. If it were possible for this effort to have been accomplished by two Eastern pundits, then it would have been. But this is exactly the way it should be, and it is for a very definite reason.

"They are here, now, at this exact time, to accomplish something very specific for the world. And it is our responsibility to help them in whatever way we can. It is our obligation to see that we assist them however they desire, and we should make available to them any information they would like to know. And that includes anything that was previously considered to be only appropriately taught to men."

It was at this point in the priest's speech that he appeared to look directly at the pundit who had been so negative toward the girls, as he concluded his message.

"We should all be *so grateful* that these girls are here at this time."

With those words, he motioned for the girls to come forward and, gesturing that two empty seats should be moved closer to him, indicated that Andrea and Sara should sit with him for the remainder of the evening.

This seemingly small gesture was actually very heavy with significance, and far exceeded anything the girls could possibly have imagined happening. Just the idea of two Western females being allowed to sit next to the head priest at his table was such a large break with a very strict tradition that Andrea and Sara had to make a concerted effort to act as casual as possible and not display the inner tumult they were both feeling.

It was obvious, even though the girls tried not to look at him directly, that the priest who had been so negative toward them was shifting uncomfortably in his seat.

The remainder of the evening passed as though in a dream, so great was the contrast between the feeling of appreciable warmth now being projected toward them by the group, and the discomfort of their previous days. The only distraction to their enjoyment were the sharp looks being directed toward them by the priest who had been such a nemesis. Though everyone else appeared greatly moved by the speech the head priest gave and was now beaming at the girls as though seeing them for the first time, he appeared grim-faced and most obviously displeased.

After the event was concluded, the girls excused themselves and went to their room to pack for their trip home the next day, all the while marveling at how wonderful everything turned out after all. Several priests had approached them and offered their services for any information the girls might like access to, as Ravi looked on proudly. Since he had been so kind and helpful from the beginning, Andrea and Sara demurred when the priests offered their help and said that Ravi had already been assisting them and had offered to continue to do so. He was so pleased, and the girls had a great friend in this forward-thinking young man.

The next day, as they were waiting outside for their dad to pick them up, the girls were surprised to turn and find that the priest who had been so difficult was actually approaching them. He didn't look overly happy to be doing so, and Andrea and Sara had no idea what to expect. As it turned out, and to his credit, he was making an attempt at something that was extremely difficult for him.

"So," he breathed, uttering the word with apparent effort as he drew up to where the girls were standing in the driveway. "I understand what it is you are trying to do now, and I think it is fine. I mean," he hesitated, then went on. "I think what you are doing is fine."

With that, he turned on his heel and walked away.

The girls looked after him for a moment, and if they were expecting him to turn around and indulge in a warm, effusive goodbye gesture, they would have been sorely disappointed. He never even looked back. He had delivered his message, and that was that.

From the girls' standpoint, his few words actually meant a great deal. To earn even the grudging respect from such a difficult adversary was far more rewarding than the expected approval of a friend.

When their dad pulled up in the car just a few moments later and asked them if they were ready to go, they looked at each other and laughed a little at the significance of his question. Climbing into their seats, they sat back and fully relaxed for the first time in the past ten days.

Yes, they were definitely ready, and what an amazing journey it was turning out to be.

chapter twenty

MANY PEOPLE, observing the way events have unfolded for us, comment on how serendipitous it seems that so many elements came together in such an apparently effortless manner. The way each situation has seemed to casually drift toward the next, they have said, is striking in its deliberateness. As examples of this phenomenon, there is the fact that the Sanskrit books were in our house to begin with because of my interest in Eastern medicine, thus giving Andrea access to a language that would change all of our lives. Then Andrea, at a very young age, realizing she needed a partner, looked to Sara, who was able to just "magically" assume that role. Robert's involvement in music certainly seems a fortunate occurrence, since that fact allowed for the natural progression of mixing Sanskrit and pop music in such a unique fashion.

The spontaneous conjunction of events, when looked at as a whole picture, seems truly amazing and we are endlessly fascinated by the elaborate attention to details. Someone (certainly not us!) is very meticulous in making sure that things unfold in specific ways.

I wrote earlier about the ways in which our endeavors are supported as long as we adhere to a specific path. I referred to an opposite reaction that could also occur whenever we attempt to do something that is not part of our "life path," but I have not expanded on what happened to us in those instances. This seems a good place to do so.

There have been many difficulties encountered on this journey, and those obstacles have been as instrumental as the joyful events, if not more so, in helping us gain a greater understanding of the abiding love that Divine guidance offers us. It is easy to see Divinity when all of life is flowing just the way we'd like it to. It is far more difficult to see a clear path when the obstacles threaten to overwhelm.

Many people have asked if Robert became so fully involved in music *because* of Shanti Shanti, and when that question arises, we tend to look at each other with an underlying awareness of the irony. The actual story is so much more complex and challenging than that of a dad who was simply doing music to accommodate his daughters' interest in Sanskrit! In truth, there were many times we might have wished it were as simple as that, but then, I suppose, we would have missed out on a clear opportunity to experience the truth of "strength in adversity," and the way even the most difficult situations can be just an opportunity waiting to happen.

The truth is, Robert loved music from the time he was a small boy, and he never really had a desire to do anything but pursue that interest. Even while we were living in Los Angeles and he was working at the TV station, his thoughts were always focused on his true path. When I first became pregnant with Andrea, it was no hardship for me to stop performing music. Not so with Robert. He always carried a cassette tape of some of his songs around with him, much the same way a photographer might carry a camera, or a painter a sketchpad.

His perseverance eventually paid off, because a casual meeting with a record company while we were in L.A. resulted in an offer for a distribution deal for an album. Everyone he told was tremendously excited for him with regard to the offer, but to my surprise he was less than elated with the whole prospect. When Robert finally made me sit me down and read the contract's fine print, I understood his hesitance.

Though at first glance the offer was every artist's dream, on closer scrutiny the contract looked more like every artist's nightmare. Even though Robert would write, produce, and record all of the songs for the record, if he signed that particular contract, he was basically forfeiting all creative license for his projects from that point forward. In addition, a huge percentage of any sales after distribution costs had been met (and this figure would be totally out of our control) would be allocated to the distribution company. We had heard far too many horror stories from people in the recording industry to not see that the fulfillment of this contract would be a painful lesson for us, and a blessing only to the company.

It was a depressing scenario, because the choices seemed so limiting. This was about the same time we found out that I was pregnant with Sara, and we made the decision to return to Reno to have our second child. I was homesick and wanted the familiar around me now that I was once again carrying a baby.

Robert brought his potential contract back to Reno with us, and all the frustration it symbolized. He was in the middle of finishing his album and would have to commute back and forth to Los Angeles to complete it. Stephen Stills, Andy Kaufman, Nicolette Larson, and June Pointer were all guest artists on his record, and long trip or not, the album had to be finished. Robert also knew he would soon have to make some sort of decision about what to do with his potential contract, but for the time being, everything was put on hold while the record was finished.

With Sara's arrival came a time of intense searching. Robert wanted to do music, and I wanted him to do what made him happy. There is an Indian word, *dharma*, that is uniquely descriptive. It means, roughly, our "calling" in life, or our unique life gift that we must fulfill. Music was definitely Robert's dharma, and we both knew it. The question was how to pursue that gift and still honor those things that were important to us in our daily lives. We both wanted to raise our children in a smaller, quieter environment than Los Angeles, and as much as he liked recording his music, L.A. studios left a lot to be desired.

Months of talk about alternatives to the traditional "big business" approach to music ensued, and all the musicians and artists we knew had thoughts to contribute. I don't know quite when it happened, but at some point during all those months of mental combing, a little idea began to take root. Somewhere along the line, the concept of building our own recording studio and attracting our own distribution deals started to form. What a great thought! Do the business side of it ourselves! Have control over the creative process! What a wonderful idea! (It was, but it was also missing certain crucial elements, which we would soon discover.)

And so began an odyssey that would result in Robert and me gaining enormous business experience in the music industry. But we were going to earn some bumps and bruises and a few black eyes along the way as well. Looking back at all we learned, however, I wouldn't change a thing, because at the end of this experience, we knew exactly what we could not ever do again. (And knowing what *not* to do can be just as valuable, if not more so, than knowing what *to* do.)

From conception to completion, our recording studio would take about two and a half years. There was financing that had to be arranged, investors to be found, and research into the feasibility of building a recording studio so far away from the musical epicenters of Los Angeles, New York, and Nashville. Our goal was to attract artists who wanted to work and create, and our own experience had been that it could be hard for musicians to finish an album when distractions like parties, groupies, and drugs were ever-present. We wanted to do something truly groundbreaking in this regard, so we set out to create an environment where artists could be at their creative best. Our studio would have live-in accommodations and be a full-service recording experience. Though we had no intention of making it so at the beginning, by the time the completion date arrived, our studio was the largest of its kind in the Western United States.

The artists came, and music filled the Victorian-style resort studio. We had everyone from Merle Haggard to White Snake, to a myriad of clients in between. Politicians came to record advertising and promotional spots for their campaigns, and artists came to do their music.

It was the fulfillment of a huge dream, or so we thought at the time, but the amount of work quickly became daunting. We had underestimated the demanding personalities of the artists we were destined to attract, and our lives quickly turned into a three-ring-circus! Our policy was "no drugs," and our desire was to provide a healthy, creative working and living environment so everyone could function at their optimum best. Unfortunately, that also meant we had many hours to fill for restless musicians who were far from home and had nothing but fun on their minds. Music, for quite a few of them, ran a far-distant second in importance.

The studio's reputation spread, and soon we were receiving contracts from a multitude of record labels, such as Warner Bros., CBS Records, Epic Entertainment, Capital, Motown, etc. Before long, the word was out that we were able to help musicians work more efficiently and could, therefore, get the actual album projects done in "record" time (read: save the labels lots of money!). That reputation also meant that companies began sending more and more of their "bad boys" to record with us, and the record labels started treating us as though, through our studio, they had found the boarding-school equivalent for recalcitrant students!

Meanwhile, our lives were becoming inexorably entangled with the very elements that were a contributing factor to us leaving Los Angeles in the first place! We had two small daughters, and the last thing we wanted was for them to see the efforts we had to go through to make sure it was records that got made, not drug deals, when artists came to our studio in Reno.

Sometimes it just became too much to deal with and, contract or no contract, the rock group was sent packing because they had decided to ignore our standard house rules. I remember one time in particular, a recording group from Epic, ignoring warning after warning, finally found themselves on a plane back to L.A. Robert was fed up and, ignoring their dire threats of "You'll be hearing from our label," was relieved to see them go, even though we knew it meant we'd suffer from the termination of their contract. Sure enough, within hours, a very heated representative from their label was shouting through the phone lines from L.A. at Robert, "How dare you? Who do you think you are? Do you know who *we* are?"

Robert was an immovable rock. Tired of the shenanigans, he refused to budge. Imagine our surprise when, opening the door a week or so later, we found these same musicians, bags in hand, standing on the studio's front porch.

Their faces looking extremely sheepish, they reminded me of naughty little boys who finally realized they'd pushed their parents too far and were reaping the consequences.

"We're sorry, man," the lead singer said contritely, when Robert came to the door. "We want to finish our record, and we won't do anything else that'll break the rules."

Apparently the label had realized that if *we* didn't record the album, someone down in L.A. would have to, and that prospect was far less appealing than an abject apology. Life went on, and their album was finished, on time.

Not everything went quite so smoothly or ended on such an upbeat note, however. I'll never forget coming in one day during a long recording engagement with a rap band, the members of which were forever doing things we couldn't have imagined when we wrote our "house rules," much less have known how to handle once they occurred.

As I walked into the reception area in the morning, I looked up the staircase to the rooms where the bands slept and saw, to my absolute horror, three young girls in Catholic school uniforms coming down the stairs. The looks on their faces told the whole story, and I imagined a whole world of trouble descending on us when their parents found out what happened.

I'm sure my voice sounded every bit as strained as my nerves were as I asked, "What are you girls doing here at this time of the day? Aren't you supposed to be in school?"

I managed not to groan aloud as I was hysterically trying to calculate their ages ... fifteen, sixteen!?! Oh, my God.

One of the girls gave me a snide look and said, unnecessarily, "We didn't go today."

Even as they tried to argue with me, insisting that they had to wait for "the boys" to take them home, I gave them the most serious lecture that, in my current state of acute distress, consisted mostly of half-finished sentences.

"What is the matter with you ...?"

"Do you want to ruin your ...?"

"What are your parents going to ...?"

I didn't know what else to do but scold furiously and get those girls off the premises before "the boys" got up and complicated this situation even more. So, the girls were unceremoniously placed in a cab and sent on their way.

A no-visitors-no-matter-what rule was inaugurated, for this particular group, on that very day.

To say our studio attracted an eclectic mix of clientele does not do justice to the humorous situations that arose the longer we were in business. I remember one particular episode when a rock group, coming down the hall on their way to the studio, found themselves face-to-face with a group of political aides and their candidate for the United States Senate. I had just come out of a side door as both groups were heading down the hall in opposite directions and, realizing we had a pending train wreck, tried to re-direct traffic.

I was too late to affect anything, though, and suddenly everyone was standing at an impasse in the narrow corridor. Rock musicians with bare chests and pierced nipples, in a direct face-off with a sea of blue suits and starched white shirts. They all just stopped for a full minute, and stared.

Finally, a low chuckle ran through the hallway, starting from someone who was standing next to the aspiring Senator, and suddenly everyone seemed to get the joke. With haphazard grins on faces from both groups, and amazing aplomb all around, half of them politely moved to the side and let the others squeeze by. I just shook my head and closed the door.

After several years in business, the uncomfortable realization dawned that we were running a recording studio so artists could do their music, but the one musician who had been the driving force behind the effort was too busy running the studio to even think about his own music! Poor Robert. He had been struggling so hard to create a wonderful environment in which to produce music, he was too busy to realize that everyone was doing music except him!

Something had to change, and it had to change right away. We had investors, so we couldn't just walk away from the business. It had taken years to develop the reputation that justified having all these recording artists coming to Reno, and Robert had been instrumental in building that good business capital. What to do, then?

The problem was simple: we had created a business that required a huge investment of time and energy to keep it going, and if we stopped, so would the business. Our two investors would not have been happy with that development, having no musical or recording business experience on their own, so we were left with a dilemma. What could we do so that the business would continue to run, but we wouldn't have to spend every waking minute either dealing with a raucous group that was currently there or soliciting record labels to send us the next group?

That was when the idea of forming a record label in Reno became relevant. The thought was that if the studio were also the home of a vital recording label, revenues would be more consistent, and we could have some portion of our lives back! (This was one of those places where, when circumstances aren't optimal to begin with, but the decision is made to dig in even deeper ... one is eventually going to end up knee-deep in you-know-what!)

Coincidentally, this was the same time when the Milli Vanilli debacle was occurring on the world music stage. The word was out that they had not really sung their own songs, and the proverbial "poop" had hit the fan. It was tossed around and eventually decided by the "money people" that our idea of developing an actual record label in Reno was cogent. The suggestion that we take Milli Vanilli and get them to actually sing on their own album was spawned, and since the millions of Milli Vanilli fans, especially in Europe, were absolutely rabid to hear them sing, it was felt that the idea might actually work.

So began a period of absolute, undeniable agony. If we thought we had seen problems before, once Milli Vanilli came to live at our studio, a whole new definition of the word "difficult" began to evolve. One of them was French, the other German, and not only did they not sing, we had a very difficult job just understanding them most of the time! We had to bring in a linguist from the university to work on their English pronunciation. Writers were brought in, directors for the music video, physical trainers, masseuses, musicians, and still more musicians, helpers, aides, aides to the helpers, and on and on and on.

It was all I could do on one particularly exhausting, frustrating day to not start laughing out loud when a "gofer" approached me about our inadequate selection of "shoe creams."

"Shoe creams?" I asked, determined not to show my irritation. "What is wrong with our shoe creams?" I didn't actually know what shoe cream was, but I was too tired to inquire and figured the answer would clarify itself.

"They want a creamier color. This one's too white."

The assistant, a young, eager girl, was doing her best to irritate me by making this request seem like the most important thing she had done that day, and she was glowering at me impatiently, all the while waving an open jar of the offending "shoe cream" so close to my face I thought I might wind up with some on my nose. Fortunately, at that very moment, I was paged to a phone call, so was spared from having to react in a more civil manner than I felt I was actually capable of mustering at the time. I hurried off to catch my call, leaving her fuming and fretting over the unfairness of it all. All I could manage to think was, "When did life become so bizarre that 'shoe cream' moved to the top of the priority list?" It would have been funny if it hadn't been so true.

We finally managed to start the actual recording process, and everyone literally held their collective breath while we waited to see if after all this work, Milli Vanilli could actually sing. I think they were very aware of the pressure because the stress was running high, but no one could make this stage of the process any easier for them than what it was. They needed to be able to sing, and it had to sound good, period. No amount of hype or spin could gloss over their first "real" album, and what people would eventually be hearing on tape and in live performances.

After the first few days, it was apparent that people were starting to relax. The boys sounded surprisingly good, and the material was catchy.

The next hurdle was the making of the video. A top director was hired, and the publicity machine started to slowly gather momentum. Inquiries for bookings on the Arsenio Hall Show as well as others were made, and expectations were rising as word got out that Milli Vanilli's new record was about to be released.

It was around this time that Robert and I came to the full realization that we absolutely hated what we were doing. This should have been an exciting time for us, but something about it all just didn't feel right. (Actually, it felt horrible.) This was clearly not the artistic path we had hoped to walk, and in fact, was so far removed from our initial goal that we were scarcely able to recognize it anymore amidst the detritus of other people's ambitions and aspirations.

We were surrounded by lifestyles that were redolent of behaviors and rationalizations representing a type of spiritual wasteland that felt very bleak to us, especially considering how opposed it was to the initial impetus responsible for the whole effort. We had wanted to create a more heavenly way to do music. And we'd wound up with the recording studio from hell.

It didn't appear there was much choice except to just put our heads down and get the whole thing brought to some sort of conclusion. We knew we had responsibilities and obligations, but our hearts were not engaged in the process. We were clearly fighting an uphill battle, and that reality struck home in a definitive way the night we received a call from one of our employees informing us that a member of the band was up on the roof (the building was three stories tall) attempting to buy drugs from someone down in the parking lot.

Apparently, all of our attempts to create a healthier, more dignified approach were being ignored. Robert went down to the studio late that night and did his "angry father" routine, but he came home quiet and unhappy with all that we were having to endure to just finish the job.

"There has to be a better way to do music than this," was all he muttered before turning over and trying to go to sleep.

My own thoughts were a silent prayer asking that we somehow be given a way to finish this whole mess. I knew everything would get easier if we could just get past this particular set of circumstances. (Be careful what you ask for!)

Around this time our partners, who, up to that point, had never cared anything about the actual recording business, suddenly caught the "money bug," and our silent partners became very noisy ones, indeed. Even though Robert and I were struggling to finish the album and bring the video to completion, while still adhering to some kind of reasonable budget, they were becoming increasingly captivated by all the business potential they could see looming just beyond the horizon. Large figures from calculated record sales, both in the States and abroad, started ricocheting through every conversation.

Robert and I cringed at each meeting when we saw the overly eager looks around the table, knowing there was still a lot of work ahead of us before there would be a reason to start reveling in any supposed achievements. No one was listening to us by that time, though, because the "bug" had taken such a firm hold on the partners. If I could have drawn a cartoon to illustrate the prevailing sentiments, there would have been big dollar signs flashing in the eyes of the partners as they contemplated their imagined successes.

Somewhere along the line, enthusiasm had turned into a kind of gold-rush hysteria. All common sense had vanished, and Robert and I found ourselves in the middle of a very difficult situation. People started vying for authority, and decisions were made that we had no control over, sometimes not even knowledge of, until it was too late. We wanted to scream, "STOP! SLOW DOWN!" We understood all too well, given the amount of work and difficulties we'd gone through, that this was not a guaranteed success. It was just a process, and we intuitively knew we weren't even partway down what could be a very long road.

The first crack in the dam occurred when the Arsenio Hall Show was booked at the orders of one of the partners, but there were no albums available in the stores to support the band's appearance.

Robert kept saying, "No, no, don't do a show with national exposure when you have no product. There's no point, and you'll just frustrate your audience."

By this time no one was listening, though, and the show was a miserable public relations mess. As Robert predicted, there was a huge flurry of people trying to buy the album, only to find it not yet available in stores.

But that wasn't our largest problem. Greed had eaten a hole through the fabric of our entire little enterprise. Thinking that Robert and I were somehow just not understanding the huge possibilities waiting to be realized, our partners surprised us one day by announcing they were staging a hostile take-over of the business. As was explained to us later, they felt that it was unnecessary to split the profits so many ways. They were the investors, and they deserved the lion's share of what was sure to be a flood of profits. Now that we had done all the work, the investors felt empowered by their pending success to step in and take the whole thing over.

Unfortunately for them, the record companies didn't agree, and the entire effort of the previous two years was slam-dunked before it could even get off the ground. As soon as word of the take-over spread, contracts were cancelled, and the new Milli Vanilli album was put on a shelf, never to be released.

The story of this debacle can still be seen on VH1, but that rendition chronicles just a few of the events that occurred. Two years of effort disappeared in one moment of arrogant grasping. We eventually wound up suing the partners and won a unanimous jury verdict, but the partners declared bankruptcy and went slinking out of town, leaving the studio with no business, no contracts, no record to release, and our hearts in tatters. Bankers came and asked us to step back in, but Robert shook his head miserably and explained that it would take too long to re-build the clientele base.

It took months of recuperation. Robert was devastated, to say the least. He had no idea what he was going to do for a living. We were emotionally invested in a business that had taken years for us to build up, and even though we'd grown miserable running it, we certainly didn't want someone to step in and destroy it all.

One day, about two months after the whole mess occurred, I was perusing some of my Eastern books and came across a section on something called "Jyotish," which is, I discovered as I continued to read, a type of extremely precise Indian astrology. I had never been a huge fan of astrology, but the more I read, the more fascinated I became.

Jyotish is the study of influences we experience as a result of our time and place of birth, and the case studies provided were amazing. Jyotish is used to indicate difficulties we may encounter during our lives, and ways we can strengthen those things that can be helpful to us or lessen influences that are negative.

This, I thought, might be fun, especially given what we'd just gone through, so I went off in pursuit of someone who could do a Jyotish reading for us. In my heart I knew the whole thing with the studio had some sort of deeper significance for us, but we needed to see the event from a different vantage point in order to achieve understanding.

In another example of our encounters with amazing "coincidences," it happened that two Jyotish masters from India would be visiting Reno that coming week! When I called to make an appointment, I was struck by how fortunate it was that they would be here just at this particular time. I went off to tell Robert that I had come across something that might prove interesting. He was politely agreeable, but certainly not enthusiastic, and I could tell he was just going along with me to be pleasant. I don't think he felt much in the mood for amusing diversions.

The day of the appointment found us feeling more optimistic than we had been up to that point. We'd spent the past few days looking at options for work that were different from what we'd previously considered while the stress of the situation was still so fresh. The possibilities weren't all that bad.

The further away the entire mess got to be, the more I was starting to feel a huge sense of relief that we were actually not trying to fit square pegs into round holes anymore. I knew that we could not have continued to make that particular effort work, no matter how hard we tried, because it was simply not dharmic for us. I felt that we had unintentionally stepped into an area where we shouldn't have been, and I was just beginning to experience how wonderful it felt to be back to our own lives, going down our own unique path.

The destinies of all those people from the studio were not the same as ours, and we could not make the divergent paths intermingle, no matter how hard we tried. I was beginning to think that, as difficult as it all might feel right now, we had been spared a huge amount of misery. I knew Robert would sense the inevitability of all that happened as soon as he got his bearings a bit more. An activity that I felt might directly contribute to that healing process was to define some positive changes we could pursue right now.

One of the things that drove Robert almost crazy during his years at the studio was the frustration of always needing an engineer to do the actual process of recording the music and then mixing it for a final product. If there wasn't an engineer available, or he/she had slept badly the night before, or was having a fight with a spouse, everything was brought to a dead standstill. Many times at the studio, Robert had been exasperated by the lack of control a musician had when it came time to record the actual music.

Suddenly, with all and no possibilities stretching out before us at the same time, the idea of changing things was potentially encouraging. Robert decided he was going to learn how to do *everything* that the music business entailed, beginning to end. He was going to learn how to record, engineer, and mix the music himself, something he'd never had the time or opportunity to do while running the studio.

This effort would initially open up new areas of work, but on a more personal level would satisfy a desire that had been niggling at him for many years.

Having all these thoughts as a basis for the day, we were fairly upbeat when we went for our visit with the Jyotish masters. Arriving at the address I'd been given when I called, we found a room full of people waiting for their appointments.

We were right on time, so we were ushered in. The two men were dressed almost identically in traditional white Indian garb. They were pleasant, polite, and very hard to understand, as their English was somewhat limited. I had provided the requested information regarding Robert's place and time of birth over the phone at the time the appointment was made, and now both men were intent as they looked over the information that was sitting on the table before them.

After a while, they both moved suddenly, as though simultaneously stirred from a deep reverie, and one of the gentlemen shifted in his chair and then looked up and smiled at us. He looked at the other Jyotish master, and then they both grinned as though they knew a secret. Robert squirmed a little in his chair, not quite understanding what these two strangers could possibly be finding so amusing in his chart.

"Have you had a little trouble with your business life lately?" the Indian man sitting on our right asked, his tone humorous and wry at the same time.

Robert looked at me, and we both turned and stared, surprised, at the men. How could they possibly know that? We had read in the paper that they just arrived from India a day or so before. Surely they had not had time to research each and every person who had booked an appointment with them. Besides, I realized with a start, I had only given them Robert's first name at the time I made the initial call.

"Yes, I have had some difficulties," Robert said, his voice not revealing the depth of the understatement.

Both Indian men glanced once again at the papers before them, and then looking back up at us, chuckled as though whatever they saw was vastly amusing. Robert shifted in his seat and looked at me as though to say, "What is so incredibly funny?!"

I shrugged slightly, as bemused as he was by their reaction, but smiled my encouragement for him to hang in there.

One of the men broke the quiet by saying, "Yes, you've definitely had some difficulties, but they are nothing. It is all going to be just fine. You see, you are entering the influence of Saturn, and that is the time in our lives when all that is unnecessary falls away, so we may experience the truth of our existence. This allows us to know what is truly important to us. Do you see?"

Robert immediately latched onto the words "it is all going to be fine," that being the most positive reflection we'd heard thus far on the events that had taken place.

"When you say it is all going to be fine, is that in the universal sense that everything is really, always, fine? Or do you mean, specifically, that my business life is going to be fine?"

I had to smile at the intensity with which Robert was trying to understand exactly what these two Indian men were saying. He had suffered so much in the past weeks and months because he felt a huge responsibility toward his family. It was obvious he thought that if these men knew so much about what had just transpired, they might also have a window into what lay ahead.

It was interesting how these two unassuming, middle-aged men, by virtue of their seemingly prescient understanding of our circumstances, were able to encourage confidence in a discipline that we had no prior exposure to until walking into the room several minutes earlier. The men expressed not the least bit of surprise by our reaction to their abilities, but rather focused on Robert's question.

"Yes, yes, your business life will be fine," one of the men responded, more kindly now that he saw the intensity of Robert's response. "You will just do those things that are important to you now, and everything will be fine. It was all, just … an … adjustment. But everything will be all right now."

I don't know if it was the confidence those two Eastern men evoked, or the need Robert and I had to hear something positive, but we left our appointment that day feeling lighter than we'd both felt in years. Perhaps something more had taken place in that room, like the accessing of some knowledge we were intended to hear at that particular moment in our lives, which is one of the precepts of Jyotish—we are always given knowledge at the exact time we're supposed to have it, and not one moment before. In any case, from that day on, we stopped worrying about what we were going to do to make a living, and just started doing what it was we loved to do.

And this "adjustment" would happen to include Robert eventually writing spiritual music for his daughters to record.

[c h a p t e r t w e n t y - o n e]

AROUND THIS TIME, Shanti Shanti began to attract quite a bit of media attention. Each day seemed to bring new calls for one type of interview or another, and they came from a variety of different venues, from public television to radio shows, magazines, and newspapers.

Chanting Sanskrit under unusual circumstances was beginning to be a common occurrence. Andrea and Sara found their ability to chant in uncomfortable and out-of-the-ordinary environments tested to the nth degree. The challenge of having to sit on soundstages in hard plastic chairs, while being assaulted by bright lights and stared at by the eye of impersonal camera lenses, all while trying to do Sanskrit from a "spiritual place," was becoming a regular part of life. When a "prove-it-to-me" host was thrown into the mix, demanding a quick example of the "Sanskrit magic" so he could judge for himself if it had any merit, things could get pretty uncomfortable, and at times, just plain exhausting. The rewards would far outweigh the discomforts, however, whenever the members of an audience would get to experience, for themselves, the indescribable joys of Sanskrit.

During one particular interview, when the girls were eighteen and sixteen, this particular point was clearly illustrated for all of us with a very laid-back cameraman who seemed completely bored and, in fact, not even to be listening during the taping of a brief but very beautiful Sanskrit chant. He was apparently caught off guard because, at the end of the piece, as the girls' voices trailed softly away, he suddenly erupted with a loud "Wow" in such a spontaneous and enthu-siastic way, the sound engineers had to adjust for the interference that the stage microphones picked up.

The cameraman seemed genuinely surprised by his own response and looked around at his cohorts as though embarrassed by his outburst. I'm sure the host was taken aback by his "talking" cameraman, who committed a definite no-no by not just being seen, but heard! But he seemed to be too pre-occupied managing his own response to the San-skrit to give more than a glance in the direction of the cameraman.

The host's eyes had unexpectedly welled up with tears, and, after clearing his throat several times in an effort to regain his composure, it soon became obvious to everyone on the soundstage that he was having to make a concerted effort to get the interview back on track. Another interviewer jumped in to help him through the rough patch.

Both of these people had definitely experienced the "secret" of Sanskrit, and what made it all the more wonderful was that neither one of them had been looking for or expecting any such reaction. It was amazing how completely startled they were by what they'd felt.

Time and time again, we were able to make the observation that Sanskrit was, truly, the great equalizer, the true common denomina-tor, because it seemed to have the capacity to break down all kinds of different barriers, whether cultural, social or religious, and make everyone feel like they were a party to something wonderful. For those few moments, the cameraman and the TV host shared a unique experience, and as they each struggled to understand their own responses, something very powerful was taking root.

After the show, the host couldn't stop talking about how won-derful the Sanskrit had made him feel, and how he wanted CDs to send to all of his friends. Just as the girls were preparing to leave, the cameraman tracked them down in the back of the studio, and glanc-ing quickly around as though not wanting to reveal his mission to any of his co-workers, asked if he could please purchase a CD to share with his daughter. He was so moved by the effects of the Sanskrit he could barely talk to the girls without becoming extremely emotional.

From this point on, it seemed that the extent and variety of exposure for the girls increased exponentially. It became almost comical to observe that, in the course of a single day, Andrea or Sara could take a phone call from a guru in India, do an interview for a women's publication, go to a luncheon for a group of professionals looking to lessen the stress in their lives, then do a performance for a Christian religious group, and finally end up at a dinner where the topic of discussion was how to positively influence society's youth!

At each and every encounter, Sanskrit paved the way. After even just a small sample of chanting, people would react as though they had been touched by something extraordinary, and, indeed, they had.

We've all heard the phrase, "water finds its own level," and I have truly understood this reality with regard to Sanskrit, except I would change the line to read, "Sanskrit finds every level." This observation is a reference to the apparent ability this most ancient language has to affect people from every walk of life, in a very profound way.

The reality of this phenomenon really made its presence known as a number of different religions began to solicit Shanti Shanti performances for their particular sect. At first, I have to admit to feeling a little flabbergasted at the consistently warm receptions provided by the various religious communities. I kept asking the girls, "Do they know what it is you do? Do they know Sanskrit comes from the East?"

Even though we had experienced genuine acceptance from the Catholic community when Andrea was younger, it was the seemingly heartfelt acceptance from so many totally different religions that was the impetus for my questions.

"Yes, Mom," Sara or Andrea would answer, their impatience with my skepticism evident in their voices. "They like how it makes them feel, and everyone says it gives them a clearer experience of their own lives."

The obvious question then became, for me, how could any religion not embrace that? When we have that feeling of clarity, that moment of touching something deep inside us, our prayers become a more lively expression within. Sanskrit seems to open the lines of communication, thereby allowing us to feel the essence of our own Divinity, as well as the Divine that is present in everyone and everything around us.

The girls had wonderful illustrations of the commonality of this phenomenon through their performances for many different religious groups, and each time, it was a special moment. The interesting thing was not how different each group was, though, but how similar their reactions to the Sanskrit.

As I mentioned earlier, one of the most important things to the girls with regard to the actual process of chanting Sanskrit is the necessity of having a very clear "inner connection" established in order to maximize what the audience experiences. It is very difficult for them to chant when this is not present, and both girls can, at the same time, suddenly be unable to access a specific Sanskrit line, or even be unable to chant an entire piece without great effort.

It is interesting how, when Shanti Shanti performances are held in churches or other spiritual communities, the Sanskrit seems to just flow, and the girls love to chant in those environments for that very reason. It only makes sense that when people gather together and invite God into their midst, this process, repeated many times, will have an effect on the environment, as well as on the people who are participating in the activity.

As Andrea and Sara have described it, in certain circumstances they can almost not chant fast enough to accommodate the amount of Sanskrit pouring through them. They refer to this occurrence as feeling something like the opening up of an internal faucet, from which the ancient language rushes forth.

But there can also be an amazing clarity that arises in the most unexpected of circumstances. It's not unexpected that a church environment can give rise to clear experiences of consciousness, but as was observed in the TV studio with the show's host and the cameraman, a particular setting can be a surprise with regard to the degree of response that is elicited.

A wonderful example of this occurrence came when Shanti Shanti was asked to do a closing night performance for a large financial seminar. Andrea and Sara had been hesitant when the request was made, concerned that the participants in the seminar would be getting something quite different from what they signed up for at a weekend of economic lectures. A performance by Shanti Shanti seemed incongruous, at best, but the seminar's organizer assured the girls that everyone would welcome a break from the tedium of discussing finances.

The organizer then made a suggestion that gave both girls pause. As they later related it to Robert and me, laughing at the difficulty of the request, we understood their reaction.

The conference coordinators had asked that the girls try to make their performance as "unspiritual" as possible.

To which Robert commented, "And we can do that ... how?"

The joke here, of course, is that Sanskrit is purely a "language of the spirit." The reason people from every walk of life respond so positively to its effects is that Sanskrit penetrates our inner obstacles, thereby allowing us the experience of our own unique connection with the Divine.

How, then, would one do Sanskrit without the spirituality? Well, obviously one wouldn't, because it cannot be done. So, it was decided that Shanti Shanti would give one of their regular concerts for the financial seminar, and let the cosmic chips fall where they may!

The night of the concert, Robert was up on stage frantically hooking up microphones and equipment while the very last speaker for the weekend made the final few minutes of his presentation. I watched with some amusement, accompanied by mild trepidation, as charts and graphs reflecting tax benefits rolled across the screen that stood center stage, while the large group of participants shifted restlessly in their seats. It had probably been a long weekend for them, filled with facts and figures and bottom lines, and I couldn't help but wonder what their reaction would be when the girls completely shifted the mood by walking up on stage in their flowing formal Eastern dresses and Robert picked up his guitar.

While waiting for the speaker to finish his presentation, I looked around the room at the bored, tired faces of the accountants and financial consultants as they waited for the talk to end. Whether they realized it or not, these people were all about to have a unique experience. They were going to be bathed in the joyful sounds of a very special ancient language, and that event might have broad-reaching ramifications for some of them. As I continued to wait for the girls and Robert to take the stage, I leaned forward in my chair and, resting my forehead in my hand, marveled at how strange our lives had become.

As I expected, the initial reaction as Shanti Shanti climbed the steps to the stage consisted more of a "what now?" type of response than the suppressed excitement that is normally present. The girls smiled encouragingly at the reluctant audience as the spokesperson for the seminar gave them a warm, though somewhat hesitant, introduction. (It's a dead give-away as to the general level of perplexity when an announcer's voice rises in the middle of a sentence, or at the end, as in, "And they've been studying Sanskrit? Since they were eight and nine years old?")

Gamely, Robert nodded to the girls to begin, and Andrea and Sara stepped up to the microphones. Without further ado, they launched into a very long and intense Sanskrit piece. This choice surprised me because my own instinct would have been to start with a song to "soften up" the audience, especially given that this particular group had absolutely no idea who Shanti Shanti was, or why they were performing at their financial weekend. Most of them had probably never even heard of Sanskrit!

Inwardly, I cringed a little as I looked around and saw that the people in the audience seemed to be glaring at the stage with less-than-positive expressions on their faces as the Sanskrit chanting continued to sweep over the room. One could almost hear the crowd's thoughts, generally reflected in the atmosphere as "What the - - - -?"

The girls' choice to do an intense Sanskrit piece at the beginning, however, was the correct one. After the group's initial reaction, the Sanskrit worked its magic like a master conjurer. I could see people who had been indifferent at first, refusing to even give their attention to the stage by talking and shuffling papers, gradually give in as, slowly, the Sanskrit sounds started to massage away their initial reactions of discomfort. One could visibly observe the stress in the room begin to dissolve as person after person abandoned any pretense of ambivalence and began to gaze intensely at the stage, gradually becoming more peaceful and quietly attentive.

As the girls moved seamlessly from one piece to the next, the room became vibrantly alive to the effects of the Sanskrit, and the audience seemed to get more enthralled as the performance continued. When Robert launched into a musical interlude as an introduction to a song, everyone responded with exuberance. The group-mood of just a few moments before had been disgruntled and tired, but now shifted into a brand new level of energy that I would guess few of them suspected they possessed at the end of such a long day.

When Andrea and Sara started into a particularly beautiful piece, I suspended all of my own awareness of the situation, which had been so acutely directed toward whether or not the audience would enjoy the performance, and just closed my eyes and relaxed into the experience itself. A few moments later, I opened my eyes as the piece was ending and was startled by the reaction of the crowd. People were jumping to their feet, and the applause was ringing out loudly. Most surprising of all, though, was that many of those standing had tears streaking down their faces. It made my own eyes sting to see how deeply touched the audience had been by the Sanskrit.

I once again had that now-familiar sensation rush through me of "What's going on here?" as I tried to absorb the transformation in the people at this seminar.

After the performance, Andrea and Sara were besieged by their "new fans" asking for autographs and reaching out to the girls for hugs with tearful promises to travel to "wherever Shanti Shanti is next appearing." Several people spoke of missing their various religions, saying they just experienced something they hadn't had for many, many years. One man shared that, during the performance, he "flashed on how empty and stark my life had become, driven by bank statements and bottom lines." He told the girls that he'd made a promise to himself that when he returned home he was going to make some drastic changes in his routine that would incorporate a more spiritual direction for his life. He laughingly concluded with, "Who knows? Maybe my finances will even improve if I straighten out my priorities!"

While this man was busy contemplating the updating of his spiritual portfolio, many others were congratulating the organizers of the seminar on the forward thinking that had led to an invitation for Shanti Shanti to perform at the evening's event. Suddenly, it seemed, it was a "hot idea" to incorporate some aspect of spirituality into a financial seminar! The hosts were being praised for their "groundbreaking" thinking! Imagine that.

In the meantime, we were still dealing with people who wanted to share their experiences.

"We never take the time anymore to just sit and reconnect with what's important. I called my wife and held my cell phone up so she could hear your singing. She said you sounded like angels ... but then asked why wasn't I at my financial seminar. When I told her that was exactly where I was, she said, 'Next time you're taking me!'"

Or the woman who waited until everyone else was gone, and then, her face still clearly reflecting an experience of deep emotion, slipped quietly up to tell us, "I had the most amazing thing happen while listening to the Sanskrit. It was as though my heart was bursting open with joy."

These types of reactions from people who were clearly not expecting anything to happen to them, much less something so dramatic, made us realize that there is a remarkable spiritual hunger present in our society, and it is wonderful to watch the acknowledgement of it unfold. It is a similar experience to what happens when, during the day, we're really busy and forget to stop for lunch, but suddenly some delicious smell wafts through the room, and all of our attention gravitates to our empty stomach. We had probably been hungry for quite a while, but we were so preoccupied with whatever we were doing, it took a strong reminder for us to realize just how starved we actually were.

Our daily lives are so busy that, just like the person who works right through lunch, we are distracted by our hectic lives, and we neglect the most fundamental elements necessary for our well-being. Food is as essential to our existence as our connection with the Divine. Until we receive some sharp reminder, we tend to forget how essential that bond actually is or, in fact, how intense our hunger has become.

Sanskrit seems to provide that gentle reminder of our perpetual longing for spiritual connection, and as it exerts its subtle influence on our consciousness, it serves as a catalyst, nudging us back toward our spiritual sustenance. Because all of life springs from that consciousness, it is only our preoccupation with the more superficial aspects of existence that makes us feel like we're disconnected from our own true Self. No matter what we think, we're never really far away from it. It is always very close by.

We just need to remember our hunger.

Abide in Me, and I in you. As the branch cannot bear fruit of itself, unless it abides in the vine, neither can you, unless you abide in Me.

JOHN 15:4

[c h a p t e r t w e n t y - t w o]

ONE OF THE MOST REMARKABLE ASPECTS of being allowed to experience many different religions from a personal vantage point is how peculiarly sweet and mystifying each religious expression can be. As fascinated as we were by the response that Shanti Shanti received from non-religious groups, the compelling essence of *spirit* was keenly experienced when the girls were asked to share Sanskrit with non-secular groups.

From a group of enthusiastic Mormon teenagers at a Shanti Shanti performance, to the children in a Jewish synagogue listening to the girls' CDs, to large audiences full of exuberant Catholics, to the warm, unbridled response of a New Age church, each religion brings its own unique expression to the experience that is Sanskrit.

The richness of each religion is revealed through its complexity and diversity of ideas and interpretations, but we seldom have the opportunity to experience the "inner" aspects of that spiritual expression. If we have been raised with a particular religion and continue in that practice as an adult, the closest we usually get to other religions can be through our relationships with friends or work associates that might have a different religious philosophy from our own. In such circumstances, the concept of staying "in our respectful corners" usually prevails, and we don't learn anything from each other except how to be quiet when it comes to any exchange of religious ideas and views.

If we had a negative religious experience as a child, our adult views of religion can fall within a completely secular framework. This path can give us a life with little or no religious overtones, and this can sometimes result in feelings of isolation or exclusion, particularly at religious occasions such as holidays, weddings, funerals, and christenings.

For years, at the Christmas Holidays, our family has gone to whatever class Micah is in that school year to do a "family performance." The girls give a small lesson in linguistics, tailored to the students' learning level, and then they do some of their Sanskrit chanting, which enlivens the kids in a way I can't begin to describe. Their excitement is palpable, and the girls use this opportunity to create a feeling of inclusiveness by chanting a bit of Latin, Hebrew, and, of course, Sanskrit.

Toward the end of the program, we take requests for Christmas carols, and it never fails to astonish me how eager the students are to sing, and how request follows request. Their little voices ring out and their faces strain with earnest effort as they sing the traditional songs of the holiday season. As a teacher explained to me when I commented on their exuberance, our little sing-along is sometimes the only religious expression many of them will participate in at this particular season of the year.

Thoughts of toys and "stuff" are the unfortunate focal point of this holiday for most of us, and that emphasis gives rise to a particular pining of the soul. It is so poignant to observe the children's enthusiasm over something as simple as a Christmas carol, and to realize how important it can be for parents to offer a child the opportunity to share in some type of religious experience. Silent Night can, all by itself, bring hints of a deeper world, of the sense that there is more, even beyond the story of Mother and Child.

However we do or don't engage the Spirit in our lives, there is a definite tendency to be complacent about the huge gift of opportunity that is ours for the taking. The foundation of our country, the most powerful, prosperous nation in the world, has its basis in the struggle for the right to worship God in the religion of one's choice. People endured great hardships for a liberty that we today take completely for granted, even to the point of blatant disregard. Religions can offer huge opportunities for us as individuals and as a society to grow and thrive, and they can provide the type of "support structure" that many families are missing.

People will say they're "spiritual, but not religious," as though that somehow protects them from the current attitude of prejudicial behavior toward organized religions. But the truth is those same people are only free to *be spiritual* because of all the religious people who fought for their right to say those words. It is important to remember all that was done in the honor of generations to come, so that we *could* be so blasé about our religious freedom. We are disrespectful of their efforts when we minimize the importance religion has had in human development.

It goes without saying that not all religious expression is honorable. Obviously, it is very much within the framework of our growth as spiritual beings to distort and obliterate the good intentions behind religious worship. But we need to keep our perspective. It's the old "throwing out the baby with the bathwater" scenario if we dismiss all religions as irrelevant, or not as pure or sophisticated as simply being "spiritual."

There are many adults adrift in the ocean of the modern non-religious attitude who feel a great tie to the religion they grew up with. But as many have confided to the girls, they feel they'd be labeled archaic and "old-fashioned" by their peers if they said they belonged to their Jewish Synagogue, Hindu Temple, or Catholic Church, etc. If we look quickly, we will be able to see those poor Quakers, Puritans, and Pilgrims of old rolling over in their graves! What an enormously sad testimony that is.

The point is to rejoice in our freedom to pursue God. We have the ability to belong to a church, temple, or synagogue, and to revel in the luxury of our choice. And if we find that particular path does not answer all of our needs, then we can share in some other aspect of our greater community's religious expression! We can pray, worship, meditate, and enjoy the freedom we have to be a part of such a wonderful society that allows for great opportunities for spiritual enrichment. Be generous and loving and supportive of your neighbor's involvement in a spiritual community. We should not let pettiness reside in us by diminishing our friends' or neighbors' choice for religious expression. And we should keep in mind that if our friend or neighbor doesn't seem to reflect a very positive embodiment of his or her religion, that's the individual's lack, not religion as a whole!

People regularly ask if our family practices any religion, and then seem surprised when we reply in the affirmative. We could truthfully say that we practice *every* religion, to one extent or another, because we find every opportunity to celebrate God by going to churches, temples, synagogues, and beautiful mountaintops as often as we possibly can.

The reason the ancient Vedic society constructed a language that was, in essence, a constant prayer, was because we needed then, as we do now, as much connection with the Divine as we can possibly manage to access. It is from that relationship, alone, that everything else in our lives flourishes.

...Out of the Ring of Fire

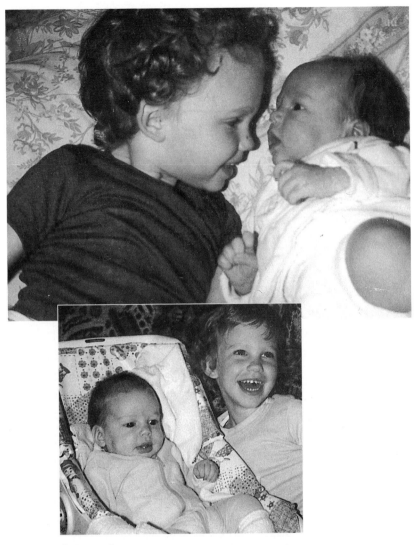

ANDREA'S CHANTING PARTNER ARRIVES

Gandharva Veda musicians
at Robert's studio

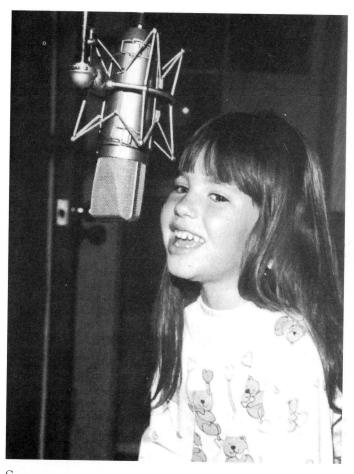

Sᴀʀᴀ ꜰɪɴᴅꜱ ʜᴇʀ ᴘʟᴀᴄᴇ ɪɴ ꜰʀᴏɴᴛ ᴏꜰ ᴀ ᴍɪᴄʀᴏᴘʜᴏɴᴇ

AND THEN THERE WERE THREE . . .

PERFORMANCE FOR
CALIFORNIA COLLEGE
OF AYURVEDA
GRADUATION

PERFORMANCE AT A TEMPLE IN PENNSYLVANIA

THE GIRLS CHANT FOR SRI MAA AND HER DEVOTEES

SHANTI SHANTI WITH DEEPAK CHOPRA

STONEHENGE

The family in Europe

Sivananda Ashram, London

THE WHITE TOWER, LONDON

AFTER A CONCERT
IN EDINBURGH

Princes'
Park
Concert,
Edinburgh

QUICK PLANNING
BEFORE A CONCERT

ANDREA RE-ENACTS
HER ROOFTOP
ADVENTURE IN
EDINBURGH

Shopping on High Street in Edinburgh with Their Uncle

[chapter twenty-three]

WE HAD NOW ENTERED a new phase of our spiritual and musical odyssey, and circumstances as well as audience demand made it very clear that the time had come for a second Shanti Shanti CD. For the last couple of years, Robert had been writing new songs, and squeezed in between performance engagements, the recording was done one song at a time. The thought was to make the release of this album a seminal event for our family, because it represented the culmination of such an enormous amount of focused effort and love.

When Shanti Shanti received an unexpected invitation to perform in London, followed by a series of requests from Scotland, it seemed the perfect opportunity to launch the "Walkin' With the Devas" album in the context of a memorable trip to Europe.

As things would turn out, we only had about eight weeks to prepare for the trip from the moment the performance dates were confirmed, but unfortunately, packing and arranging passports wasn't all we had on the agenda for those two months. The record still needed finishing touches, then it had to be mastered for production, the artwork for the cover and the insert had to be completed by the graphic designers, and finally, the whole mess had to be sent off for manufacturing.

And all of this had to happen before our departure!

Past experience had taught us, with a consistency that could have been humorous if it weren't also so extremely frustrating, that the process of being involved with something as life-changing as Sanskrit can create its own set of karmic rules. Those rules supercede all the normal boundaries that one usually counts on to support and guide specific activities, and can make reality begin to feel as unpredictable as a misbehaving child who starts to take on ever more surprising patterns of behavior. I've come to the conclusion that this is the "cosmic payment" for being allowed to participate in something so wonderful as the ancient tradition of Sanskrit. And, to put it plainly, it is also the price of admission onto a playing field that includes some pretty rough confrontations between conflicting levels of good and evil. There is the distinct possibility that the resulting clash will result in a state, for us, that most closely resembles hilarious hysteria.

I've related instances where huge problems were encountered when our family veered off our chosen path. And I've spoken of the underlying support that seemed to result when we were functioning in a "dharmic" way. The anomaly I'm now referring to is something outside all those boundaries, but also directly caused by the choices we make. The choice of this *particular path* brings with it a very unusual set of complications.

Simply put, life has a way of becoming incredibly complicated whenever Sanskrit is involved. Activities can have a very unusual quality to them, sometimes making one feel as though caught in some sort of cosmic standoff with frustrating, albeit sometimes comical, ramifications.

The closer the trip came, the more we encountered that naughty tendency in the cosmos to create absurdly gigantic stumbling blocks. It was like a test. Our efforts to take Sanskrit into a larger sphere were creating an almost predictably difficult set of circumstances, and as our days became suffused with increasingly irritating interferences, we realized we had a major battle on our hands to actually finish the album in time and get ourselves on the plane.

After encountering innumerable setbacks to the actual completion of the recording, the album was finally ready to be mastered for production, and it was with great relief that we delivered it to the mastering lab.

When we received a call from the engineer later that same day, however, saying that our album had completely melted down all of their equipment, our frustration almost got the better of us.

"What do you mean it 'melted your equipment'?" Robert asked disbelievingly, while the rest of us literally held our breath when we realized what the call was about. This was devastating news, and we saw our ability to take our new record with us to Europe quickly fading.

"I've never heard of that happening," was all Robert could manage as the engineer went on and on about the extent of the difficulties.

The engineer explained that he had never before had anything like this happen, so this experience was a first for him, too.

Apparently the employees had put the new Shanti Shanti album on to play while they were working on the settings and adjustments for the mastering process, and before they knew what was happening, "Everything started to, well, just melt," the engineer explained to Robert with a mixture of amazement and anxiety in his voice. The engineer knew that this was a huge problem since we were due to leave on the concert trip in a week or so, and there would be no time for manufacturing the CDs given the current fiasco.

After a few minutes spent in a feverish exchange of options that could be explored, the engineer finally said he'd see what he could do, but his equipment, as far as he could tell, seemed to have been "Sanskritized" and didn't appear to be responding to any commands in a normal fashion.

Well, we understood *that* phenomenon all too well, so we couldn't be upset with him or his company. We knew there wasn't much he could do beyond try everything … and hope for the best. We all said silent prayers to help him.

Two days later, the engineer called with "some good news, some strange news, and some not totally positive news" (actually, I think he probably thought most of it was just bad, but was trying to pad the reality of the situation). Apparently, when his equipment experienced its meltdown, something dramatic happened to his high-tech machinery, and he felt it tied to the Sanskrit. It made sense, he felt, because everyone in the place had been very affected by the Sanskrit while they were listening to the album, and the consensus by the other engineers was that the equipment had experienced a reaction as well!

But that wasn't all the news. The engineer continued on as Robert mentally searched through the fragments of this conversation for the "good" part.

"Now, here's where it gets weird," the engineer stated with something approaching awe in his voice. "When we all left for home, on the night of the screw-up, we locked the place up tight, and everyone was determined to try and figure out a way to get you your mastered copy in time for the manufacturing to be done.

"When we returned the next morning, the place was still locked up as tight as we'd left it, and I had the only key since my assistant was out of town."

Here the poor guy paused, as though trying to find a way to explain to Robert what happened next. Little did he realize that Robert was already steeling himself on the other end of the line for the recounting of some bizarre occurrence that he, Robert, would then have the difficult job of trying to explain. This response would soon prove to be justified.

The engineer went on with his explanation.

It seemed that the following morning everyone was startled by what they were greeted by as they filed in for work.

All of the computers in the office had been turned on and were in operation mode, and all of the boxes and containers in the business had been completely moved around.

"But," the engineer went on with elaborate emphasis, "that isn't all."

Once the engineers had dealt with all the physical changes that "mystically" occurred during the night, putting everything back where it belonged, they finally sat down to work, thinking they had a huge mess ahead of them that they were still going to have to figure out how to sort through.

Instead, to everyone's amazement, they found that the problems of the night before had apparently been fixed.

"We were able to actually get things up and running, and ... [the engineer paused here as though trying, himself, to understand his own recitation of the facts], "it looks like we'll be able to give you a mastered format to make the CDs. I have no idea exactly *how* we're able to do that, but it looks like we are."

The only real down side to the whole conversation, as far as Robert was concerned, was that some time had been lost, so they would probably have to ship our CDs to us in Europe.

The engineer drew a breath and waited to hear Robert's response. Truthfully, the news he had related was not that much of a surprise. There were so many things that happened all the time for which there was no ready explanation, we had given up trying to fill in all the blanks quite some time ago.

Robert thanked the engineer, apologized for "how weird everything seems" with regard to our project, and made arrangements for the shipping of the CDs. The engineer was waiting for more, but there really wasn't a Cliff Notes version of the strange happenings that were becoming such a regular experience for us, so Robert left it at that. He knew that after our shipment finally left their offices, their lives would return to normal and, if the engineer and the other employees thought of us at all, it would just be with a slight sense of strangeness and confusion over the inexplicable happenings.

(As an anthropological and historical side note: our current numeric system is Arabic, brought to Western civilization during the Crusades in the 11th and 12th centuries C.E., replacing Roman numerals at that time. Although the Arab civilization is credited for our current number system, they actually absorbed it from the Indus Valley Civilization, which was the dominant civilization circa 5000 B.C.. In addition, the Indus Valley peoples were familiar with binary numeric systems, and even today, starting in 1984, some software companies have used Sanskrit as their computer language because of its binary and mathematical nature. This information is not offered as an explanation for the computer anomaly, because, God knows, I've given up trying to explain anything, but rather just as an interesting aside.)

We had learned that the best way to deal with something like this was to "keep it simple" and avoid protracted explanations. In some circumstances, the subtle nuances of the situation were somehow understood by whoever was involved with us at the time, and required very little elaboration. Other times, reflection after the fact by the affected party created an astonished response. However it all played out, this aspect of the whole phenomenon wasn't our responsibility. Everyone would have their own unique interpretation, and that was as it should be.

Life, after all, creates its own magic, and no person can understand all of the details involved in the interplay. It's just for us to enjoy, and to marvel at the wonder of it all.

We did understand from this little event, however, that we definitely were going to be dealing with some volatility in the process of trying to take this trip. Our most sincere hope was that we would just be allowed to go.

As expected, each day held some new problem, but travelers everywhere experience that irritating reality, and nothing more happened after the incident with the mastering lab beyond the normal exasperating delays and difficulties. We fought through each new mini-crisis, and finally, on the day of our scheduled departure, woke to bright skies and fluttery anticipation. It actually looked like the trip was going to happen, and even though we knew we had a potential disaster on our hands if the new CDs did not make it to Europe in time for the performances, there was nothing more we could do from this end beyond getting on a plane and flying over there.

My to-do list had just about everything crossed off as we made our final preparations that day. Our flight was to leave around four o'clock that afternoon, and we had planned to reach the airport at about 2:00 P.M., so there would be no last-minute rush for the gate. Keys had been given to our neighbor, who was to care for our animals in our absence, and since it was summer, final arrangements for watering and mowing the yard were made.

We said our good-byes and, packed in like sardines with our luggage stowed around us, drove to the airport. I was excited, but I also had a little niggling sense of concern drifting through me. I put it off to traveling jitters and focused on the adventure ahead.

We had arranged for my brother Dan, who lived in Los Angeles but had resided in England for a time, to accompany us, and we certainly welcomed the extra set of hands, not to mention his knowledge of the city we would be staying in. With just our regular luggage, plus all the additional equipment we had to take with us due to the concert engagements, we knew we would truly be grateful for his help. We had all the normal paraphernalia required by five people living away from home for several weeks, but there was also an additional strain because of performance outfits, press kits, and musical instruments. In other words, we were a traveling nightmare of packing logistics. My brother was a welcome addition to our convoy, and we had arranged to meet up with him in Phoenix and continue on together from there.

We arrived at the airport already tired. There had been a lot to organize to make sure that, in the event our shipment of CDs did not reach us in Europe, we still had some fallback material packed with us. Schlepping all of our luggage and instruments and boxes around was no small task, so it was with a huge sense of relief that we finally walked through the doors of the airport, and, locating our correct airline queue, prepared to wait for our turn.

Suddenly, a disturbance at the counter caught everyone's attention. There was a man arguing with the airline employee, and the exchange of words was heated. Unfortunately, once we gathered the drift of the conversation, we realized the man probably was justified in being so unhappy. From what we were able to tell, it looked like *we* had reason to be unhappy as well.

As the man, mumbling discontentedly, gathered his luggage together and struggled to steer past the line, Robert asked him, "Are you going to London?"

"I *was*," he answered warningly. "If that's where you're headed, you have a huge problem. You'd better find another airline, and quick. Apparently the flight to Phoenix was delayed, and they've known about it since this morning, but they only called the first-class passengers to inform them. The rest of us just missed our connection to London."

We all just stood there, disappointment washing over us as we tried to fathom what this news meant to us. How could the airline have known and not called? We had to be at a performance in London! And then, it suddenly occurred to me that my poor brother was catching a flight to Phoenix even as we spoke, and if we weren't able to get hold of him before he boarded his flight, he would have no idea where he was supposed to go once he arrived in England. I had the itinerary of where we were staying! Since his layover time in Phoenix was extremely short, he probably wouldn't realize we weren't on the transatlantic flight until the doors closed and he had a chance to take a look around the plane.

Plus, there was the added stress of the fact that we had a shipment of CDs due to arrive in London.

None of this was good.

When we finally reached the counter, Robert made a huge effort to control his frustration and get to a potential solution. Unfortunately, the airline employee couldn't have cared less about Robert or any of the rest of us who were currently standing in her line. In fact, for some reason she looked as though she'd like nothing better than to make our day as miserable as possible.

Robert started off calm and reasonable.

"If you've known, all day, that the flight was going to be delayed, why didn't someone call us?"

"I was busy, sir. I did call the first class passengers."

"But we called and checked, and the flight was reported to be on time." He was still making an effort to get some cooperation.

"Yes, our computers malfunctioned and did not report the delay to the operators. Now, would you like me to arrange a room for you?"

"A room? Why would we want a room? We live here! We have to leave, for more reasons than I can name. We have to get on a plane to make our connection."

"Sorry. That's not going to happen. Did you say you wanted a room?"

By this time, Robert turned and looked at me, and I thought he was going to explode. I could feel the kids standing behind me, all of them anxious with concern and disappointment. Maybe I could make more headway with this situation.

"Miss," I began, "we have to leave today, as soon as possible. Are there other flights you could help hook us up with if this flight is going to be too late to make our connection in Phoenix?"

"No."

"No?" Now I was the one having a very difficult time restraining my impatience. I fully understood Robert's frustration.

"May I speak to a supervisor?" I asked, not visibly angry, but definitely very serious now as I realized what a mess we were in.

"Well, you could ... but by the time I page one, there will be about a 45-minute wait until someone comes to speak with you." Stony-faced, she turned her attention back to her keyboard.

That was all Robert could stand. Tossing harried instructions over his shoulder for us to follow him as soon as I could retrieve our tickets, he hoisted as many of our bags as he could carry and quickly went off to find a flight, any flight, that could get us to Phoenix.

Collecting our tickets from the surly airline employee (clearly an example of someone *not* on their dharma!), we loaded up the rest of the luggage and headed off in search of Robert. I heard the poor man who was next in line mutter something to the effect of, "I guess there's no point in my telling you I'm going to miss my flight?"

We caught up with Robert at the counter of another airline, and he quickly told us he had been able to reserve seats for us on another flight, but it was leaving in minutes, and we needed to get to the gate as quickly as possible. He told us to show the airline our identification, and then move as fast as possible, because we could still make the flight and our connection in Phoenix.

He had the girls stay with him, with the majority of our luggage, and told Micah and I to run. He wanted the two of us to get on the plane, and the three of them would follow as soon as he had our luggage checked in.

Micah and I ran through the airport and, since this was prior to the increased airport security, were able to get our boarding passes quickly and get right on the plane. We held three extra seats, stowed our carry-on luggage, and sat down to wait for the rest of my family to arrive.

Suddenly I noticed the crew making motions in preparation to closing the door, and I panicked, knowing that once it was closed, Micah and I were on our way to Phoenix, minus the rest of our family.

"Wait!" I called out as I hurried to the front of the plane. "The rest of my family isn't here!"

"Well, I'm sorry, Ma'am, but we have to depart. I suggest you return to the concourse and wait for them there. I'm sure you'll catch another flight."

The airline attendant was actually very helpful, assisting Micah and I as we hurriedly retrieved our luggage from the bins overhead, and then struggled through the narrow aisle while the other attendants waited impatiently to shut the door.

"Hurry!" one of them said, adding to the tension. "We have to close the door!"

Before I could even pause to try and come up with a different plan, Micah and I found ourselves back in the airport, sagging with exhaustion, and looking around frantically for Robert, Andrea, and Sara. What had happened to them? I thought for a frantic minute that maybe we got on the wrong plane, but then quickly realized that impossibility given that the girl at the counter had our reservations when we had checked in.

Finally Andrea came running up to us, exhausted beyond words, and informed us, in between deep gasps of breath, that the airline couldn't get our luggage checked in time, so Robert had to make arrangements for still another flight, in a different part of the concourse.

"Are we still going to make the flight to Phoenix?" I asked as poor little Micah, beyond tired by now, struggled with me to pick up our bags and follow Andrea.

"Yes, if we hurry!" With that she was off and running, and Micah and I trailed behind.

Arriving at our newest gate of departure, we found Robert and Sara holding down the fort by standing at the front of the line, Robert occupying the employee behind the airline ticket counter by regaling her with tales of our travel woes. He was buying time for us, and while she commiserated with him, he cocked his hand behind his back and motioned for us to come forward quickly. We dug out our identification still yet again, and this time, everything was handled with no additional problems.

It was all going to be just fine. Our reservations were fine, the luggage would make it on the plane just fine, and we would make our connection in Phoenix just fine. Fine, fine, fine!

We all looked at each other with enormous relief and felt huge gratitude for the wonderful airline employee who was, at that very moment, helping us fix what had seemed to be an insurmountable set of problems. She smiled at us in sympathy for all we'd been through, and then said that wasn't it wonderful that it was now all going to be ... just fine!

We sat down in the gate area to wait and try to relax. What a relief. For a while there, I had really thought we were going to be stopped from taking this trip. In retrospect, it had been almost comical, especially when Micah and I found ourselves on that plane, getting ready for departure, with no one else in the family anywhere to be found! Whew! What an experience! But now we could at last breathe a sigh of relief.

I should make a point here of trying to convey the feeling our family sometimes has of being reluctant soldiers in a battle that we know little about. It can feel as though there is a constant balance of lighter and darker energies in the world, and the longer we were involved in our own "odyssey," the clearer that impression was becoming. And the clearer it also was that we had some unsuspecting role to play. It was becoming increasingly obvious that there were forces at work in Nature beyond our most immediate comprehension, but when confronted with a day like the one I'm describing here, the battle lines seem keenly drawn. It is as though a genuine effort is being made by one side to thwart the good of Sanskrit, but the support we receive from the other side, the "good army," or the army of "light," eventually seems to balance everything out. It is just that there are times, when the battle is raging all around us and we're caught up in the fervor, that we can't be sure who the victor will be. Interestingly, though, as well as fortunately, it seems to most always come down to one particular side ... but there can be some pretty uncomfortable moments as the drama is unfolding before it is obvious to us which side will prevail! What we were about to face was definitely going to prove to be one of those experiences.

Robert went to buy something to eat because all of that running around had left everyone ravenous. We still had about ten minutes before the plane we were now due to take was even supposed to arrive at the gate, so the rest of us settled into our seats to calmly enjoy the peaceful respite before finally embarking on our huge trip. We were heady with the feeling that we had brought everything back on track. Within a short time, we'd meet up with my brother, and then it would be on to London!

As Robert came walking up with some snacks, I noticed that the airline employee who had been so helpful to us was now talking on the phone, and eyeing us with a strange expression on her face. Gone was the smile and enthusiasm of just a few moments before, replaced by a rather grim look. I was looking at her, and she was looking right back at me, straight into my eyes, while listening to whomever was on the other end of the phone. I knew we were in trouble.

A second later, with her eyes focused on our small group, the airline employee picked up the microphone and began to speak. Her words fell like big, fat drops of rain on our European parade.

"If I may have your attention, please. We have been informed that Flight 826, to Phoenix, is to be held at our gate here in Reno for an undisclosed period of time." A series of moans and groans issued forth from the waiting area. Our little group was too stunned to respond.

"Apparently," and here she looked at us specifically, as though to apologize for whatever it was she was getting ready to say, "some sort of noxious, potentially poisonous cloud is laying over the exact area of the Phoenix terminal where flight 826 is due to disembark, so Phoenix control is asking us to hold this flight until further notice. Thank you for your cooperation."

Noxious cloud? The exact area of the terminal where our plane had to go? Arrrghghgh!

The employee walked over to us, her face totally perplexed, and said, "I have no idea what is going on. They just called us, and the only flight departing from our airport that is affected is the one you're going to be on. What are the chances of that?" She laughed a little nervously, probably remembering what Robert had told her about what we'd already been through.

We smiled back at her through gritted teeth, trying not to break down and cry, and thanked her for her concern. Robert patted her on the arm in reassurance.

"It's just too weird, isn't it?" she asked.

Yes, we assured her that, indeed, it *was* too weird. We then looked at each other in misery as she went back to her post at the counter, where disgruntled passengers were waiting for more of an explanation. "Noxious cloud" was a little vague for them. Not to mention weird.

We wound up waiting in the airport for about four hours. By that time, we had obviously missed our flight and had no luck trying to connect with my brother. We left messages on his cell phone, as well as with his roommate, hoping he would check in once he arrived in London. We imagined his confusion when he had got on the plane to Europe, only to discover we were all AWOL.

At this point, we just had to let everything go. We could feel that we were definitely fighting against *something* trying to keep us from leaving on this trip, and our only hope was that whatever positive influences there were out there, they were rooting for us and working to make sure we prevailed. We wanted to share Sanskrit with audiences in Europe, and we hoped that there were other energies or forces that wanted us to do that as well. It was feeling more and more as though we were sitting smack in the middle of a raging battle.

Finally the announcement was made that our plane was due to depart, and the airline employee beamed at us once again as she made the announcement. We were too tired to do more than just smile back weakly. We stood up and started to gather our luggage together.

But then, wait! Oh, no! She's picking up the phone again. And she's getting that same, really strained look on her face, and she's glancing at us nervously as she listens with the receiver pressed tight against her ear.

We automatically put our luggage down and sat back in our seats. We didn't even have to hear the announcement to know we'd had yet one more obstacle laid across the tarmac.

"Ladies and gentlemen, I'm afraid we've received yet another delay," she announced into her microphone. One passenger actually turned around and with frustration dripping from every word asked, "Are you joking?"

The airline employee continued on, a look of painful resignation on her face, "I'm sorry, but apparently a series of local forest fires encircling the area have made visibility difficult, and they're asking the pilots to wait until some of the smoke clears."

Please don't think I am exaggerating any part of this, or indulging in complete flights of grandeur with respect to the way this all unfolded. It truly did seem as though we were watching opposing armies fighting some kind of bizarre battle over whether or not we were going to be allowed to go to Europe, with first one side winning a skirmish ... only to lose the next.

And back and forth it went.

Meanwhile, we sat in our seats, digesting this latest announcement, and no one said a word. And then, suddenly, probably because none of us could possibly be any more exhausted or frustrated or annoyed, we just started laughing, and the laughter rolled through us as the absolute ridiculousness of the entire day was experienced in its entirety.

A good laugh must have been exactly what we needed, because it seemed to have a centering effect, and we even managed to get the rest of the passengers involved in the humor, though why they thought they were laughing, I really have no idea. At any rate, we continued to sit in the waiting area, all of us feeling more than slightly bemused by the absurdity of our day, but also completely resigned to the fates at this point.

For a long time afterwards we sat and stared out the window at the plane ... our plane ... the one that was *supposed* to take us to Phoenix. And eventually, just about the time we had started to think that the whole trip was going to be a bust, and we were never, ever going to be allowed to leave, a serendipitous breeze came up ... and began to disperse the smoke.

The beleaguered airline employee once again picked up the mike and, this time, not daring to look at us, announced that they'd been cleared to start boarding the plane.

As our plane finally took off and began its much anticipated climb toward our destination, we all looked in silent awe at what appeared to be an actual ring of fire completely encasing the valley. It was awesome and terrifying at the same time. I'd never seen anything like it in my whole life, and it left me feeling like we were departing the scene of a huge war, and we were even now gazing down at the remnants of the battlefield, which consisted of smoke and fiery tongues of flame, reaching toward us as our plane struggled to climb out of the inferno.

I sat back in my seat and closed my eyes. My exhausted mind took hold of a phrase from an old Johnny Cash song that kept repeating itself in my head, in silly chorus ... "that ring of fire, that ring of fire."

Micah turned in his seat next to me, and nudging me with his arm said quietly, "Mommy, do you see the ring of fire? It looks like we're flying out of hell, and right into heaven!"

And I thought we were just trying to get to Scotland.

. . . AND THEN, EVERYTHING CHANGES

[c h a p t e r   t w e n t y - f o u r]

OUR ARRIVAL IN LONDON was accompanied by a huge feeling of relief and triumphant success. After a twenty-four-hour stay in Phoenix with temperatures that hovered at a sizzling 117 degrees, and all of us wilting from the heat but forced to wear clothes intended for a much cooler climate, we could scarcely allow ourselves to believe that the 747 we finally boarded was not some shimmering apparition sitting on the tarmac, but a real plane bound for Europe.

Though we were weary and a bit frayed around the edges by all we'd been through in the past two days, it was still a glorious feeling, some twelve hours of flight-time later, to look out the windows of our plane and see the green, pastoral vision that is England unfurl beneath us. We were a group picture of happiness over the realization that we were here at last. In Phoenix, I was afraid that the pleasure of our trip was going to be somewhat diminished by all we'd been through, but I underestimated our resiliency!

My brother was waiting in the concourse, trying for a little levity by holding up a sign with "FORMAN" printed on it in large letters. He looked relieved to see us. We had connected with him before we left Phoenix and learned that he checked into the flat we had rented in London with few problems, following the instructions we'd left him on our myriad messages. In fact, he told us as we waited for our luggage, it all had probably worked out for the best since he'd been able to get everything situated before our arrival, and now all

247

we had to do was walk through the door to our rented home-away-from-home, and relax.

We decided at the very beginning of our reservation flurry some eight weeks ago that a flat, or apartment, was definitely the way to go, rather than hotel-hopping. We wanted the privacy and autonomy that comes with a live-in sort of arrangement, not to mention the added bonus of a kitchen and spacious rooms. We weren't disappointed by what we saw when we walked through the front door.

First off, the flat was in an older building that oozed European charm. A centenarian, at the very least, she was an elegant old thing with wrought-iron trim and flower boxes, and had stood solidly against the passage of years, with an air of having seen a great many things but been impressed by few. As we would soon find, most of the old buildings in both England and Scotland, of which there are a great number, possess an inordinate amount of what could only be called "attitude." Indomitable, at the very least, and considering how long many have stood against the ravages of time, their "air" of fortitude is certainly justified.

The inside of our building had been thoughtfully refurbished, with soothing light tones of white and tan, as well as a fully functional kitchen. No dishwasher, but everything else we could possibly need. The tiny refrigerator, which I thought at first to be a renter's anomaly but which I quickly found was the normal size, took a little getting used to. I finally realized that the English don't "stock up" like we do, shopping for a week of meals at a time, but rather on a schedule that is more reflective of day-to-day appetites.

In Britain, where food has always been picked fresh daily, the people's connection to what they eat and where it comes from is clearer than it is in our country. Even though the U.S. is beginning to take advantage of the re-emergence of "farmer's markets" in the summertime, overall we tend to be more concerned with time, I think, than most Europeans are. This could have to do with historical perspective and the difference in the ages of the individual countries. We are new, and young, and a bit brash, while the English seem to be more tempered in their presentation, perhaps in much the same way that an older person tends to be less impatient than members of the younger generation!

The time for the girls' London debut was upon us faster than we would have preferred, and our extra-long stay in Phoenix had adjusted our itinerary. It was not a huge performance, but large enough to be considered a perfect-sized audience for a first-time event.

The performance went well, and, since the CDs had arrived in London without a hitch (!), the evening was considered a success. We were starting to feel as though whatever had been constraining us, and inhibiting our efforts, was starting, at long last, to let up.

Later that evening, when we were all winding down at the flat, the girls mused about the cultural differences in audiences—the reserve of the British audience, juxtaposed against the normal American response to one of their performances. Usually, the girls reach a certain portion of the evening where they ask if anyone has any questions about the songs, the Sanskrit, etc. American audiences can't wait for the question portion of the night to begin, and hands fly up before the girls can even finish the sentence.

The English audience, though, had no questions, which the girls found surprising, and certainly different from what Shanti Shanti was accustomed to. They were exceedingly warm and polite and welcoming, but they asked no questions.

Afterwards, however, when the performance was over and Robert, Andrea, and Sara had said their goodnights from the stage, things changed completely. Now it seemed the audience had lots of questions! Everyone waited politely to the side of the stage and then filed up, one by one, to ask something that had obviously been on their minds during the performance. Finally Andrea asked one courteous young gentleman why he hadn't just asked his question during the performance. He blushed and looked sheepishly to the side, as if to say, "Oh, I couldn't do that!" He then said something about not wanting to appear "impolite." The girls thought everyone's elegant manners absolutely charming, and a total cultural delight.

The evening was deemed a success, and our "European tour" had begun.

* * *

We go to Westminster Cathedral, and arrive just in time for services. This place is truly so beautiful, the mind and heart can't take it all in. Gorgeous marble everywhere. We take communion with hearts full of joy. Everyone is transported.

We do the London "tourist thing" and have a ball. Since the whole family has such a strong love of most things historical, a visit to each new place is like meeting up with an old friend. The Tower of London, Buckingham Palace, Regent's Park, Parliament—all feel completely magical with the weight of history that surrounds them. We try and take time at every stop to absorb a little of each location's unique and ageless charm. Even though we snap lots of pictures, I decide to journal my way across England and Scotland to keep the flavor of our adventure with us long after we return home.

We walk back across the bridge after a relaxing, panoramic ride on the Eye, and buy some roasted candy peanuts, hot from a vendor's pan. They smell unbelievably good, and the vendor smiles as he watches us catch the scent and then descend on him with coins eagerly jingling. We think the peanuts cannot possibly taste as good as they smell, and we're right, they don't! Munching hungrily as we continue across the bridge, we're so happy we don't care. We probably would have devoured them even if they'd been toasted sawdust. We're in London, and it's a glorious day!

There are black transom cabs everywhere, and they are so quaint that they make the London streets unbelievably picturesque. Sitting at a light and discussing plans for the day, I notice Micah staring at the cabbie in the car next to us. The man is staring back at Micah and smiling big as you please, and then, suddenly, holding out one hand, he reaches over with the other and appears to pull the top of his thumb right off! Micah jumps, startled at first, and then as the cabbie winks at him and puts the thumb back on, and then off again several more times, Micah bursts out laughing and asks me how the man is doing that! I had been watching the cabbie as well, and have to admit he startled me too, with his little bit of street theatrics, but it was fun to see how much enjoyment they were both having, the cabbie making wry faces and wriggling his large moustache up and down, and Micah laughing, and then both of them exchanging hellos as we stop at the next light.

There are a dozen such vignettes that seem to occur each and every day we're here, and each one freeze-frames in the mind, an event to be savored once we're back home again.

We find ourselves doing a lot of walking, and one of the things that strikes us as amusing are the big, bold letters painted at each street corner which caution pedestrians to "LOOK THIS WAY," followed by a large arrow pointing in the direction the traffic is coming from. Because the English drive on the opposite side of the road from us, it is easy enough for a tourist to approach a corner, look in the direction we're used to seeing traffic come from, and, seeing it is clear, step blithely out into the street. This is a huge mistake, because pedestrians in London are not regarded as something to be treated with consideration or concern. The traffic speeds around whatever poor soul is trying to cross a street as though he or she is an impediment to the rights of the cars! If a pedestrian is in the intersection and the light turns red, don't expect to see him or her continue to casually stroll to the other side of the street. When the light changes, everybody RUNS!!

The bold lettering, painted right on the street at every crossing, made a great effort to guide jet-lagged tourists such as ourselves to LOOK THIS WAY. Considering how many times we almost stepped out into the street anyway, my brother joked that the only thing missing was the word "STUPID" at the end of each warning.

The day for our departure from London and our trip to Bath arrives. It is a huge effort to get all our bags and equipment out of the flat, packed into two cabs, and through the train station, where we then have to find our correct platform. We don't want to miss our train and we've been told that they run *on time*! (We discover this to be an area that is a clear exception to the more relaxed concept of "time' earlier mentioned. "Late" in a European train station means that a train is running two minutes behind schedule!)

The English countryside rolls past and we are transported to a different time and place: the sight of farms laid out in neat rectangles with ancient stone fences for borders and then, off in the distance, a crumbling castle peeking over the top of a rise in the landscape. We're on our way to Scotland but will first spend a couple of days in Bath, as we want to see nearby Stonehenge. Bath, the town's name, is reflective of where we derive the name for that particular part of our *toilette*. The Romans had a fondness for the soothing waters of the area and built lovely bathhouses in which to enjoy their rejuvenative powers.

We are staying at an old home that has been turned into a bed and breakfast, and we have no idea what to expect. B & Bs are fun because they give the traveler an opportunity to share a more home-like atmosphere than the average hotel can offer, at the same time allowing one to experience more of the "flavor" of a particular area. But it can also be a bit of a grab-bag experience, since you're never quite sure what you're getting until you actually arrive at your destination.

The cabbie pulls up in front of a beautiful old stone home that is the epitome of understated elegance. The discreet B & B sign swinging gently on the front lawn assures us that this is, indeed, the place we reserved rooms at so many weeks before. We can scarcely believe our good fortune.

The house looks so delicate and refined, we feel somewhat awkward to be such a huge group. We have what is starting to seem like "tons" of very awkward and cumbersome baggage. I'm sure it's just my imagination that the house seems to draw back a little as we make our way clumsily down the delicate walkway, trying but failing to stay off the exquisitely manicured lawn! I can almost hear the resigned sigh of "tourists" as we raise the knocker on the door to announce our noisy arrival.

The door is promptly opened by a very proper, very English gentleman. He has perfectly silvered hair and is wearing immaculately pleated khakis, a light pink shirt, and a lovely ascot which is tied elegantly around his neck and sports a flawless knot. He takes one look at our group, blanches slightly, and then moves his mouth in such a way that one automatically thinks of the phrase "stiff upper lip," even as he steps aside and invites us in.

We immediately start apologizing for everything as we glimpse the elegant Victorian entry, and I am painfully aware of the delicate décor and the home's fragile beauty. All I can think of is we must look a bit like the proverbial bull(s) in a china shop to this gentleman, as everyone is shifting about uncomfortably, trying to make room for our feet amid the sea of bags, guitars, and other belongings. We are the epitome of awkwardness, somehow, with regard to everything concerning our presence—our abundance of luggage (it seems crass and uncouth to have so much luggage with us in these dainty and elegant surroundings), the size of our group, and the lateness of our arrival (we're not really late, but there's just something about this gentleman that makes one feel like an apology would always be in order, no matter what!).

After very formal introductions are made all around, our host informs us that we should call him Gordon, and invites us to make our way upstairs to our rooms. He indicates that we should go ahead of him, and we all reach down as though with one reflex and start to pick up as many bags as we each can carry.

"Excuse me!" comes a clipped voice from behind us. We all turn around and Gordon is standing in the entry, arms akimbo, looking at us as though we've all just stripped naked and painted ourselves purple!

"We do *not* allow ladies to carry baggage in this house, if you please."

I have to admit that we all hesitated, making the mistake of thinking he must be joking, or maybe that he does not see that we are all completely capable of carrying our own luggage upstairs, ladies and gents both. Not to mention the fact that we have so much luggage to carry that it would mean a gazillion trips up and down the stairs if just the "gentlemen" did the carrying.

I laugh a little and assure him that no, we're just fine, we are big, strong girls, and we can all help carry the luggage.

His voice takes on an air of righteous indignation as he quietly but firmly replies, "No ladies shall now, or ever, carry their own luggage as long as I live in this house. Now, if you please, ladies. Put down the bags and we'll carry them up the stairs in no time, won't we, gentlemen? And Master Micah, you can carry more than that one small bag, surely?"

With that, Gordon picks up two large bags and starts his way up the stairs, glancing back at the other "gentlemen" with an encouraging nod and a clipped "Come on, now, this way."

Andrea, Sara, and I look at each other, and it is with great effort that we don't dissolve in laughter, and instead affect a dignified attitude as the men (and boy!) struggle with the bags we've just been ceremoniously relieved of. Watching the luggage bang into their legs as they heft their loads clumsily up the stairs, while we "ladies" stay at the bottom, trying our darnedest to be the epitome of the refined representation of the fairer sex we've been pronounced to be, is really an exercise in cultural restraint.

Within a few minutes, the luggage has been hauled upstairs, and we are divided into groups and shown to our rooms. Robert and I are given a beautiful room, pure English country décor with rose chintz everywhere. The girls and Micah are happily ensconced in the third-floor attic, which is a huge blue and white hide-a-way that they all pronounce as "perfect" the minute they see it. My brother has a room that is delightfully comfortable, but it also happens to be very, very pink. Pink walls, pink linens, pink bedspread, pink, pink, pink! He also has his own (pink!) bathroom, just as the rest of us do, but his is teeny, tiny, with a sloping ceiling. Dan soon discovers that he can't stand at the sink because he hits his head on the ceiling, and the room is so shallow, the door can't be shut when he sits on the commode unless his legs are extended out into the bedroom. We all commiserate with him, but no one volunteers to trade rooms!

Gordon had explained earlier, after showing everyone else to their rooms and then finally my brother to his, that this "particularly pink" room was generally reserved for the young ladies in any group, but because every room in the house was already occupied, this room would have to be his. My brother did his own admirable version of being stiff-lipped and assured Gordon that his room was just perfect. Gordon's quiet dignity and scrupulous manners rendered the thought of complaining about *anything* absolutely ludicrous.

After we've had time to explore our rooms a bit, we decide to walk down the road and into town for a bite to eat. It is at this point that Sara, who, like the rest of us, is extremely fatigued from all the traveling, starts down from her shared room on the third floor. I'm not exactly sure what happens next, but one minute Sara is starting to walk down the stairs, and the next thing I know she is catapulting past where I'm standing on the second landing. As she sails by, she's doing a sort of graceful falling and sliding combination that, to me, as I stand watching in horrified fascination, seems to be occurring in slow motion! When she finally reaches the bottom, she hits the floor and then suddenly springs up, as though pulled upright by invisible puppet strings. It all happens so fast that it is a full thirty seconds before I realize that none of these amazing maneuvers I've just witnessed has been done on purpose. Sara looks at me in embarrassed surprise, and for a moment, I just stare back, too shocked to respond. Suddenly, we both start to laugh. It starts low and quiet, somewhere deep inside of us, but then it builds and builds until we're both holding our aching stomachs. Tears stream down my face as I try and focus on her broken explanation of how she fell down the steps, and then tried to get up before anyone could see her. She's obviously fine, with the exception of her bruised ego, but it is a full five minutes before we can get it together enough to continue on downstairs. I turn back to grab a jacket from my room before we reach the bottom, but still catch Gordon's voice, remonstrating with Sara to not "play" on the steps. I hear Sara quietly start to explain, but then stop and ... just ... apologize!

Breakfast at a B & B can be an unexpected highlight of a trip. There's something indescribable about sitting down with total strangers, early in the morning, at the same table, that can make for very interesting dining. Add to this the fact that we're in Bath, England, and our tablemates are visiting from a small town in northern Scotland, and you have a fascinating potpourri of possibilities.

Gordon appears, all pressed and proper, ascot in place, and inquires as to our choices for breakfast. This is a pleasant surprise, since other B&Bs we've stayed in had a set menu with no variations. We all reach for the little menus that are propped in the center of the table.

After a moment or two in which Gordon passes around the table with a delectable pot of steaming coffee, we all decide on our choices. Andrea and Sara love oatmeal and decide to try something exotic sounding. "Whiskey oatmeal" is featured as the house favorite, and Andrea asks me what I think that will be like. I shrug and say that it has to be like a flavoring, as opposed to the real thing, since it's offered to minors as well as adults. Andrea nods her agreement and orders the whiskey oatmeal, accompanied by a nod of approval from Gordon over her "excellent choice."

I inquire where the "staff" is that does the cooking. The aromas wafting through the house by this time are making our stomachs growl with anticipation.

He laughs and says, pouring more hot coffee, "Oh, there's no staff. It's just my wife and me."

In a surprisingly short period of time, we all have a delicious-looking meal sitting in front of us. We haven't spoken much to the Scottish couple yet, beyond the initial introductions, as everyone seems more interested in giving their full attention to the lovely breakfast that we've just been served.

I notice that Andrea and Sara are staring at their oatmeal, but making no motion toward eating. When Gordon leaves the room for another plate of buttered bread, I lean over and quietly inquire as to why they're just sitting there instead of eating.

"Mom, this is really whiskey!"

I look at her steaming bowl, and sure enough, her oatmeal is floating in what appears to be a pool of hot whiskey, with a large pat of butter melting slowly in it. I look at Robert and he looks at Sara's bowl, eyebrows rising as he leans down for a sniff of the aromatic concoction.

"Yep. That's whiskey, all right," he states unnecessarily.

Not sure what to do, we wait until Gordon returns. I notice the Scots are watching us with amusement, and I wonder if this is a well-known prank that is fun to play on unsuspecting Americans who are dumb enough to order "whiskey oatmeal."

This notion is immediately dispelled when Gordon returns, however. He seems genuinely perplexed at our surprise that "whiskey oatmeal" is, in fact, w-h-i-s-k-e-y o-a-t-m-e-a-l. He smiles, as do the Scots, over our concern that the girls are going to be consuming so much whiskey along with their oatmeal.

"It's good for them. It's cold in this part of the country, and that dish will stick to their ribs. We eat it all the time."

I feel more than see, since I'm turned toward Gordon, the Scots nod enthusiastically at this declaration, and I privately think that this must be why they seemed so enthusiastic at the prospect of breakfast this morning!

Not quite knowing what else to do, since this is, after all, the breakfast Gordon has served the girls and it would be inconceivable to leave it uneaten, they both pick up their spoons and gamely give their meal a try.

As they stir the whiskey and butter into their oatmeal, I try not to blanch at the sheer volume of alcohol swimming in their bowls.

When the girls spoon up their first bites, I wait for the expected signs of distaste to register on their faces. Instead, their spoons return to the bowl for a follow-up, and in another moment or two they are too busy eating to do more than just nod their delight.

I hear a deep voice, with a thick Scottish brogue, from the end of the table. "It's hot, so most of the alcohol has gone. Don't worry."

At least, I think that's what has been said. I truthfully only understood about every third or fourth word, unaccustomed as my ears are to his particularly thick accent, so I look to Robert, but he's looking back at me with a face that tells me he understood even less than I did. I don't bother to look at the girls because they're in whiskey oatmeal heaven, but Micah, who has been watching the entire exchange, is smiling at me as though in silent challenge to respond to the man's remark.

Thinking it would be rude to not comment in return, I gamely forge ahead, half hoping he just nods in response to anything I might say so that I don't have to embarrass myself by not being able to decipher his answer.

"Are you on vacation?" I know, for sure, that a nod would work here.

"Aye. On a tuur, doon frooom Fife." The husband and wife both look at me expectantly, and I try not to choke on my swallow of coffee. Robert is now grinning at me with eyebrows raised, and nodding enthusiastically at the Scots as though to encourage them to continue on.

"You're on a tour?" I am determined I can do this. I'm not exactly sure that was what he said, but I figure I have to start someplace. When the husband nods and responds with a resounding "Aye," I feel a tiny sense of triumph.

"And wha arrrr yu doon in Bath?"

The wife just nods and smiles as her husband asks this. She is not eager to contribute to this conversation, and I vaguely wonder if it's because she is more entertained by watching the look of confused concentration on my face as I attempt to translate what has just been said.

"Our daughters," and I nod at Andrea and Sara, who look up from their oatmeal long enough to smile and wave their spoons. "They are doing Sanskrit and music concerts in England and Scotland."

I'm thinking this is a fortuitous incident actually, because we've been excited about seeing the Scottish reaction to Sanskrit since it is the basis of their beloved Gaelic, but we thought we were going to have to wait until we made it all the way to Scotland to experience it.

But the Scots are glancing at each other, then back at us, with a look that could only be described as perplexed.

"Sanskrit? Wha is that?" The Scots are quite a handsome couple, and the husband is a big fellow, tall and robust, with reddish-blonde hair and sparkling blue eyes. They are both looking at me expectantly, and I, in turn, look at the rest of my family. I had not expected that people from such a direct Gaelic lineage would not know what Sanskrit was, and the surprised reaction from my table-mates tells me I'm not alone here. We were thinking Scotland was going to be a Sanskrit breeze, but if these people, who seem well educated and presumably well informed, have no idea what it is, we could definitely be in trouble.

Andrea picks up on this fact immediately.

"You've never heard of Sanskrit, then?" she asks.

"No. Wha is it?"

I jump back in and explain that it is an ancient language that is the basis of all the Gaelic languages, thinking that might jog his memory.

"Oh. So, wha doo yu du?" The Scot has apparently tired of the language discussion and has now turned his full attention toward Robert as he asks this question. I start to think this might turn out to be fun after all. I watch as Robert silently works to translate the question, then, to make sure, sort of asks it again.

"What do I do?"

"Aye."

Robert beams at the man because he's so pleased to have gotten the question right. The Scot looks back at Robert, waiting for a response.

"Oh," Robert remembers that the point of the question was not to see if he could translate it, but to get a response. "I do music."

He smiles again at the Scot, but now the Scot is the one with the perplexed look.

"Muusic. Thas wha yu du fur a livin?" he asks, disbelief underlying the question.

"Well ... yes," Robert has definitely heard the tone and realizes, somehow, in some sort of male shorthand form of communication, that he has come up short with his answer, so he tries a question of his own.

"And what do you do?"

"I'm a managerrr at a larrrge minin companee," the Scot answers proudly, pulling himself even taller in his seat. His wife pats his hand and smiles her approval. There's definitely a bit of a tone to his voice that says, "Now, *that's* a decent living, man!"

I find this whole exchange to be an extraordinary amount of fun. Robert's face reddens a bit at the large Scot's unspoken intimation that doing "music" for a "livin'" is an unmanly occupation. The Scot reinforces this notion by looking up a couple more times at Robert and just shaking his head.

The remainder of breakfast is eaten quietly.

* * *

We realize that we are going to be celebrating Andrea's twenty-first birthday here in Bath, but we've been so harried, there hasn't been the time or opportunity to actually plan anything. We find a small store downtown that has a variety of candles and ancient maps and books that we think she might like, so Robert and I go on a mad buying spree for the few moments we find ourselves alone, while the rest of the group is engaged elsewhere. We're not quite sure how to pull together a little celebration, given that we're in the middle of a trip, so we just hope something will work itself out.

After an enjoyable dinner at a restaurant recommended by Gordon, we decide to return to the B&B so Andrea can open her presents. As we open the entry door of the old home, we are greeted by soft lamplight and good smells. There is not another soul around, so we start to head upstairs. It is a few seconds before we realize that the music we hear, lilting softly in the background, is one of our Shanti Shanti CDs. The entire atmosphere of the place, at this moment, is truly like something out of another time, and we all pause on the staircase, soaking in the ambience, and feeling enormously fortunate to have such thoughtful hosts.

Continuing up the stairs to the landing, we find that any concern we might have had over Andrea's birthday was completely unnecessary. There is a bottle of champagne and six crystal flutes waiting for us on a silver tray, accompanied by a lovely note wishing her a very Happy Birthday.

Not wanting to wake the other guests, we are quiet in our exclamations of surprise at Gordon's excellent sleuthing skills, vaguely recalling that we must have made some mention of Andrea's birthday when we first arrived, though none of us remember it as anything more than a quick reference. We decide to take the champagne and glasses downstairs to the parlor to be enjoyed in style, and Robert and I gather her gifts together and bring those downstairs as well.

The parlor is decorated in the most tasteful combination of white and dark woods, with lovely floral chintz-covered sofa and loveseat, and luxurious draperies setting off the elegant windows. As we all walk in carrying the champagne, glasses, and presents, it suddenly seems like the most perfect place for a birthday celebration.

After all the presents have been opened, the birthday toasts made, and Andrea has had a wonderful celebration for her twenty-first birthday with all of us, we finally just sit back on the plush upholstery and revel in the pleasure of the evening. It is wonderful and spiritually renewing to have this quiet time to bask in the warm glow of simple family joys.

*   *   *

There is one last destination on our itinerary before we depart Bath for Edinburgh, Scotland. We discover that Stonehenge is just a short trip by car, forty-five minutes through rural England, which is wonderful because we had planned to see the ancient stones but didn't realize they were so close to where we were staying. We decide we should be driven rather than drive ourselves, because none of us can really get a handle on the left-side of the road, right-side of the car phenomenon!

The ride is beautiful, even though we're all a bit cramped together in a small sedan. We marvel at the beautiful rolling farmland passing by, mile after mile of idyllic green pastures, interspersed with thatched farmhouses and clusters of sheep that look as though they've been painted into the scene for effect.

About thirty minutes into our drive, I start to feel a bit sick to my stomach, and a little further on, I find myself rubbing my ears to try and hear the conversation in the car.

"Are we climbing in altitude?" I ask our driver.

"I don't think so, ma'am."

He is a great driver, careful and attentive, but he doesn't waste a lot of effort on idle conversation.

The closer we get to our destination, the sensation of discomfort I'm experiencing increases exponentially. The nausea is absolutely overwhelming, and the sensation in my ears has turned into a roar of sound that is so loud, I can barely think. The worst part, though, as I look up and see Stonehenge standing in the near distance, is that the feeling in my head is so bad it seems almost as though it is going to explode. I'm having a hard time metabolizing just how awful the symptoms are that I'm experiencing, but what I do know for sure is that I desperately don't want our one chance to see Stonehenge affected by them.

I manage to croak out something to Robert like, "What is going on? I'm feeling terrible."

He looks concerned when he glances at my face, which I assume, based on how I'm feeling, is three shades lighter than white, but he assures me I'll feel better as soon as we get out of the car. I am hugely relieved when the driver puts his blinker on and finally turns into a parking lot on the side of the road.

The first thing that surprises me, even given how bad I'm feeling, is that we've stopped in the middle of nowhere. I don't know what I expected, but not anything quite so desolate. There are no towns within sight, no public buildings, no farmhouses, no nothing. The location feels weirdly isolated, and I can see the stones standing like solitary sentries a little ways off in the distance.

I am out of the car the second it coasts to a stop, and I pull in deep breaths of the bracing country air. I *will* myself to feel better, but even though we're no longer driving, but standing on solid ground, the discomfort is continuing. The sound in my ears is not growing quieter with the cessation of movement, but louder, which I didn't think was possible given the decibel level of the roar I'm already experiencing.

Robert takes my arm and urges me to walk with him, hoping the distraction will help to level out whatever is going on. As I look around, trying to take my mind off the discomfort, I'm surprised to see that the stones are across the street (which is more like a country lane) from the parking lot where we're currently standing. The driver has told us to walk down the ramp to the entrance, where we can purchase our passes to get into Stonehenge proper.

The whole place feels eerie, really, and the sensation of isolation from any other signs of normal daily life is a bit overwhelming. If one blocked out the cars from any direct line of vision, as well as the people milling around, and just gazed across the field toward the stones, it could be any time in history ... a thousand years ago, as easily as today. It is as though this vista has always looked exactly this way—the huge stones standing alone in the middle of barren acres of windswept fields, waiting.

We walked down the ramp and were delighted by the lambs frolicking in the field right next to the parking lot. England can present such a spectacle of contradictions. The sight of the lambs innocently playing, and on the opposite side of the lane, Stonehenge, standing so stolidly and dramatically eloquent in its ancient silence, gave me a good case of goose bumps. I already had such a variety of uncomfortable distractions to deal with, I was surprised I could feel anything more on a sensory level!

We bought our passes and then were directed to walk through a tunnel that passed under the road and follow the path, which would rise back up to ground level a short distance from the Stones. I was still queasy, but the roaring in my head seemed to get a little better as we walked through the tunnel. We were all excited to see the Stones, and while walking through the protection of the underground passage we also felt a bit relieved to be secluded from the bitter wind whipping across the fields.

Reaching the end of the tunnel, we stepped out into the open grassland surrounding Stonehenge. I stopped for a moment to get my bearings and found myself trying to figure out why, suddenly, I was having a hard time focusing my eyes. Our small group passed by me and started to head off toward the circle. I shrugged it off to the contrast between the relative darkness of the tunnel and the stronger light outside, and assumed my eyes would quickly adjust.

As I started to follow my family, I was buffeted by the strong, cold wind, but no one else seemed that bothered as they pulled their jackets more tightly around them and continued to walk. Even though I did the same, I was feeling a growing sense of discomfort the further I walked. The closer I got to the Stones, the more I realized it had nothing to do with the temperature, or the wind.

The nausea and the roar in my ears had returned with a vengeance.

It reached a point where I was feeling so debilitated, I did not think I could continue any further, which was infuriating given how much I'd always wanted to see Stonehenge. Now, here I was, just a few hundred feet from the actual circle, and all I could do was stand on the path and tremble with discomfort, unable to even make my feet move so I could get a closer look.

Robert looked back and saw me standing just a hundred feet or so from the tunnel entrance, so he turned around and came back to see what was amiss. Micah had been watching me, concerned, and now hung back as though to wait, but the girls and my brother were already at the Stones.

"What's wrong? What are you doing?" Robert asked, looking from me to Micah for an explanation.

"I think Mommy's head hurts," Micah answered, a reasonable assumption given that my hands were holding the sides of my head.

Robert glanced to where the rest of the group was now waiting and motioning us to come along.

"Are you sick?" he asked.

"I don't know what's wrong," I answered honestly. "The roar in my head is so loud, I can barely hear your voice, and it's a weird sound, like nothing I've ever heard before. The nausea is back, too, and I can't see very well."

I realized that I had just named a ridiculous number of problems, and he gave me a look that said, "Is that *all?*" I knew this sudden, dire illness I was experiencing sounded preposterous, and I also knew how much Robert had been looking forward to seeing Stonehenge with me. As an ardent history buff, this was an archeological wonder he'd always wanted us to visit. And now I was having some kind of physical meltdown.

"Linda, we have to see the Stones. You'd never forgive yourself to have come this far, and then miss getting to see them up close."

I knew he was right, so I gathered together all my inner strength and determination, and literally gritted my teeth against the overwhelming discomfort. Taking Micah by the hand, I started to march us in the direction where Andrea, Sara, and my brother were standing.

The problem was, the closer I got to the Stones, the worse I felt, and the roar in my head was now beginning to take on more of the characteristics of an actual sound, with a pitch and tone unlike anything I'd ever heard before.

Everyone was waiting for us impatiently, and as soon as we approached, Sara put a camera in my hand and ran over to stand with Andrea and Micah so that I could snap some pictures of them in front of the Stones. They had a hard time holding their smiles with the wind whipping their hair and clothes, and by the time I finished, their cheeks were rosy from the very chilly, and for us unexpected, August temperatures.

One of the other tourists commented on how it was a shame that we couldn't actually approach the Stones and instead had to stay on the path. Vandals from years past had apparently necessitated the restriction of visitors, in order to preserve the integrity of the historical site, and it did seem sad that where once people had been allowed to actually touch the Stones, we could now only look.

But, truthfully, the last thing in the world I wanted to do was to get any closer than I already was. Something about the entire environment was having a very unsettling effect on me, and this sensation wasn't confined to the physical symptoms I was dealing with. At the first opportunity, I made my excuses and saying I'd meet everyone after they finished looking around, turned and walked/ran back toward the tunnel.

Once I was inside the underground passage, I felt better almost immediately. For one thing, it was warm in there, and protected from the wind, and as I looked around, smiling at the tourists making their way past me, I suddenly found myself wondering why I'd been in such a hurry to get back down here. The sound in my head had receded somewhat, not to the point of disappearing, but it had definitely cut back to where I could hear people talking as they passed by. My overall discomfort level had improved substantially.

After about ten minutes or so, during which time several people stopped to ask directions (in a tunnel!), and I was continuing to feel considerably better, I started to assume that whatever physical malaise I had been dealing with was now beginning to pass.

Finally Robert came down the passage with Micah in tow, and both of them were begging me to please come back up one more time and see the Stones with them.

"This place is so incredible," Robert said. "Now that you've had a chance to warm up a bit, you'll enjoy it more this time."

He and Micah each took one of my hands, and back through the passage we went. Emerging from the tunnel again, I looked at the surrounding countryside and the beautiful configuration of the Stones, and was struck once more by what an incredible place this is. The Stones were so awe-inspiring, standing in sharp relief against the panorama of field and sky, I couldn't help but want to draw closer. I walked resolutely toward the circle once again.

But before I could manage to take more than a few dozen steps, the roar in my head was back, only this time it came on with such a fury that I found myself overwhelmed to the point of actually being a little frightened. Before Micah and Robert even realized what I was doing, I had turned around and was making my way back to the underground passage. I could vaguely hear them calling to me, but it was as though from a great distance, and I knew I had to return to the relative comfort of the tunnel while I still had the capacity to do so. This time, it had really been difficult for me to see when the sound in my head took over. My vision narrowed until there was just a pinpoint of light in the center of my eye, and my peripheral sight became non-existent. I actually had to feel the walls of the tunnel with my hands to guide myself inside.

Once I was safely in the passage, the sound mercifully receded again. This time, though, I had the presence of mind to try and objectively observe the episode. The discomfort didn't disappear altogether, but it became more tolerable. My vision cleared, and the nausea, which increased as soon as I'd stepped out of the tunnel, eased a little as I stood in my underground sanctuary and drew in a series of deep, steadying breaths. Apparently, and inexplicably, I was having some sort of reaction to the Stones, but I seemed to gain insulation from whatever was affecting me as soon as I stepped underground.

I was so disappointed, and confused as well. I was unable to enjoy the spectacle of Stonehenge, because there was something about this environment that was deeply affecting me, and even interfering with my ability to see! And what on earth was that horrendous roaring sound in my head that increased in intensity the closer I got to the Stones?

As I stood in the protective tunnel, I grew determined to understand this. The problem was that I found it difficult to think clearly enough to make much sense of anything. I still had all the same symptoms in the passage, just not so intensely, but it made my ability to discern what was happening almost impossible. The only thing I knew was that the symptoms did seem to worsen the closer I got to the Stones, but I had no idea why. I had never heard of such a thing happening, and no one else seemed to be having any difficulty. People were coming and going through the passage, as easy as could be, and I watched a bit enviously as they went about their business, navigating the tour so effortlessly.

When the rest of the group decided to come find me, I was wandering around the little gift shop, looking at all the Stonehenge souvenirs. The first words from my brother and Andrea as they came through the door to the store were strangely reassuring.

"Mom, I'm really sick to my stomach. Should I get some Tums or something?"

And then from my brother, "I have a bit of a headache, and some nausea. Do you have any herbs in your purse?"

As though it had suddenly occurred to her to ask, Andrea said, "What was wrong with you back there? Was it just the cold?"

"This place makes you feel really weird!" This was from Micah as he walked into the store with his dad. I certainly was in no position to debate that sentiment.

After we all piled back into the car and assured our driver that Stonehenge was as incredible as we'd been told (he was looking at me curiously, so I must have still been a little "green around the gills"), we headed out of the parking lot and onto the main road. The roar in my head started growing louder again as we drove past the site, and the feeling of nausea became so intense I thought I was going to have to ask the driver to stop.

By this time, I was starting to experience some genuine apprehension about my ability to make it all the way back to Bath. As the driver accelerated, though, and we sped on down the road, I felt a corresponding reaction that caused my sense of concern to lesson. As we pulled further and further away from the site, and I watched as the Stones recede into the distance, I had the sensation we'd just passed through some sort of invisible curtain. The symptoms decreased rapidly until they were only a faint memory.

While I was at the Stones, it was as though I heard something reminiscent of a million mosquitoes buzzing in my ears, but as we drove further away, the sound of those million bugs became several hundred thousand, then a thousand, then a hundred, and so on, until a few miles down the road the sound disappeared altogether, along with the overwhelming nausea and vision problems.

There has always been much speculation with regard to the reasons Stonehenge was built to begin with, and a lot of that has centered on conjectures that the circles of stone were established as some sort of portal of energy. Whether that's true, or whether there is some other explanation, it is well accepted in even the most conservative scientific communities that there are areas on the Earth where magnetic fields are stronger, and these areas can create unusual phenomena. Stonehenge was erected many, many eons ago, and the exact reason for its existence has never been fully understood. Speculation, no matter how popular, is still not certainty.

I, however, certainly experienced *something* while we were there, and though I have no real understanding as to what actually occurred, I do know that even looking at pictures of the area still bothers me. I can remember most acutely the sound I kept hearing as I tried to approach the Circle, and the corresponding response in the rest of my body.

I suspect that one day we will re-discover exactly what it was that our ancestors found so magical about that lonely place, in the middle of the wind-swept fields of southwestern England.

[c h a p t e r t w e n t y - f i v e]

OUR TRAIN RIDE TO SCOTLAND turns out to be quite long, about five hours, but the trains are so comfortable and the countryside so beautiful that the time just flies by. The cars are not crowded, so we sprawl out and relax. After a while, and at about the point we calculate to be somewhere near the border between England and Scotland, we ask the porter when we will actually be in Scotland.

His brogue is intense as he says, "Soon."

How will he know exactly when, we ask him.

"I'll feel it herrre," the porter replies, rolling his rrr's as he lays his right hand over his heart.

This is a good introduction for us to the passion that is Scotland, and we all smile at the sweetness of his gesture. That, however, will be the last warm, fuzzy thought we have about anything Scottish for quite some time.

Arriving at the depot, we hail the cab and give the driver the address for the bed & breakfast we've booked for the next week or so. The pictures we'd seen of the house at the time we made our reservations made the place look like something out of a Scottish dream. Our reaction, when the cabbie pulled up and stopped in front of a building, was that it didn't resemble any of the pictures we'd poured over when making our reservations six weeks before, so we just sat in our seats and waited for him to drive on. When we realized he was not going anywhere and wanted us to disembark, we immediately pulled out the crumpled piece of paper that contained our reservation confirmation, and double-checked the address. Unfortunately, it seemed to coincide with the numbers swinging back and forth on the shingle in the front yard.

"Is this it? Are you sure?" Robert asked, hoping that there might be some part of this whole Scottish-address thing that we didn't quite get. Maybe the shingle was an advertisement for a place further down the street?

"This is the place," the cabbie assured us, and jumped out to help expedite our departure since we still didn't seem anxious to get out of his cab. Within thirty seconds or so, he had all of us and our luggage piled on the sidewalk. With the money for the fare in his hand he gave us a little jaunty wave and drove away down the street.

The house didn't look terribly inviting, more like something out of a scary movie, but it was 7:30 in the evening and we were exhausted, so we picked up our bags and headed for the front door.

After several rings of the doorbell, a young girl finally answers and, after we give our names, moves aside to allow us to step inside. She then hands us a couple of keys and points to the staircase that curves steeply up to the second floor. We look at the old, narrow stairs, then down at all of our bags, and think longingly of Gordon and his outdated code of chivalry. It won't be the last time we think nostalgically of the hospitality of Bath.

"Do we just go up?" I ask the young girl, as I realize she's heading off down the hall to the "private quarters," and there's a good chance we won't be seeing her again tonight.

"Yeh, and brrreakfast is at 8:30." This is said with a thick Scottish accent, followed by a little flip of her hair as she turns and disappears through a door.

We all look at each another, and try our best to put a good face on the situation.

"Well, let's go look at the rooms," Robert says as he heaves three or four bags into his arms and starts the steep climb.

We all follow, and are actually pleasantly surprised to find our rooms are not terrible. They are clean and adequate, though certainly not luxurious, but they seem like they'll do. Once we've washed up, and changed out of our traveling clothes, we feel renewed and more confident. We decide to venture down to the old part of Edinburgh, and check out the Arts Festival.

High Street is made up of cobbled stones, left over from the time when Robert the Bruce and Mary, Queen of Scots, walked around Edinburgh. The street is lined by gothic-looking buildings made of grayish-black stone and brick, and the ambience is so old that one feels the drama of hundreds of years of history pulsating in the air.

We were told by the people responsible for arranging our trip to Edinburgh that we should go to High Street on our arrival, and mix and mingle with all the other artists attending the Festival. Robert was advised to bring his guitar to get a feeling for the acoustics that he would have to deal with the following day, when Shanti Shanti was due to perform.

We had come Edinburgh to participate in Scotland's largest cultural event, which takes place throughout the entire month of August. Artists come from all over the world to share their own unique talents. Among many other venues, there is a film festival, as well as a musical extravaganza with every type of musician imaginable from bagpipers to Highland percussion groups. Theatre and performance exhibitions abound.

The more we looked around, though, the less we were able to understand exactly where Shanti Shanti was ever going to fit in with all of this commotion, and the longer we walked the streets, the more Edinburgh started to seem like a madhouse than the home to the world-renowned Arts Festival that we were expecting when we booked the tour.

Andrea and Sara search out and find the registration office, and go in to speak with someone while the rest of us wait outside. A carnival atmosphere permeates the area, and we look around dubiously as we try and picture exactly how Sanskrit chanting can possibly be done in this environment.

The girls return a moment later, and their faces tell the whole story. The news is bleak. Apparently, the organizers have booked Shanti Shanti to perform on this street in the midst of this loud, cavorting mass of humanity, the following day. The women Andrea and Sara talked to in the office conveyed, proudly, how they had arranged an extra-special place on High Street just for the girls, and, in fact, they even suggested that Shanti Shanti do a bit of an impromptu appearance right now to get a feeling for the crowd!

We were all flabbergasted. This was impossible. How could the girls possibly chant Sanskrit with the amount of hubbub going on here? And how was Robert supposed to be able to play his music? He couldn't hear himself think, let alone tune and play his instruments! The worst part, as the girls related it, was the fact that the organizers thought everything was just great. Andrea and Sara didn't have the heart to tell them that they had no idea how they were ever going to be able to perform here!

Robert suggested that maybe he should go back to the bed & breakfast and get some electrical support equipment to help out with the sound problem. The volume of the crowd was so high that an acoustic guitar would be drowned out.

But no, the girls informed him, that wouldn't be possible, because no electronic sound was allowed on High Street, in deference to the antiquity of the surroundings.

Actually, the surroundings were in great part responsible for the level of pandemonium we were dealing with in the first place. The tall, stone buildings lining the narrow cobbled street acted as great big mirrors for sound, so that each noise bounced off a million hard surfaces and reflected right back at the people in the street, including us, where we stood contemplating our dilemma.

The girls decided they would be troopers about the whole situation. As their rationale went, if all these other people could sing and dance and mime and act, Shanti Shanti could stand and do a little Sanskrit. I think, present in their decision, there was also a bit of a desire to see if they could, in fact, hold up under such extreme circumstances.

Robert, shaking his head in dismay the whole time, opened his guitar case and reluctantly took out his twelve-string Martin. This was obviously not at all what he had in mind when the girls were asked to come to Scotland and do Sanskrit.

The decision had apparently been made to do a mini-concert right where we were standing, seeing it was so difficult to move through the crowd and this seemed as good a place as any. Besides, that was exactly what all the other artists appeared to be doing.

Robert tried hitting a few chords, but found he could hear almost nothing, so he just shrugged his readiness at the girls. Looking up from their preoccupation with the guitar, Robert, Andrea, and Sara—who a moment before had been surrounded by people as tightly packed as an army of ants—suddenly found themselves standing in the middle of a human half-moon which had been effortlessly created around them. Apparently, when the crowd noticed Robert take out his instrument, people responded in one continuous, flowing stream of movement by altering direction slightly to accommodate the new activity. Now Robert, Andrea, and Sara looked out at the portion of the crowd that had stopped in anticipation of some new performance, and the people were looking back at the three of them expectantly, waiting to hear what they had to contribute to the whole acoustic circus.

If it hadn't been so bizarre, it would have been funny. Robert, Andrea, and Sara could not possibly imagine how their relatively small, "unplugged" sound was going to be able to cut through the mayhem. But gamely, they started into one of their songs, and the waiting crowd stood and listened politely, clapping enthusiastically at the end.

Slightly encouraged, the girls then started into a Sanskrit piece but found they practically had to shout in order for people to hear above the din in the street. Both girls said later how surreal it was to stand in the center of a medieval city and be literally shouting the *Vedas* at the crowd, while the Scottish voices passing by were raised in a variety of conversational choruses, in open competition for sound space.

After they had done a couple more songs, the girls and Robert ended the abbreviated performance by yelling their thanks, and the crowd applauded back in appreciation. How it was that they managed to have heard anything Robert and the girls had done was totally beyond me, but something must have gotten through, because suddenly an older Scottish gentleman broke away from the group and walked straight up to where the three of them were standing. He was a bit aggressive in his attitude, and I saw that when Robert glanced up and noticed the man descending on them, his expression grew a little wary. As the man drew nearer to them, though, he was muttering something under his breath that sounded gruff, but must have been a compliment, because he then proceeded to fling some Scottish coins into the guitar case Robert had left open earlier.

This action apparently inspired others in the crowd, because people began walking up, and also with exaggerated aggression, threw coins into the case. The girls and Robert were dumbfounded. This was certainly a first! Scream-chanting Sanskrit for their performance, and then having to try and decipher the crowd's peculiar gestures of appreciation.

We all finally decided it must be a unique Scottish way of expressing approval. It wasn't the act of putting the coins in the guitar case that was so perplexing to us, but rather the almost angry way in which the delivery was made!

After this rather strange cultural exchange was over, and Robert had taken all the money from his case and laid his guitar inside, we adjourned to a relatively (!) quiet corner to try and decide what to do.

We could all agree on the fact that there was no way Shanti Shanti was going to perform in this particular venue, and there were a number of reasons why it couldn't possibly work. Number one, and most important, was the fact that Sanskrit is a spiritual language and must always be treated with the utmost respect. Street chanting for large, rowdy crowds was not the way to deliver the sublime gift of Sanskrit.

But now we were left with a huge dilemma. As we started to head back to the B & B, there was a prevailing mood of disappointment, because the festival on High Street was where Shanti Shanti was booked to perform, and, technically, that was where they were due to appear tomorrow. However, neither the girls nor Robert felt like they could really face the mayhem again, and they also did not know what options there were.

On impulse, before we left the actual festival area, Andrea slipped back into the festival offices to try and speak to someone about an alternative venue. But a few moments later, when she came back out, she was shaking her head and it was obvious that she'd had no luck. The woman she spoke to was very nice, Andrea said, but didn't understand what the objection was.

"Just shout louderrr," was the woman's advice. "They'll hearrrr ya!" There weren't any other places available for performances either, Andrea discovered, because everything else had been completely booked up months before.

So, it was High Street or nothing.

We left the medieval part of the city with heavy hearts. Even though we intuitively felt that everything would eventually work out, we were too fatigued right at the moment to try and think about how, exactly, that feat was going to happen.

It was late by the time we reached the B & B, and after our evening on High Street, the ramshackle old place seemed even more off-putting than it had earlier in the day. No one seemed to be about, so we slipped quietly upstairs to go to bed. A good night's sleep seemed the only solution at this point. It had been an extremely long day.

The kids' bedroom was right next to Robert's and mine. As we walked up the steep stairs to our rooms, we were surprised that there didn't seem to be another soul in the place.

"Where is everyone?" I asked Robert.

He shrugged and said, "I don't know. Maybe we're the only guests."

Somehow that notion wasn't terribly surprising. We had yet to meet our landlady, and the only other person we'd spoken to was the young girl who'd unceremoniously handed us our keys and then turned on her heel and left. The place certainly was not a good representation of warm Scottish hospitality, which we'd heard so much about, so the thought that we were the only guests at this inn seemed a definite possibility. What was a bit unsettling about that particular scenario, however, was the fact that we'd been told by the cabbie who'd driven us here that the town was completely full because of the festival, with every place totally booked. If we were the only guests, and the rest of the place was empty, that did not speak well of our choice of accommodations!

Everyone hugged each other goodnight, and Robert and I left the kids to climb sleepily into their beds while we retired to our small room next door. I said something about hoping the beds were even half as comfortable as the ones in Bath, and Robert mumbled something about being so tired, it wouldn't matter since he could sleep on a wooden plank if he had to.

In another strange twist of circumstances, my poor brother had wound up having to take a room somewhere down the street, at an associate's of our innkeeper, as his reservations had been mixed up. I hoped his room was at least tolerable.

Just as we settled into bed, I realized I had left our little clock in the kids' room, which we needed because we had to be up early to try and sort through the High Street problem. Since there didn't appear to be anyone on the premises to talk to about a wake-up call, an alarm was all we could rely on. Our jet lag was better than it had been in London, but we still couldn't be sure of waking up on time, so I dragged myself out of bed to go retrieve the clock.

Opening the door, I look around our floor, and seeing no one about, step into the hallway in my nightgown. The doors to our rooms were huge and made of solid wood. From the looks of the knobs and hinges, they appeared to be at least a couple of hundred years old. I grab the door before it can swing heavily shut, deciding at the last minute that Robert should get out of bed and help me move one of the suitcases into the kids' room. Our room is so cramped it is hard for me to even get to the door, and it occurs to me that the girls will need some of the things from the suitcase in the morning anyway.

He mumbles something about having been almost asleep, then climbs slowly and clumsily out of bed. I assure him that this will take just a moment, but he balks when he realizes that I expect him to step out the door and into the hall in his underwear. Even though I assure him that no one's about, Robert glances around cautiously anyway, and then, still grumbling, steps into the hallway with the suitcase.

I have to push on the door to keep it from closing heavily on his back while he maneuvers the piece of luggage out the door, and I then try to lean over, just as Robert steps completely into the hall, to knock on the kids' door. At the exact same instant my knuckles make contact, I realize that I've somehow just let go of the door to our bedroom. Which, in a moment of suspended terror, I realize is a huge problem, since our key is on the nightstand inside. Robert sees what I've done, and as though in slow motion, we both turn and try to reach out to stop the door from closing. Too late, we can only watch in horror as it slowly slams shut in our faces.

Robert does not say anything. He just looks at me, looks down at his underwear, then back up at the door. I can't believe what I've done and neither, apparently, can he.

"Why did you do that?" he asks me with deceptive calm.

"I don't know," I mutter, frustrated and unbelievably tired. "I'm so sorry. But we can't worry about that now, we have to figure out how we are going to get back in." I decide that a pro-active approach is the best move, considering the fact that I pulled my husband out of a warm bed and the only reason he's standing in the hallway in his underwear right now is because of me.

I knock, once again, on the kids' door and wait a few moments while I hear stirring inside. Finally Andrea answers the door, half-asleep, but she doesn't appear to be the least bit surprised to find me standing in the hall in my nightgown, and her dad in his briefs.

"What?" she asks.

"Your dad and I," I begin to explain, but then stop when I see the look on Robert's face. "Actually, I," I amend, "locked us out of our room, and now we can't get back in because our key is inside."

Andrea doesn't even bother to look surprised. She reaches around to the bed behind her, grabs a blanket, and hands it to me ... and then she shuts her door.

I sputter my indignation and knock again on her door. Robert reaches over and, still not speaking to me, takes the blanket and wraps it around his waist.

Andrea opens the door and again says, "What?"

I think the "what" is pretty obvious, but she looks exhausted and in no mood for her parents' misbehavior at this time of night. The other two are sound asleep in beds behind her.

"Honey, we're stuck out here in our night things. You can't just leave us like this."

"Mom, I am so tired, I'm practically asleep on my feet. You and dad are going to have to work this out on your own. There is no room for you to sleep in here. We're so crowded now, no one would get a good rest." With that, she softly but firmly shuts the door once more.

I turn around to Robert to express my dismay over where we've failed as parents, but *he's* looking at me with eyes that are so tired and full of irritation and recrimination that I don't say a thing. He apparently cannot believe that I have locked us out of our room on our first night in Scotland, and I'm sure I will never hear the end of this, at least once he is rested enough to express the full extent of his annoyance.

"There has to be someone in charge who stays here overnight, doesn't there? And they have to have keys to all the rooms, don't they?" I ask, even while I study the offending locked door of our bedroom for some sign of vulnerability that we might to able to take advantage of. I discover that the saying "they don't build them like they used to" could have been strictly referring to door construction from the previous centuries, because there's no possible way to get back inside. I turn my attention to the staircase and the dark entry down below.

"You should try to find someone." I really only say this to him because assigning tasks to our husbands when we, the wives, are fresh out of ideas is something we do very well. He gazes down at his blanket-clad bottom half, and then refusing to even look at me again, turns and heads off down the stairs. I have heard no sounds from anywhere else in the building, so I fully expect it will be an errand of futility.

Robert reappears at the bottom of the stairs a couple of minutes later, and as he starts the steep climb back up, I can see he has a sheet of paper in his hand.

"What is that?" I ask eagerly, and my voice sounds like a stage whisper in the cavernous old building.

"This," he responds as he reaches the second floor, breathless from his efforts, "is our landlady's phone number. Apparently there is no one here tonight."

"But we can call her!"

I'm thrilled that we still might salvage a few hours of sleep this night. The reality of our circumstances is daunting, at best. We are in a strange place, in the city of Edinburgh, Scotland, and it's the middle of the night. We don't know a soul, and there doesn't appear to be anyone around to help us. A phone number seems to me to be a very welcome thing.

I knock on the kids' door again, and this time it's much longer before the door swings slowly open.

"What?" We've obviously pulled Andrea from such a deep sleep that she's actually weaving a bit on her feet.

I hold up the piece of paper that I've taken from Robert's hand. "We have a phone number!" I announce in a victorious whisper. Robert doesn't share my exuberance, and I can't begin to understand why. Surely this is progress!

Andrea steps aside and we go into the bedroom. Micah and Sara stir as Robert sits down on Andrea's bed and dials the phone. While he's waiting for someone to answer, he decides to share with me the reason for his lack of enthusiasm.

"You know, it's really late at night, and we've never even met the person who owns this place. I don't think a phone call from two dim tourists who've locked themselves out of their room in their underwear is necessarily going to inspire anyone to come down here and help out."

I respond that he is crazy, no one would leave two guests, no matter how dense (!) their behavior, to spend the night on the landing in their underwear. I wait confidently while the phone continues to ring.

Someone finally picks up, but my optimism is somewhat dampened when Robert has to repeat himself several times to make himself understood. It occurs to me that I may have overestimated the strength of our position.

Several minutes of apparent miscommunication between Robert and the person on the other end of the line pass, during which there are repeated attempts on my husband's part at what first sounds like cajoling, but which quickly turns to unabashed bribery, and I think, toward the end, I even start to hear him resort to flirting. When Robert finally hangs up the phone, it is obvious that nothing he did has made any difference.

"Well?" I ask unnecessarily, since the answer is pretty obvious from the look on his face. "Did you talk to the owner? Is she coming?"

"Yes, I talked to the owner, and no, she is not coming. At least not for several more hours. She is at a party, and she says she never goes out, but she's out now, and she has no intention of coming back anytime soon."

I can't believe this news, and my response feels shrill even though my voice is still a whisper.

"What? She won't come? Did she understand that we're in our underwear?"

"Yes, she understands that, and she doesn't seem very concerned. She was mostly irritated that I was interrupting her party."

After several more minutes of frustrated disbelief, while all three kids, fully awake now, are looking at us miserably, I suggest that he call back.

"Tell her we'll pay for a cab to bring the key across town," I suggest. "There's no way she won't agree to that." I am confident that I have stumbled upon the perfect solution. The woman wouldn't have to leave the party, and we could still get into our room. Unfortunately, I was not taking into account the recalcitrance of the Scottish disposition.

Robert reluctantly re-dials the number. "She's going to be really mad" is all he mutters as the phone begins to ring again.

Obviously, the line is picked up because he quickly begins explaining the idea about putting the key in a cab, and he's speaking very rapidly, as though the person on the other end is responding with impatience. I keep interrupting with "What is she saying?" because I can't tell which way the conversation is going.

Finally he says, "OK, well, thank you," in a disappointed but resigned tone of voice. Hanging up the phone, Robert turns to me and, using his best Scottish brogue, imitates the woman's decisive tone.

"No, she can't send the key, because the key is herrrre, in a cabinet, and she has to come and unlock the cabinet that holds the keys, and the cabinet is in her prrrrivate quarrrters, and we can't go in therrrre."

He delivers this with a combination of irritation and grudging humor, but the situation is really pretty bleak, considering our level of fatigue. We look at each other in tired misery, and then remember our kids, who are all observing the entire fiasco from the comfort of their beds.

"Well, we'll just go out and sit on the stairs until she comes back. It probably won't be that long," I say, glancing at Robert, who shakes his head dismally.

"It sounds like three or four in the morning, if we're lucky" is his response, as he gathers his makeshift "skirt" around him and gets up to follow me out into the hall. If we can't sleep, we have to at least leave the room so Andrea, Sara, and Micah can. If we all tried to bunk down in their small room, we'd be packed in so tightly no one would rest well.

We shut their door behind us and sit down dejectedly on the stairs. It is going to be a very long night.

We have only been sitting on the steps for a few minutes when the door suddenly swings open, and out walks Andrea. She has a very determined look on her face, and I instinctively know that she is going to say something I am not going to like.

"There's a window in your room, right?" she asks, all business now, with previous signs of sleepiness completely gone. She is pulling a jacket on over her pajamas, and I think, with increasing wariness, something about what she's going to suggest isn't going to be good.

"Yes, we have a window," Robert responds wearily, not understanding the significance of the question.

"And I think I saw a roof under your window, am I right?" Andrea asks, tying on her tennis shoes as she's speaking.

Robert finally catches my sense of alarm. "There is a roof under our window, but Andrea, this is a really tall, old building. The second floor is more like a third floor, height-wise."

"If you boost me up on the roof, I can crawl along the tiles until I reach your window, and," Andrea pauses as though something has occurred to her that she hadn't previously considered. "Is the window locked?"

"No," I respond, answering her question but refusing to consider what she's suggesting. "The window is not locked, because it's warped, so I just left it open. It's why our room was so cold. But, Andrea, listen to me," I am speaking to her back now, as she heads down the stairs with concentrated resolution. Robert is following her, barefooted, with his blanket still wrapped haphazardly around his waist. Neither of them even hesitates in their steps, and I know that means that he and Andrea are now on a mission.

"You guys! Stop!" I command to no one because they're not even listening to me now. "This is insane. Andrea, you aren't a climber, you're afraid of heights!"

If my goal is to inject some common sense into this potential disaster, it isn't working. They are both at the front door now, feverishly planning their escapade. Robert has tied his blanket around him and tucked the ends under, so it might even pass for a longish kilt in the half-light of the moon, but I am still in my flimsy nightgown and have no desire to venture out into the night. Still, my impulse to keep them from doing something so insane drives me to follow them out onto the front stoop.

"Robert, you know this is incredibly dangerous! That is a really, really steep roof. She could slide right off." As I speak I am looking in the direction of the tile roof that I am frantically gesturing toward, and seeing the actual height and steepness alarms me even more. Unfortunately, I am the only person who seems to care. And I am already convinced this is a bad idea.

"I'll be right underneath her if she falls, and I'll catch her," Robert tells me in a reassuring voice, as they both disappear around the corner of the building, and I am left standing on the small porch in my nightgown.

I am anything but reassured. Feeling unbelievably frustrated that they have left me alone with my worries, I turn to go back inside when suddenly an idea dawns, and I run up the stairs as quickly as I can. Reaching the top floor, though, and seeing the locked door looming in front of me, I literally smack my forehead with the palm of my hand as the full impact of my own stupidly registers. Some crazed impulse had made me think that I would be able to see what they were doing if I just looked out our window. But, of course, in order to do *that*, I would have to be able to get into my room. And the only way I could get into our room . . . was if our door wasn't locked in the first place! In which case, none of this would be necessary! Andrea would be asleep in her bed, and not climbing around on the roof of a two-hundred-year-old Scottish inn, during the middle of the night, in a valiant attempt to get her parents back in their beds, so she can go to sleep.

I sink down dejectedly onto the top step and wait in a state of undiluted terror. Visions of my eldest daughter on the roof cause my heart to palpitate. This is making everything else we've dealt with since deciding to take this trip look downright tame. Why couldn't that woman have just left an extra key, or better yet, why couldn't she have been here to greet us earlier that day and warn us that a locked door in Edinburgh meant you weren't going to get any sleep that night, because *no one* would be around to help you open it? Scotland was not my favorite place right at that moment.

I don't know how much time passed because the stress probably made it seem longer, but suddenly I hear a loud thump, and then a rolling thud and an "ouch" from the other side of the door. Before I can scramble to my feet, Andrea is swinging open the infernal door and standing victoriously in our room. She is smudged with dirt from head to toe, and is rubbing her elbow gingerly, but she is in one piece, and I could not possibly be more relieved. Just then Robert comes bounding up the stairs behind me.

"Is she in? I couldn't see her anymore, but for a minute, I thought she had slid back down the other side," he announces, breathlessly. And to think I had actually doubted him when he said he'd have it all under control. Silly me.

"What did you do?" I ask Andrea. Now that she is safe and sound, except for a few scrapes and bruises, I can tell that the whole escapade is going to wind up as some sort of huge Scottish adventure by the time we get back home.

"A little boy asked his mom if he could take us home," Andrea laughingly relates as we stand the table back up that crashed to the floor when she fell through the window. "And the mom said she was going to call the police!"

Oh, good, I thought. On top of everything else, there was the possibility we might still have the police to deal with tonight. But, no, Robert explains, apparently the woman and her little boy were charmed by their plight and had just watched in fascination as Andrea went clamoring up onto the roof.

"I told her we locked ourselves out of the room," Robert said.

"How did you not fall?" I ask Andrea, even though I don't really want to know the gory details. It was enough that she had come through it with just a little dirt on her, and I knew I'd be seeing her on that steep roof in my dreams for many nights to come.

"Well, that's just it. I almost slid right off," she admitted, extremely proud of her Spiderman exploits. "And Dad was really scared, but suddenly I just had this thought that if I could make myself let go of what I was holding on to, since the tiles were all coming off and I was going to fall anyway, I could catch the wire dangling from the overhang and swing over to the next eave."

I really couldn't believe this.

"I had this rush of 'I'm going to be just fine' flood through me, and I just let go. And it was so cool, I could swing out and grab the wire and it was perfect. I don't know how I did that, though, because it was really scary." And then, almost as though she just now remembered, "And I do hate heights."

Robert added his own version of how terrifying this whole adventure had looked from his position on the ground, what with tiles sliding down and almost hitting him where he was standing. I thought I'd never heard anything so insane in my life.

"You could have been really hurt, Andrea," I state this emphatically, while wiping some of the dirt off her face and arms. I don't want this event to be a precursor to some new laissez-faire attitude with regard to dangerous situations. "That was so unsafe. You should have just come back down. We could have waited until our landlady got back; broken bones would have really ruined our trip considerably more than a lost night's sleep."

"No, it wasn't like that, Mom. I normally would never have done anything this crazy, but *at that moment,* it was a completely sane thing to do. In fact, I had this incredibly clear experience of being absolutely safe, that what I was doing was correct. I would never court disaster, because that's just not me, but I can't quite describe the feeling I had up there."

I should have known better than to be concerned that this activity heralded a trend. Andrea *was* a very cautious person, but she had also always been something of a warrior with regard to pursuing things she felt strongly about. She met almost every obstacle she had been confronted with in her life with as much confidence as though she'd received a clarion call-to-arms. When faced with seeming adversity, she had a marvelous way of connecting with something deep inside that helped guide her through the difficulty. Her adventure on the roof that night underlined for me how determined she was about not giving in to fears when something felt correct. And though what happened was a silly exercise from most perspectives, when looked at from a certain angle, it was a wonderful metaphor for what I had seen her clearly display in other, more important situations. Andrea had the clear ability to just let go ... and trust, when the situation demanded it.

We all crawled off to bed then, tired and a little buzzed from all the activity. The landlady still was not home, and it felt like a huge gift to be able to curl up in our bed and relax when we could have still been hanging out on the stoop in our sleeping attire.

The next day, Robert and Andrea had to go out and take pictures at the "site" of their nighttime escapade. Robert boosted Andrea back up onto the roof, and she stayed at a safe height so he could take some snapshots. The landlady had disinterestedly inquired this morning how we had, in fact, managed to unlock the door to our room, and sensing from her irritable attitude that she would not have found any aspect of the adventure the least bit amusing, we opted to merely say, "Oh, we just got the door to open." She didn't inquire further, and we didn't provide any additional explanation.

Now, however, with Andrea up on the roof for a photo re-enactment, it seemed we just didn't know when to quit. Who should happen to walk out into the small courtyard to hang up some clothes? Well, our crabby landlady, of course.

As I'm watching all of this unfold from the safety of our bedroom window, in a state of disbelief at their bad timing, Robert goes ducking around the corner with his camera before the woman spots him, leaving Andrea perched right above the landlady's head in a crouched position on the roof. She holds her breath, not daring to move, while the woman jerks the pins from the hanging bag and impatiently starts pinning the damp clothes along the line. At one point, Andrea has to stifle an attack of nervous giggles when the woman is standing directly under her, and a tile that Andrea is sitting on starts to slide loose. We aren't quite sure exactly how this woman, who has not been the personification of hospitality up to this point, would react to finding one of us perched on her roof, but knowing there are no rooms left in Edinburgh, Andrea and Robert are inspired to be as surreptitious as possible.

After the woman goes back inside, Andrea vaults down from the roof, onto a wall, and then slides safely to the ground. She and Robert go rushing back up the stairs and into the room where I'm standing, and they're red-faced with a combination of terror and hilarity.

Whatever else we might say about Scotland, we certainly have not had a boring minute since we arrived.

[c h a p t e r t w e n t y - s i x]

AFTER RECOVERING FROM OUR LATEST near-catastrophe and fortifying ourselves with a hearty Scottish breakfast, we set out to confront the problem of how Shanti Shanti was going to manage to do a performance on the infamous (or so we had named it in our own minds) High Street. Following last night's rooftop adventure, we'd all had a semi-restful sleep, but now, the following morning, we were still facing the same problem as yesterday. In fact, if anything, the girls were more adamant than ever about not going back to the festival at all if it meant they had to scream Sanskrit just to be able to perform!

We decide we should try and experience a little more of the actual city of Edinburgh, since what we had been able to see up to this point has been so filled with revelers attending the festival as to make it almost impossible for us to get any real feeling for the place. We are also hoping to stall a little for time, in hopes some brilliant light bulb of an idea will go off over one of our heads, giving us an indication of what our next step should be.

We take a cab to downtown Edinburgh, and the driver regales us with stories about "Sean" ("Connery," he explains in answer to our puzzled looks, a bit irritated that we don't automatically know who he means) and how he, the cabbie, has driven "Sean" about town quite a number of times. The actor must spend quite a bit of time in Edinburgh, because a couple of other drivers we encounter during our stay have their own stories about personal adventures with 007.

Walking the streets of the city is a bit like a 3D hike through an episode of "Gaelic Adventures" on the travel channel. Scottish brogues assail us from all sides, and at times it is difficult to know if someone is genuinely irritated with you or instead just making a passing comment. The Scots can be very brusque and straight-spoken, and after a while, you can find yourself actually liking the trait because you always know exactly where you stand. No beating around the bush, a Scot will just come right out and tell you.

Sightseeing pleasures aside, we are all still feeling very concerned about the pending performance that afternoon. Walking along, we spot a beautiful park nestled against the base of some steep cliffs, and it is filled with gorgeous flowers and decorative wrought-iron fencing. We glance up, and at the top of the cliffs, dominating the park, is the medieval castle that sits at the end of High Street. It is perched where it has stood for hundreds of years, overlooking Edinburgh as a timeless sentinel for the city below. We are dazzled by the sight of the jutting stone cliffs, positioned as they are as such a grand backdrop for the beautiful old Castle. We decide to take advantage of the scenic location to stop and rest our feet.

Before we even manage to sit down, however, Sara looks across the park and spots something that makes her eyes light up.

"What is that?" she asks, and we all turn in the direction she is pointing. We see what we missed before while we were caught in the enjoyment of the view. At the very base of the cliffs is a huge outdoor amphitheater, and even as we stand there watching, a musical group walks out onto the enormous stage, picks up their instruments, and starts to sing and play. The amphitheater provides a fascinating contrast to the rugged cliffs and the medieval castle above. What a glorious place to be able to perform.

"What is this place, do you think?" Andrea asks this question as though we've all been part of a conspiracy to hide something from her. "Is this connected to the festival?" And then she voiced another question that we were probably all thinking right along with her. "Why aren't we performing here?"

She had been talking with a kind of stream-of-consciousness delivery, as though mesmerized, as we all were, by the sight of the beautiful park with the huge amphitheater tucked at the base of the cliffs. When she reached the last line, however, the actual implications of the question made her voice rise with frustration.

"I don't know if it's a part of the festival, but there's a lot of people in the audience here, so it's possible," Robert said. He hadn't actually caught the tone in her voice and was still sort of dreamily staring at the beautiful spectacle.

"I want to perform here." Sara made the declaration very simply and to the point, and her voice was quiet with determination.

"You want to perform here?" Robert now seemed to have been pulled out of his reverie by the intensity in Sara's tone. "Are you crazy? If this place *is* connected to the festival, every single act has been booked solid for the last six months. We wouldn't have a chance of getting in."

Realizing that what he'd just said was absolutely true, the rest of us started to continue on down the street, but Andrea and Sara stood glued to the spot, staring at the huge crowd and listening to the wonderful acoustics as the music from the band bounced off the cliffs and reflected back to where we were standing.

"This is where Scotland should hear Sanskrit chanted." Andrea made this statement so quietly I had to lean a little back toward her to make sure I was hearing correctly.

I knew where this was going. Visions of rooftops and falling tiles went flitting through my head. What did I say a little earlier about Andrea seeming to just "know" when something was right? Maybe it was more akin to plain old stubbornness!

"Andrea, your dad's right, you shouldn't focus on this right now. We have to go back up and deal with the High Street problem. This isn't something we can make work for us this visit. Maybe we can try and come back next year, and book the spot way in advance. We can find out what the criteria is for appearing at this venue."

Before I had even finished the last sentence, Andrea had grabbed

Sara's hand, and the two of them went running off toward the amphitheater. The rest of us stood looking after them stupidly, until Andrea turned around and shouted back at us, "We're going to perform Sanskrit here! Come on, Dad!"

Trying to be the voice of reason, Robert looked at me and shrugged his ambivalence about their effort. "There's no way we're going to get in here on this short notice, but maybe they can make inquiries for next year."

Saying this, he then turned around and followed casually in the direction they had just run off in. My brother Dan, Micah, and I waited for their return. I really didn't want them to get too focused on this beautiful place as a possible location for a performance, only to then have to return to the reality of High Street. It would make the inevitable seem that much more difficult.

We waited in the park for about ten minutes or so, and my brother bought Micah a snowcone while we bided our time until they returned. Before Micah had a chance to do any real justice to his icy treat, I heard—before I saw—the two girls running through the crowd and up the slope of lawn leading from the amphitheater to where we were standing. With barely suppressed glee, Andrea and Sara, grinning from ear to ear, were running toward us and calling, "Guess what! Guess what!," making such a sincere effort to control their excitement that it was obvious that *something* had happened. I looked behind them and saw Robert following several paces back. He had a somewhat baffled expression on his face.

"Guess what!" they both repeated again, breathlessly, as though in their excitement they'd forgotten how to say anything else.

Then Sara started off. "OK, you're not going to believe this."

And then Andrea, "This amphitheater is where . . .

And Sara, ". . . the festival does its big performances!"

And again, Andrea, "And they are totally booked!"

I wasn't quite sure if they were both a bit addled from the barometric pressure of the northern latitudes, but that sounded like exactly where we started off. Robert had now reached the group, and was nodding and smiling, which just added to the confusion.

"But," Sara managed to get out before Andrea interrupted again.

"… they have had a cancellation from a group that missed their flight from France," Andrea interjected, still speaking in a breathless voice, though now it was just due to suppressed excitement.

"And," Sara continued for her, "we told them we could fill the spot."

I was finding all this way too much of a coincidence to actually believe. There had to be a catch. Robert finally spoke up, seeing my look of obvious disbelief.

"It's true, they need an act, and they need it right now. They said it was good luck that we just happened by at that particular moment, because they had only received the notice of cancellation a few minutes before. They had no idea what they were going to do to fill the space."

"We have to give them a CD to hear us, and some press to show them a record of past performances." As Andrea said this, she was rifling through Robert's travel case because it contained extra CDs and copies of press. He had carried it along this morning in anticipation of trying to bargain with the festival coordinators on High Street about a quieter place for them to perform. This opportunity completely eclipsed any and all thoughts of a High Street performance.

"What about the High Street people, though? Aren't they going to be miffed at having you change venues without going through them?" I asked this as the thoughts went running through my mind, but I wasn't deeply concerned about the answer. It was obvious from what we'd observed last night, there were so many performers on High Street that the coordinators would have very little difficulty filling the girls' spot. I also realized how incredibly fortunate it was that we had happened by at just that moment. Even if the High Street people had learned of this cancellation, the likelihood of them helping us change venues was almost non-existent, as occupied as they were with their own overwhelming responsibilities. It was also clear that the coveted performing spot at the amphitheater would probably have been quickly and happily filled by another eager group, if not for the girls acting on the impulse they'd had.

"We shouldn't get our hopes completely up yet, though," Robert cautioned. "The 'powers that be' still have to listen to the CDs, and go over the press. They told us to check back in about an hour."

We passed the time by grabbing a bit of lunch at a restaurant nearby. We were all a little anxious, and didn't have huge appetites. Now that the possibility of performing Sanskrit at the base of the cliffs of Edinburgh had reared its head, all other possibilities paled in significance. This was truly a location worthy of the goal we had come here for, which was to present Sanskrit to Scotland, in an atmosphere that was perfect for the presentation of this ancient spiritual language. We waited impatiently for the verdict.

At the appointed time, we made our way back to the huge park, and Micah, my brother, and I once again waited outside while Andrea, Sara, and Robert went into the offices. We didn't want to all go in and overwhelm them with our enthusiasm.

A few short minutes later, they came back out, and I was dismayed to see they were walking this time instead of running, and talking quietly among themselves. My mind immediately started to look for a way to make this seem like a positive result, but could come up with nothing as I kept envisioning what Sanskrit would have sounded like, echoing off the cliffs of Edinburgh.

"So?" I asked, as they walked up to us. "They didn't like the CDs?"

No one answered until all of them had come up level with where our little group was waiting, and then Robert responded quietly.

"No, they liked the CDs."

"So, they don't think you can do the amphitheater? Do they think you need a bigger band?" I asked.

"No, they thought we would do just fine," Robert responded, still in that same quiet voice.

Then, as though the girls couldn't stand it any longer, Sara burst out, "We're performing here this afternoon! They loved the CDs, and said they couldn't believe how fortuitous it was that we stopped by right at the moment we did."

"They said we should have been booked here to begin with,"

Andrea added, her face reflecting excitement and something else I couldn't quite identify. It was apparent she was extremely affected by the realization of the bizarre number of "coincidences" that had come together to bring about this particular result.

"They also said we shouldn't have been put on High Street anyway. If they'd known what it was we did, they would have automatically placed us on the amphitheater roster. They didn't see our initial application, or this is where we would have been all along."

When Robert spoke again, it was clear that they were all reeling from having just witnessed, first-hand, a pretty remarkable cosmic demonstration.

"This is so completely strange. Apparently we didn't come to Scotland to perform on High Street at all, but there was some point for us to understand here. All we had to do was stumble in this morning, at the exact 'right time,' and everything would automatically fall into place, like a line of dominoes. It's too weird for words."

We all stood there in the park, with the crowds milling closely around us, and felt a little stunned by the delicate but determined deliberateness of fate. A cancellation here, a walk through a park there, a casual glimpse of a stage, an impulse to follow the improbable desire to perform on that stage by going and talking to the people in the office. What an elegant arrangement of casual components this had turned out to be!

There was not a great deal of time to stand around and more deeply explore the phenomenon, because one of us glanced at a wristwatch just then. We realized that we had very little time to go all the way to the B & B to pick up the equipment Shanti Shanti would need to do a performance, then make it back here in time to get set up. There was also the matter of talking to the High Street people and explaining the situation. We certainly didn't want our actions to come off like those of a fickle high school prom date that cancels because of a better offer from someone else, so as we dashed to catch a cab, we considered how best to explain the situation to the festival organizers so we wouldn't be offending anyone.

As Andrea pointed out, once we were in the cab and on our way across town, it was not exactly our doing (!) that things had worked out this way. When we submitted our application to perform at the festival, we had not been given a choice of venues, but if we had, we most certainly would have requested the amphitheater. Closer scrutiny of the actual conversation, however, enabled Andrea to remember that by the time we filed our registration, the festival told her that all of the venues were completely booked except the High Street one. Our only chance of performing in the amphitheater was based entirely on a series of cosmically organized coincidences, and we had been unwitting accomplices in that plan!

Once we reached the B & B, we rushed upstairs to gather together all of our belongings, including the musical equipment (guitars, cords, etc.) that would be needed, plus CDs for anyone who might want to purchase one after the performance. Andrea and Robert slipped off to a quiet corner to find a phone from which to call the High Street people. I made a last check of our rooms, and bid our landlady goodbye since we would be going right from the performance to the train station.

By the time we were ready to hail a cab to take us back downtown to the amphitheater, everything was well in hand, and our reputation with the organizers was still intact. Apparently, the consensus of the festival office was that, indeed, Shanti Shanti should have been at the amphitheater all along, and the woman they spoke to was delighted to hear of our success. With a hearty "Good Luck!" and assurances that there were scores of people waiting for performance spots and not to worry, we set off in another Scottish cab ("Do you know Sean?" asked the cabbie) to do the appearance.

Up to that point, we were so focused on the tremendous good fortune that allowed even the possibility of Shanti Shanti to perform at such an auspicious location that the *reality* of performing *at such an auspicious location* had not really penetrated our awareness. As the cab dropped us off and everyone picked up something for the trek to the amphitheater, the actuality of the situation began to dawn.

"That is a huge stage," Sara said, as she packed the box of CDs down the stairs, looking at the amphitheater the whole time.

"And that's a huge crowd," Andrea supplied, as she juggled their outfits with one arm and guitar cords with the other.

Robert looked at the stage, the crowd, then back at me, and quietly said, as though underlining his own concerns, "Be careful what you wish."

I knew that meant that we had all been so caught up in the absolute magic of the morning, we really had not taken the time to absorb what the fulfillment of our desire fully entailed.

Shanti Shanti had never performed at a venue quite as intimidating as this. They had performed for an ample crowd when they opened for Patch Adams at a large auditorium, and there had been other big performances, but there was something so awe-inspiring about the beauty and drama of this particular location, with its backdrop of jutting cliffs and the magnificent castle looming overhead, that made the performers who were currently on the stage seem very small and insignificant, indeed.

There was no time for further introspection because the minutes were clicking by, and Andrea and Sara weren't dressed yet in their performing outfits. Robert also had a lot to do with regard to sound checks, etc. We finally found a festival employee who must have taken in our rather frazzled appearance and overloaded arms, because he walked us straight to the artists' dressing area and took Robert off to talk with the stage managers.

The girls and I looked around, and we all smiled in glee at the way everything suddenly became transformed. From the moment we stepped into the backstage area, which was large and somewhat open to traffic with various stage employees walking in and out, the entire "vibe" changed.

"Are you Shanti Shanti?" a petite, young, dark-haired girl asked as we started to set our things down.

"Yes," Sara answered, and before we could think of what we should ask next, she turned and said something quietly to another girl who was standing close by. They both then looked at us and, smiling broadly, scooped up all the clothes and other accessories and motioned for us to follow them into another part of the downstairs labyrinth of rooms.

"Well, then, Shanti Shanti, we need some information about you, so that we may introduce you properly from the stage when it's your turn to perform." This comment came from the second girl, and it was spoken in a lovely, lilting British accent that had just the slightest hint of a rolling "r" thrown in.

"Mom?" Andrea turned to me, and I knew what was coming before she even said it, so I reached for my pen and some paper. Meanwhile, both girls started to change their clothes, watching over their shoulders for any intrusion on what was only a partially private dressing area.

At one point, while they were still changing and I was doing the writing for the introduction, a couple of young men in stage technician get-ups came wandering in, and Sara zipped up her skirt quickly while I made broad comments about the girls being "not quite ready." Even though the atmosphere was very intimate and convivial, I could still feel the girls desired some semblance of privacy in which to finish changing their clothes.

"What's that?" the one guy asked as they proceeded to walk right through the room. Then, seeing both girls rather glaring at him as they reached around to try and button the backs of the outfits, he realized their discomfiture and smiled graciously.

"That's fine, no worry. We'll just slip through and leave you alone."

As both young men started to walk up the steps to the first level, one of them whispered to the other and nudged him lightly with his elbow. The guy who had spoken turned then and asked, "Are you the Shanti Shanti girls, then?"

At their affirmative nods, he and the other guy broke into huge smiles. "Good job on those CDs! Outstanding! Welcome to Scotland!"

With red faces, both young men turned then, and ran the rest of the way up the steps.

The girls looked at me and laughed slightly with a combination of nerves and amusement, then quickly returned to the task of getting dressed. The young men had been attractive and engaging, and the Scottish accent delightful, but stage jitters were building, and the constant stream of people through the dressing area wasn't helping. The girls and Robert had started a tradition some time before of spending five or ten minutes in meditative silence prior to each performance, to add clarity and focus. Sara muttered to me while I combed the back of her hair that it didn't look as though there was going to be a time or place for that luxury in these current circumstances.

The stage call arrived long before we realized it was time, and the "Five Minutes" announcement caught us completely off guard. I have no idea what I expected, but it was evident what it was the festival people expected. There was no time for second-guessing anything. Shanti Shanti was set to perform, and the stage people assumed we would know how to do everything we were supposed to do, with little or no fuss.

It was really a great learning experience for all of us, but most specifically for the girls. When the five-minute call had been made, the reality of the situation took on a rather dramatically different dimension. There was no going back now, and the ephemeral quality of the day suddenly took on a real shape and form. Providence could only intercede up to a point, but now Shanti Shanti's own efforts and abilities would have to move into focus. This was no time for the faint-hearted.

With a last good-bye kiss, and a frantic "Come on!" from Robert at the top of the stairs, Andrea and Sara rushed off. I went out to sit in the front with Dan and Micah, who were patiently holding a place for me close to the front of the stage.

"How'd it go?" my brother asked as I collapsed, exhausted, into my seat.

I smiled and nodded my answer because, just then, the music from the loudspeakers soared so that I couldn't hear much else. As two emcees walked out onto the stage, I was struck again by how very big the stage was. It almost swallowed up the two ladies who were now standing center-stage, and they looked tiny against the amphitheater backdrop.

"Ladies and gentlemen, we are proud to present a very special treat from America ..."

As they spoke, both women's voices rang with charming Scottish inflections. I listened as one of them read the impromptu information about Shanti Shanti I had written just moments before, and then as the other one added some personal comments based on the girls' CDs and press packet. I was filled with a feeling of complete joy. What a huge gift for Shanti Shanti to get to share Sanskrit with Scotland, in such an incredibly wonderful way.

"... And let's have a huge round of applause for **SHANTI SHANTI!**"

With that, the audience burst into a huge, warm welcome, and Andrea, Sara, and Robert walked out onto the stage. When the men in the audience spotted the girls, whistles and catcalls broke out, and Andrea and Sara smiled in return. Which prompted more whistles. As reserved as the Scottish people we'd encountered had been up to this point in our visit, so were they now equally outspoken in their appreciation. I couldn't help but wonder what in the world this crowd would think of Sanskrit!

Robert hit a few chords on his guitar, and they started into their first song. The audience sat in rapt attention, and even clapped along on the choruses. The sight of the three of them on the stage was pretty spectacular, but then my brother nudged me and motioned for me to look up, and as I followed his gaze, I saw they were also being magnified in huge relief on a screen above the stage.

I found myself wishing the three of them could see what they looked like from our vantage point. I thought of the girls' very first entry into performing and chanting Sanskrit, with their small living-room appearances in friends' homes. That inner memory juxtaposed itself against the drama of the spectacle before me. The whole thing produced an indescribable sensation. We were clearly not responsible for any of this, and I could only sit there feeling a sense of infinite gratitude for the presence of grace I felt swirling around us on that spectacularly beautiful day in Edinburgh.

There was a moment when my euphoria was challenged, however, and I had a definite, though temporary, experience of trepidation when the girls actually started into their first Sanskrit piece. The crowd looked puzzled as the strange sounds echoed across the stage, and I felt an unspoken, collective question ripple through the audience that was an eerie echo of what the Scottish man had asked us that morning in Bath: "Sanskrit, wha' is that?"

My brother even turned to me with a questioning look on his face, as if to say, "Do they like it, or not?" Before long, though, it was apparent that the crowd was starting to be infected by the profoundly powerful experience of Sanskrit, and they were enjoying the sensation.

After Andrea and Sara finished chanting, and the audience responded with warm enthusiasm, the girls went on to talk about the origins of the Scottish Gaelic language and how Scotland's own mother tongue reached back to find its origins in the ancient language of Sanskrit. Heads nodded in understanding, and the girls then demonstrated Latin and how closely that language relates to Sanskrit, and there were more nods and small shouts of encouragement.

Andrea and Sara spoke briefly about some of the positive effects of Sanskrit, and then, while the audience was still digesting this brief mini-intro, they launched into an even older piece of Vedic chanting that was particularly beautiful and melodic.

At first there was a strange, almost physical shift in the attitude of the audience that felt to me as though the crowd had just inhaled sharply in response to something that surprised them. Then, suddenly, the sounds of the Sanskrit words took on a peculiarly haunting quality, and the actual nature of the tones and words seemed to somehow become altered. I didn't know quite what was happening, but then my brother, obviously making the same observation that I was, pointed to the cliffs. I realized that for some reason, the longer the girls chanted, the more a remarkable kind of vortex of sound was being created. As the girls continued to perform, the resonance of the Sanskrit words floated over the people in the audience, where they sat intently listening, and then, because the amphitheater seating was situated on a steep incline, the words would hit the angle of the hill behind us and ricochet back toward the cliffs. What I was hearing, and what my brother had observed, was that the cliffs were serving as a kind of reflective surface, thereby making the amphitheater a gigantic reverberation of sound. After hitting the cliffs, the pure evocative tones were shot back directly at the audience until the entire area became a giant encapsulation of cosmic intonation. Where the girls left off and the reflection off the cliffs began became indistinguishable, and as the chanting rolled over the crowd, emanating first from the stage, then again from the cliffs, to finally disperse over the downtown area of Edinburgh itself, the experience of the "Sanskrit buzz" was palpable. The audience was caught in an explosion of bliss, and the city itself was literally being bathed in Sanskrit blessings.

As the girls finished, everyone in the entire area remained perfectly still for several moments, and then, suddenly, a roar of applause burst forth from the crowd. The emotion reflected in the thunderous ovation reached out to Andrea, Sara, and Robert, where they stood smiling on the stage in a kind of tidal wave of uninhibited joy.

My brother looked at me and smiled, then practically shouting into my ear to be heard, said, "Well, we got to experience Sanskrit in Scotland."

And most important of all, I thought, as the response from the crowd continued on and on, Scotland got to experience Sanskrit.

[c h a p t e r   t w e n t y - s e v e n]

By the time we left the amphitheater, and were on our way to the train station, we were all still riding on a wave of Sanskrit bliss. The performance had been such an incredibly fulfilling experience to be a part of, and as we walked down the street, it was as though we were all floating along in a wonderful sort of hazy after-glow. It had been a spectacular trip, and the girls had been given an incredible opportunity in which to share their joy, but it was now time to go home.

As we made our way along the sidewalk of the busy main street, people had to move slightly to accommodate our large group, and our even larger amount of gear. Periodically someone would turn and stare as we went schlepping through the crowd, loaded down with luggage, but none of us minded a bit because we were still reveling in our own cocoons of quiet happiness. It had been an amazing day.

What occurred next is such an extraordinary incident that it has taken all of us a long time to try and put together the pieces in such a way that we are accurately capturing the event. The following description is the closest I can come to what actually happened that day, and it is based on the collective recounting of circumstances that everyone experienced.

As we approached a busy intersection—three lanes of traffic going in both directions, converging from all four streets—we stopped to rest our hands and legs for a moment before starting the trek across the wide street. We could see the train station from where we stood, so we relaxed a little. It looked as though we were going to make our departure time just fine.

As we stood on the corner, watching the traffic whiz by and waiting for the light to change, I happened to glance over and see a little boy, who looked to be about four years old, staring at our group from where he was sitting on his dad's shoulders. Catching my gaze, he looked at me and smiled, and I smiled back, charmed by his cherubic face. With his red hair, blue eyes, and rosy cheeks, he was the quintessential adorable Scottish boy. After a moment, his gaze shifted to the girls, and I wondered if perhaps his family had been in the audience at the amphitheater, because he seemed to be staring at them so intently.

The light changed, and we all picked up our bags and started across the street. We didn't want to get caught in the middle of this busy street when the light changed, loaded down as we were. Drivers in Edinburgh had about the same tolerance level for pedestrians as they did in London. I said something about having to hurry a little, and everyone picked up their pace even as the light started to flash its warning from the other side of the street.

Suddenly a voice rang out, rather loudly, calling something I couldn't understand, and hurried though I was, it startled me because the voice so clearly contrasted with all of the other street noises. I looked around quickly, not cutting my pace, but I couldn't tell where the sound had come from.

"Girls!" The voice rang out again, but this time I caught what was being said.

Based on the fact that I saw every head in our particular group swivel slightly, side to side, it was obvious they had all heard it as well, and were also trying to figure out the source. Strangely, no one else in the crosswalk with us responded, but it seemed that *we* all had heard that voice with crystalline clarity, which made no sense given that the traffic was whizzing by at a numbing speed, and the city street was bustling with activity.

We were now at about the halfway point in the intersection, and still walking at a brisk clip, even as we continued to glance around to see who had called out.

"Girls!"

This time there was no mistake. The voice was coming from behind us, and I paused for a moment, as did everyone in our group, all of us stopping and turning around to look behind us. There was the little Scottish boy on the street corner, still sitting on his father's shoulders, and now he was grinning at us with a huge smile of delight.

I realized that he must have recognized the girls from the performance and was trying to say something to them.

And then his little voice called out again, even as we all stood in the middle of the street, and the other pedestrians continued to trudge on around us.

"CONGRRRRATULAATIONS TO YOU GIRLS!" As he said this, his face was literally glowing with delight, and his words reached out to where we were all standing in the crosswalk, a little mesmerized by his joyous intensity.

As we stood there, looking at the little boy, a simultaneous shift seemed to occur in our collective perception. We all saw the little boy as he continued to smile at us from his perch atop his father's shoulders, but suddenly everything else around us started to slow way down and take on the qualities of a dream. The sounds of the bustling traffic became strangely muted. As I stood looking at the little boy and his father, they appeared crystal-clear to me, but the rest of the people around us, as well as the cars driving by, faded into soft focus.

Nothing was moving at the normal pace, and as I watched the cars pass by, it was as though I were suddenly experiencing everything from some place outside the usual boundaries of time and space. When the little boy called out to us, his voice had sounded so sweet and strong, and it was strange to me, even at that moment, that what he was saying could cut through all the other sounds of the busy city street. This fact made no sense, given that he didn't seem to be speaking loudly enough to do so.

As he sat looking at us, his little round face was suffused with an expression of such pure delight and joy that we couldn't help smiling back at him. Some of the people in the crosswalk with us, still moving with a kind of slow, disjointed flicker across my vision, turned and looked at us, also smiling, and then continued on past, to be swallowed up in the crowd.

Suddenly, as quickly as it had started, everything snapped back into its "correct" place, but the way the transformation happened just added to the strangeness of the experience. For a fraction of a second, all of the cars and people seemed to stop completely, but then, in a barely perceptible shrug of movement, life resumed its normal pace. Or rather, I assume it was normal, but it was hard to tell since I was feeling anything but.

As reality righted itself, the delayed recognition that we were still in the middle of the street seemed to dawn on all of us simultaneously. I glanced up and found that the light had changed, and the sound of the traffic was suddenly loud and throbbing again as the cars veered around us. It was apparently a moment before our limbs were able to respond normally, though, because none of us seemed able to walk very quickly as we tried to get out of the crosswalk. In retrospect, I remember my legs felt heavy and lethargic, as when one wakes from a deep sleep. It took a herculean effort for us to force ourselves to continue walking to the other side of the street.

Once we finally made it to the sidewalk, though, we all came to a dead stop and turned to look at each other.

"*What in the world just happened there?*" my brother asked, his voice shaking a little and his forehead covered with a fine sheen of sweat.

"What on earth ... was ... that?" Andrea asked, not bothering to answer Dan but just voicing her own version of the only thought we were all having. We could do little more than look at each other and gape, somewhat stupidly. Everything looked so normal right now, but that had certainly not been the case a few moments before. Each one of us had the same question in our minds, but no one had a ready answer.

For myself, I could only stand and look at the street, even as the crowds continued to surge around us. What *had* just happened here? I looked back across the street but could no longer see the boy and his father. My gaze then went to the street itself, and as I tried to reconstruct what occurred, I found I could not tie it to any experience I'd ever had in my life.

What I felt right then, as I stood on the corner with my family, was first and foremost a type of euphoria, but it was dampened somewhat by the overwhelming sense of confusion over whatever we had collectively experienced. I wasn't the slightest bit worried or scared, just totally perplexed. The most prominent feeling, however, was an overpowering sensation of Divine fullness, as though I had received some sort of heavenly transfusion.

It was apparent from the looks on everyone's faces, as well as the stunned demeanor, that we were all sharing a similar response. I looked at Robert and he smiled slightly, wryly, and I knew we were both thinking the same thing … we had all just had one of those "God things!" But this was a rather spectacular incident, given that we'd all experienced it together, and under such unusual circumstances.

Finally, concern over missing our train surfaced in our thoughts, and we realized we were going to have to reserve further discussion about this incident until we were safely on board. Walking resolutely, if a bit unsteadily, toward the station, we all kept checking the impulse to launch into a commentary on what we'd just been through, and instead focused on reaching the station.

Once inside, we checked our tickets, found the correct platform, and arrived just in time to climb aboard and take our seats. We all sat quietly until the train pulled out of the station, and then, as though responding to a single impulse, we turned toward one another, intent on sharing our thoughts. The rocking motion of the train was lulling, but the urge to talk overrode every other sensation, including fatigue.

"That was the weirdest thing I've ever experienced in my life," Sara volunteered first. It was a place to start. The rest of us nodded our agreement.

"When that little boy said the whole 'congratulations' thing, it was like I could feel the totality of his happiness inside myself," Robert said.

Again, everyone nodded.

Finally, Andrea expressed what we'd all experienced, and she did it in a way that reflected some larger, universal understanding of the entire event.

"It was as though, for just a minute, we all got to experience some aspect of the entirety of the joy that Sanskrit brings. Like a sort of microcosm of what all those people, together in the stadium, were feeling during the performance."

"And that little boy was the embodiment of that experience." This came from Sara.

Yes. That was exactly what it felt like, I thought, sitting back in my seat. The train continued to roll along, taking us back to London. As I tried to sort through my impressions, it was as though I had an overwhelming need to reflect on the whole episode while it was still fresh in my mind and heart, and glancing around, I noticed a similar desire reflected in the attitudes of my seatmates. Everyone had become uncharacteristically quiet, and the silent memory of the incident sat pulsating between us.

It was as though we had all somehow been given a glimpse into a dimension that was beyond our normal perceptions. For that brief moment, we'd been immersed in the experience of the fulfillment that resides in the spirit of Sanskrit, and it had taken us to a place outside the normal continuum of time and space. Whatever the exact explanation for what occurred, there was one thing we knew for certain. We had all, in one way or another, been changed forever by what took place in the middle of that busy city street in Edinburgh.

As I looked out the window at the lovely countryside speeding past, I saw everything, as though in an overlay, that we had gone through in the past months, to be in Scotland right at that moment in time. And then I saw, in a changing kaleidoscope of images, all that had transpired through the years to bring us to that particular point in our lives.

I turned and, looking at my family, realized that it all came down to a single thought.

Everything we had ever done, or would ever do, in any of our lives, would always be a continuation of one specific, eternal experience. All of life was just ... one of those "God things."

OUR RETURN TO THE UNITED STATES found us with a profoundly different perspective on the odyssey that had been our lives up to this point. We had all "gotten" it, finally, and now there was almost a feeling of urgency with regard to taking the next steps on our path. We realized that we had an intense need to share our experiences with as many different people as possible. And we had to do so in such a way that they would then also have the opportunity to experience the Magic of the Divine. In other words, they would ideally get to have their own version of the "God thing."

It is so easy to get lost in the mire of life, and so difficult to find a way out of the mess. One aspect of our group epiphany was the realization that, with just a little boost—such as what comes from the deeply spiritual experience of Sanskrit—most of us can tap into the support and benefit of the cosmic connection that gives our lives intense meaning and true fulfillment. Without that connection, one's existence can feel very one-dimensional and superficial, because the whole point of life appears to be centered round its development. When we pursue the spiritual by making it as much a part of our day as eating and sleeping, the benefits are immeasurable, and indescribably wonderful.

For those who doubt this assertion, the line "what do you have to lose?" comes most quickly to mind. Without God, our perception is that we are simply a temporary flutter of consciousness on the surface of the vast universal plane. With God, we are eternal. And we get to share in the perpetual joy of Infinite Love, even while we are bound to this earth and all of its challenges. It's an answer that seems to be a bit of a no-brainer! If only all of life's decisions could be this easy!

Returning home was wonderful, and our dogs and cat, after giving us the silent treatment for about ten minutes as punishment for leaving them, were thrilled to have us back. Everything was the same, and yet nothing was. We were certainly different, enriched and changed by the entire experience. We knew, from a place deep inside our hearts, that it was our true dharma to share the understanding we had gathered. We had to pass on the realization that all cosmic beings have the ability to participate in the "exercise of expectation," when it comes to life's infinite possibilities. Embrace the Divine, and watch how everything changes.

The vision of us leaving Reno, during what was a very rocky beginning to our trip, and flying up through the smoke of that literal ring of fire, has stayed with me, and periodically I revisit that scene in my mind. It has become, for me, a sort of living metaphor when everyday things become difficult or trying. We can find, sometimes, that having to fly through a ring of fire before we reach clear skies allows us the benefit of contrast and adds to our appreciation of the clear blue horizon. As long as we keep our vision clearly focused on our goal, the flight goes a little easier, and we may even find we're not so afraid.

A very wise man once said that, in life, there are actually only two emotions, those being love and fear, and everything else we experience is just an offshoot of those two basic expressions. If we think about that statement, especially the way it applies to ourselves, we will find there is huge wisdom in those words. For our family, it has been a profound experience to watch how the presence of God in other people's lives has the power to take away fear, while it effortlessly supports love. If we all use the everyday presence of God as our touchstone, everything else becomes infinitely easier.

The ancient sounds of Sanskrit help make that vibrant Presence more accessible to us by allowing us to see that particular expression as just one of the many brilliant gifts of creation. For the ancient Vedic civilization, each spoken word was a gift to God, and by simply speaking and hearing Sanskrit, all of life became a prayer. This meant that through the process of just living and communicating, each person was building a strong foundation for peace and happiness, and, God knows, we could certainly use a little of that in our busy lives today. And how wonderful for all of us that Sanskrit is once again becoming lively on the level of world consciousness.

If we think we don't have time for prayer or meditation, we can remind ourselves how much time unhappiness and discontent consume when they're residing in our lives. Anytime is a good time for touching the foundation of our Being, and each small act of remembering the nature of our true Selves enriches us beyond measure.

From our family's perspective, we don't really know how this all came to be; daughters manifesting a language they shouldn't really know; a father who is the driving force behind music that enriches the expression of the language so much that people everywhere are singing in Sanskrit; a son who is happily discovering he has his own unique role in the cosmic family puzzle; and a mother who has to somehow find a way to write it all down so people can share in the odyssey with us!

What we do know is that we have to trust in something larger than ourselves to help us through all this, and, since we don't know how we got here to begin with, it would be the epitome of silliness to think we have much to say about the direction from this point on!

The one thing that can certainly be said of this whole story is that it reflects the reality of every person's life, which is simply that *we are all living within the realm of Divine possibilities. The magical Mystery is a constant for us all, if we just remember to look.*

It will be interesting to see how the saga continues.

[a b o u t   t h e   A u t h o r . . .]

LINDA FORMAN is a Certified Ayurvedic Specialist, writer, teacher, and motivational speaker on the subject of stress management and its connection to mind/body health. She has been a student of meditation, Eastern philosophies, and healing modalities for the past twenty-five years, and has also run a successful full-time Ayurvedic practice. In addition to these pursuits, she has an extensive media background in television and radio. She wrote for the "History of America" series hosted by James Whitmore. Linda lives in Sparks, Nevada, with Robert, her husband of twenty-seven years, and their three children, Andrea, Sara, and Micah. As the mother of the sensation that is Shanti Shanti, her main focus over the past years has been the captivating challenge of the integration of her family's everyday life with their pursuit of the Divine.

[about the CD...]

This book contains a special Shanti Shanti gift CD to give the reader the ability to share in the unique and wonderful experience of Sanskrit. We hope you enjoy listening to it as much as we enjoyed making it.

1. GANESH PRAYERS
This is a prayer to the aspect of God that removes obstacles from our path, and is an adaptation of an ancient Rig Veda prayer. It has been put to a melody composed by Shanti Shanti.

2. VEDIC LULLABY
Written by Robert, this is a song to the Saintly Mothers of the universe, and it is also a sweet prayer intended to be shared with all mothers in their special roles throughout creation.

3. ANGELS INSIDE
This song is to the guiding angels that are within us, loving us, at all times.

4. SHANTI MANTRA
From the Krishna Yajur Veda; a regional interpretation. This is a prayer asking for peace and blessings from all aspects of the universe.

5. STAY WITHIN THE LIGHT
This is a song written around the healing mantra, Triumbaka, from ancient India.

6. DURVA SUKTAM

This piece is from the Krishna Yajur Veda and is a prayer for guidance and protection against evil and sin.

7. SONG OF COMPASSION

By the renowned leader of India, Shankara, this song is an expression of the heart and of deepest compassion. It is an offering to the gurus and Masters of the Ages....

8. WALKIN' WITH THE DEVAS (*Live in Scotland*)

Recorded at the concert in Scotland, at the base of the cliffs of Edinburgh.

CREDITS
Ganesha Publishing (BMI)
Blue Halo Productions

Produced by Robert Forman
Mixed by Robert Forman

Mastered by John Polito at Audio Mechanics, Burbank, California
English lyrics and music by Robert Forman (BMI)
Sanskrit lyrics by Shanti Shanti (BMI)
Textual Sanskrit arranged by Shanti Shanti (BMI)
Vocals by Shanti Shanti, Robert Forman, and Micah Forman
Harmonium and violin by Andrea Forman
Tamboura and cello by Sara Forman
Drums by Beau MeLei
Bass by Mario Gusman
All other instruments by Robert Forman

ॐ
Shanti Shanti

Now that you read the story, experience the magical sound of Shanti Shanti

- Shanti Shanti
- Walkin' with the Devas
- Three
- Dreaming in Real Time

Companion CD to "Dreaming Real Time"

AVAILABLE AT FINE MUSIC STORES.

www.shantishanti.com

BlueHalo   New Leaf Distributing Company